MERCEDES-BENZ
G - WAGEN
WORKSHOP MANUAL
1979- 1991

OWNERS EDITION

COVERING ENGINES
Petrol M - 102, 110 & 115 - 4 & 6 Cyl.
Diesel OM - 602, 603, 616 & 617 - 4, 5 & 6 Cyl.

BROOKLANDS BOOKS LTD.
P.O. BOX 904, AMERSHAM,
BUCKS. HP6 9JA. UK
sales@brooklandsbooks.com

ABOUT THIS MANUAL

This 'Owners Edition' workshop manual covers the Mercedes-Benz petrol and diesel powered vehicles known as the G Class or 'G-Wagen' short for Geländewagen (or cross country vehicle). The G-Wagen was initially developed as a military vehicle from a suggestion by the Shah of Iran with the civilian version being introduced in 1979. Universally known as the G-Wagen it has also been sold under the Puch name in certain markets.

This manual has been compiled for the practical owner who wants to maintain their vehicle in first-class condition and contains comprehensive step-by-step instructions to enable them to carry out the bulk of their own servicing and repairs. With easy-to-follow instructions and hundreds of illustrations to amplify the text, many aspects of service, overhaul and repair are within the scope of an owner with a reasonable degree of mechanical aptitude.

Some operations, however, demand more skill whilst other jobs require the use of special tools and, in some cases, testing facilities and techniques that are not generally available. Only you can judge whether a job is within your capabilities. Whilst we do try to assist the reader to ensure that the information is correct it is obviously not possible to guarantee complete freedom from errors or omissions.

Information found in the driver's handbook is not necessarily duplicated here. It is not possible within this volume to cover every aspect to be found in the manufacturer's own workshop manual which is of greater size and complexity. However, it should be consulted if more detailed information is needed.

Always remember that you are responsible for your own safety, and that of others, when working on a vehicle. Particular care should be taken with safety related systems like the brakes and steering. If in any doubt professional advice should be sought. Never work under a vehicle unless it is properly supported (a single jack is not enough). Care should be taken with power tools and potentially harmful fuel, lubricants, solvents and sealers. These should always be stored in labelled, sealed containers. Always obtain your spare parts from an officially appointed Mercedes-Benz dealer.

With care and common sense the practical owner can make an excellent job of maintenance and overhaul. You will be adding to your knowledge too, knowing more about what needs to be done even if it does, in some instances, have to go to a professional repair shop.

The Mercedes-Benz G-Wagen range of vehicles are built with care and precision. Given regular servicing and maintenance they will provide long and reliable service.

ISBN 9781783180547   MBGWH

BROOKLANDS BOOKS LTD.
P.O. BOX 904, AMERSHAM,
BUCKS. HP6 9JA. UK

Mercedes-Benz
G-WAGEN

ENGINES COVERED - PETROL & DIESEL
300 G, 240 GD, 230 G, 280 GE, 230 GE,
250 GD, 300 GD
2.3, 2.4, 2.5, 2.8 & 3.0 Litre

CONTENTS

Introduction, General Information	4
616 and 617 Diesel Engines	10
Lubrication System	48
Cooling System	54
Clutch	65
Manual Transmission	68
Front Axle and Front Suspension	72
Propeller Shafts	79
Rear Axle and Rear Suspension	80
Steering	84
Brake System	88
602 and 603 Diesel Engines	98
M115 and M102 Petrol Engines	134
M110 Petrol Engines	163
Diesel Injection System	176
Petrol Injection System	183
Electrical System	189
Carburettor Fuel System	193
Servicing and Maintenance	195
Fault Finding Section	198

0.	INTRODUCTION

Our 'Owners Manuals' are based on easy-to-follow step-by-step instructions and advice enabling you to carry out many jobs yourself. This manual will give you the means to avoid delays and inconveniences which may result from not knowing the correct procedures for carrying out repairs, which are often of a comparatively simple nature.

Whilst special tools are required to carry out certain operations, this manual shows you – whenever possible – how to improvise or use alternative tools. Experience shows that it is preferable to use only genuine parts since these give the assurance of a first class job. You will find that many parts are identical in the various makes covered, so our advice is to find out before purchasing new parts and suggests that you always buy your replacement parts from an authorised dealer.

0.0.   General Information

Four-cylinder, five-cylinder and six-cylinder engines are covered in the manual, having in common a diesel injection and injection pump, a carburettor or a fuel injection system, as listed in brief below:

300 G, 3.0 litres: Five-cylinder diesel engine with a performance of 88 B.H.P. (64.5 kW). Engine type OM 617 is fitted.

240 GD, 2.4 litres: Four-cylinder diesel engine with a performance of 72 B.H.P. (53 kW). Engine type OM 616 is fitted.

230 G and 230 GE, 2.3 litres: Four-cylinder petrol engine with carburettor. Engine type M115 with carburettor with a performance of 90 B.H.P. (66 kW) or 102 B.H.P. (75 kW). From approx. 1982 model 230 GE with the same engine, but with fuel injection. Performance 125 B.H.P. (92 kW) without catalytic converter or 122 B.H.P. (89.5 kW) with converter.

280 GE, 2.8 litres: Six-cylinder engine with fuel injection and a performance of 156 B.H.P. (114.5 kW). Engine type M110.

230 GE from 1985: Although the model identification has not changed and the performance with and without converter has not changed, the successor to engine type "M115" is fitted. The new engine is of type M102 with fuel injection as fitted to other MB models.

250 GD from 1988: The original 240 GD is now fitted with a five-cylinder diesel engine. The engine belongs to type "OM602" and has a performance of 84 B.H.P. (62 kW). Since model year 1991 the engine has a performance of 94 B.H.P. (68 kW).

300 GD from model year 1990: Based on the "OM602" engine (an additional cylinder has been added) a six-cylinder diesel engine has been fitted with a performance of 109 B.H.P. (80 kW). The engine is of the type "OM603".

The vehicles covered in this manual are fitted with a four- or five-speed manual transmission or an automatic transmission.

0.1.   Vehicle Identification

You will know the location of the type identification plate, giving you the vehicle type, chassis number, permissible maximum weight and the permissible axle load on front and rear axle.

The engine number can be found on the positions shown in Figs. 0.1 and 0.2, given as an example. In the case of the "OM602" diesel engine the engine number is stamped into the cylinder block near the injection pipes on the L.H. side of the block, as shown in Fig. 0.1. In the case of the four-cylinder petrol engine you will find the engine number at the position shown in Fig. 0.2., shown here in the case of a "M102" engine.

Fig. 0.1 – The engine number of a diesel engine can be found at (1).

The code numbers and letters must always be quoted when parts are ordered. Copy the numbers on a piece of paper and take it to your parts supplier. You will save yourself and your parts department delays and prevents you from ordering the wrong parts.

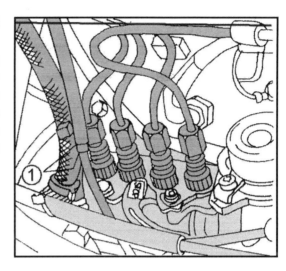

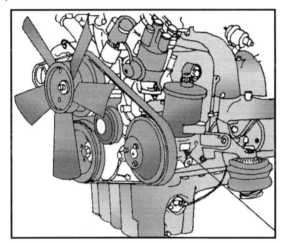

Fig. 0.2 – The engine number of a petrol engine (M102 shown) can be found at the position shown.

0.2.   General Servicing Notes

The servicing and overhaul instructions in this Workshop Manual are laid out in an easy-to-follow step-by-step fashion and no difficulty should be encountered, If the text and diagrams are followed carefully and methodically. The "Technical Data" sections form an important part of the repair procedures and should always be referred to during work on the vehicle.

In order that we can include as much data as possible, you will find that we do not generally repeat in the text the values already given under the technical data headings. Again, to make the best use of the space available, we do not repeat at each operation the more obvious steps necessary - we feel it to be far more helpful to concentrate on the difficult or awkward procedures in greater detail. However, we summarise below a few of the more important procedures and draw your attention to various points of general interest that apply to all operations.

Always use the torque settings given in the various main sections of the manual. These are grouped together in separate sub-sections for convenient reference.

Bolts and nuts should be assembled in a clean and very lightly oiled condition and faces and threads should always be inspected to make sure that they are free from damage burrs or scoring. DO NOT degrease bolts or nuts.

All joint washers, gaskets, tabs and lock washers, split pins and "O" rings must be replaced on assembly. Seals will, in the majority of cases, also need to be replaced, if the shaft and seal have been separated. Always lubricate the lip of the seal before assembly and take care that the seal lip is facing the correct direction.

References to the left-hand and right-hand sides are always to be taken as if the observer is at the rear of the vehicle, facing forwards, unless otherwise stated.

Always make sure that the vehicle is adequately supported, and on firm ground, before commencing any work on the underside of the car. A small jack or a make shift prop can be highly dangerous and proper axle stands are an essential requirement for your own safety.

Dirt, grease and mineral oil will rapidly destroy the seals of the hydraulic system and even the smallest amounts must be prevented from entering the system or coming into contact with the components. Use clean brake fluid or one of the proprietary cleaners to wash the hydraulic system parts. An acceptable alternative cleaner is methylated spirit, but it this is used, it should not be allowed to remain in contact with the rubber parts for longer than necessary. It is also important that all traces of the fluid should be removed from the system before final assembly.

Always use genuine manufacturer's spares and replacements for the best results.

Since the manufacturer uses metric units when building the cars it is recommended that, these are used for all precise units. Inch conversions are given in most cases but these are not necessarily precise conversions, being rounded off for the unimportant values.

Removal and installation instructions, in this Workshop Manual, cover the steps to take away or put back the unit or part in question. Other instructions, usually headed "Servicing", will cover the dismantling and repair of the unit once it has been stripped from the vehicle it is pointed out that the major instructions cover a complete overhaul of all parts but, obviously, this will not always be either necessary and should not be carried out needlessly.

There are a number of variations in unit parts on the range of vehicles covered in this Workshop Manual. We strongly recommend that you take care to identify the precise model, and the year of manufacture, before obtaining any spares or replacement parts.

Std.: To indicate sizes and limits of components as supplied by the manufacturer. Also to indicate the production tolerances of new unused parts.

O/S: Parts supplied as Oversize or Undersize or recommended limits for such parts, to enable them to be used with worn or re-machined mating parts.

U/S: O/S indicates a part that is larger than Std. size U/S may indicate a bore of a bushing or female part that is smaller than Std.

Max.: Where given against a clearance or dimension indicates the maximum allowable If in excess of the value given it is recommended that the appropriate part is fitted.

TIR: Indicates the Total Indicator Reading as shown by a dial indicator (dial gauge).

TDC: Top Dead Centre (No. 1 piston on firing stroke).

MP: Multi-Purpose grease.

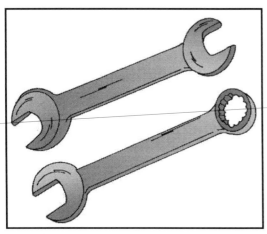

0.3. Recommended Tools

To carry out some of the operations described in the manual we will need some of the tools listed below:

Fig. 0.3 – A double open-ended spanner in the upper view and an open-ended/ring spanner in the lower view. Always make sure that the spanner size is suitable for the nut or bolt to be removed and tightened.

As basic equipment in your tool box you will need a set of open-ended spanners (wrenches) to reach most of the nuts and bolts. A set of ring spanners is also of advantage. To keep the costs as low as possible we recommend a set of combined spanners, open-ended on one side and a ring spanner on the other side. Fig. 0.1 shows a view of the spanners in question. Sockets are also a useful addition to your tool set.

A set of cross-head screwdrivers, pliers and hammers or mallets may also be essential. You will find that many bolts now have a "Torx" head. In case you have never seen a "Torx" head bolt, refer to Fig. 0.4. A socket set with special "Torx" head inserts is used to slacken and tighten these screws. The size of the bolts are specified by the letter "T" before the across-flat size.

Fig. 0.4 – A graduated disc is used to "angle-tighten" nuts and bolts. "Torx" head bolts are shown on the R.H. side.

Circlip pliers may also be needed for certain operations. Two types of circlip pliers are available, one type for external circlips, one type for internal circlips. The ends of the pliers can either be straight or angled. Fig. 0.5 shows a view of the circlip pliers. Apart from the circlip pliers you may also need the pliers shown in Fig. 0.6, i.e. side cutters, combination pliers and water pump pliers.

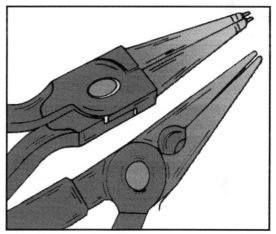

Fig. 0.5 – Circlip pliers are shown in the upper view. The type shown in suitable for outside circlips. The lower view shows a pair of pointed pliers.

Every part of the vehicle is tightened to a certain torque value and you will therefore need a torque wrench which can be adjusted to a certain torque setting. In this connection we will also mention a graduated disc, shown in Fig. 0.4, as many parts of the vehicle must be angle-tightened after having been tightened to a specific torque. As some of the angles are not straight-forward (for example 30 or 60 degrees), you will either have to estimate the angle or use the disc.

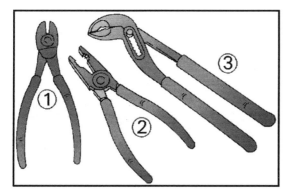

Fig. 0.6 – Assortment of pliers suitable for many operations.
1 Side cutter
2 Combination pliers
3 Water pump pliers

Finally you may consider the tool equipment shown in Fig. 0.7 which will be necessary from time to time, mainly if you intend to carry out most maintenance and repair jobs yourself.

0.5.   Before you start

Before you carry out any operations on your vehicle it may be of advantage to read the following notes to prevent injuries and damage to the vehicle:

General Information

- Never carry out operations underneath the vehicle when the front or rear is only supported on the jack. Always place chassis stands in position (refer to next section). If no chassis stands are available and if the wheels are removed place one wheel on top of the other one and place them under the side of the vehicle where you work. If the jack fails the vehicle will drop onto the two wheels, preventing injury.

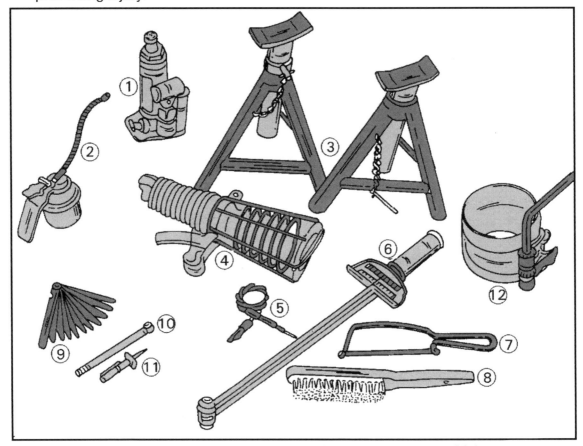

Fig. 0.7 – Recommended tools to service and repair your vehicle.

1 Hydraulic jack		7 Small hand saw
2 Oil can		8 Wire brush
3 Chassis stands		9 Feeler gauges
4 Electric hand lamp		10 Tyre pressure gauge
5 Test lamp (12 volts)		11 Tyre profile depth checker
6 Torque wrench		12 Piston ring clamp band

- Never slacken or tighten the axle shaft nuts or wheel bolts when the vehicle in resting on chassis stands.
- Never open the cooling system when the engine is hot. Sometimes it may, however, be necessary. In this case place a thick rag around the cap and open it very slowly until all steam has been released.
- Never drain the engine oil when the engine is hot. Drained engine oil must be disposed of in accordance with local regulation.
- Never allow brake fluid or anti-freeze to come in contact with painted areas.
- Never inhale brake shoe or brake pad dust. If compressed air is available, blow off the dust whilst turning the head away. A mask should be worn for reasons of safety.
- Remove oil or grease patches from the floor before you or other people slip on it.
- Do not work on the vehicle wearing a shirt with long sleeves. Rings and watches should be removed before carrying out any work.

- If possible never work by yourself. If unavoidable ask a friend or a member of the family to have a quick look to check thats everything is OK.
- Never hurry up your work. Many wheel bolts have been left untightened to get the vehicle quickly back on the road.
- Never smoke near the vehicle or allow persons with a cigarette near you. A fire extinguisher should be handy, just in case.
- Never place a hand lamp directly onto the engine to obtain a better view. Even though that the metal cage will avoid direct heat it is far better if you attach such a lamp to the open engine bonnet.

0.6.   Dimensions and Weights (typical)

Overall length: .... 395.5 to 459.5 mm, depending on model year
Overall width: ....1700 mm
Overall height: .... 1925 to 1990 mm, depending on model year
Wheelbase: .... 2400 or 2850 mm
Front track: ....1425 mm
Rear track: ....1425 mm
Kerb weight: .... See Operators' Handbook

0.7.   Capacities

Engines:
- Oil and filter change – 616 and 617 engines: ....6.5 litres
- Engine dry – 616 and 617 engines: ....7.5 litres
- Oil and filter change – 602 and 603 engines – Five-cylinder: ....7.5 litres
- Oil and filter change – 602 and 603 engines – Six-cylinder: ....7.5 litres
- Engine dry – 602 and 603 engines – Five-cylinder: ....8.0 litres
- Engine dry – 602 and 603 engines – Six-cylinder: ....8.2 litres
- Oil filter and filter change – M115 engine: ....6.0 litres
- Oil and filter change – M115M engine: ....6.5 litres
- Oil filter and filter change – M115 engine: ....6.0 litres
- Oil and filter change – M102 engine: ....5.0 litres
- Engine dry – M102 engine: ....5.5 litres
- Oil and filter change – M110 engine: ....6.0 litres
- Engine dry – M110 engine: ....7.0 litres
Cooling system: ....Refer to section "Cooling System"
Transmission: ....1.6 litres
Rear axle: ....1.6 litres

0.8.   Jacking up the Vehicle

To prevent damage to the underside of the vehicle, apply a jack or chassis stands only to the points specified below. Under no circumstances place the jack underneath the following sections of the vehicle when the vehicle is lifted: under the body sidemembers, parts of the steering linkage, the propeller shaft, the engine or transmission, the fuel tank or the suspension arms.

If a mobile or hydraulic jack is available, place it underneath the front or rear axle tube. We recommend to have a helper to observe the operation, as the vehicle is fairly high. If both sides of the vehicle are lifted, first lift one side, place chassis stands underneath the vehicle and then lift the other side. Again a helper is recommended. Apply the handbrake and place blocks (for example bricks) to check the front or rear wheels in question.

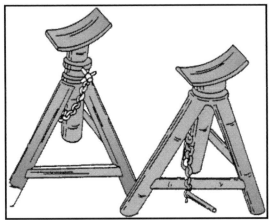

Fig. 0.8 – Three-legged chassis stands are the safest method to support the vehicle when work has to be carried out on the underside of the vehicle.

Before jacking up the rear end of the vehicle engage the reverse gear.

Always make sure that the ground on which the vehicle is to be jacked up is solid enough to carry the weight of the vehicle.

Chassis stands should only be placed on the L.H. and R.H. sides under the side of the body without damage to the paint work. Use chassis stands of the construction shown in Fig. 0.8, but again make sure that they are strong enough to carry the weight of the vehicle. Make sure the vehicle cannot slip off the stands.

Note: It is always difficult to raise a vehicle first on one side and then on the other. Take care that the vehicle cannot tip-over when the first side is lifted. Ask a helper to support the vehicle from the other side. Never work underneath the vehicle without adequate support.

1. 616 and 617 DIESEL ENGINES

Note: The remaining engines are covered at the end of the manual.

1.0 Main Features

Fitted Engines:
- 240 GD: ....OM 616, four-cylinder
- 300 GD: ....OM 617, five-cylinder

Injection Order:
- Four-cylinder: .... 1 - 3 - 4 - 2
- Five-cylinder: ....1 - 2 - 4 - 5 - 3

Arrangement of cylinders: .... In line
Camshaft: .... One overhead camshaft
Arrangement of valves: ....Overhead
Cylinder bore: ....91.00 mm
Piston stroke: ....92.4 mm

Capacity:
- 240 GD: ....2404 c.c.
- 300 GD: ....3005 c.c.

Compression ratio: ....21.0 : 1

Max. kW/B.H.P. (DIN) (variations are possible):
- 240 GD: .... 53 kW (72 BHP) at 4400 rpm
- 300 GD: .... 64.5 kW (88 BHP) at 4400 rpm

Max. Torque (variations are possible):
- 240 GD: ....13.7 kgm at 2400 rpm

- 300 GD: ....17.2 kgm at 2400 rpm

Crankshaft bearings: 5 (4-cyl.), 6 (5-cyl.)

Cooling system	Thermo system with water pump, thermostat, cooling fan, tube-type radiator, 617 engine with viscous fan clutch.
Lubrication	Pressure-feed lubrication with gear-type oil pump, driven with chain from crankshaft. With full-flow and by-pass oil filter, with and without air-oil heat exchanger.
Air cleaner	Dry paper element air cleaner.

General Information

This section covers the engines fitted to models 240 GD and 300 GD, fitted in general to the end of model year 1987. From model year 1988 (250 GD) or from 1990 (300 GD) the next generation of diesel engine is fitted.

1.1.   Engine – Removal and Installation
1.1.0   REMOVAL OF THE ENGINE

The engine and gearbox should be removed as a single unit out of the engine compartment. The gearbox can then be removed from the engine. We would like to point out that the total weight of the power unit is approx. 200 kg and a suitable hoist or crane is required to lift out the assembly. The following instructions are given in general for all engines, but depending on the equipment of the vehicle some differences may be encountered. The engine bonnet must be placed in vertical position or can be removed to prevent damage to the paint work. The vehicle must be placed on chassis stands when necessary. Proceed as follows:

Fig. 1.1 – The protective panel for the radiator is removed from below the vehicle.

- Disconnect the positive battery lead from the battery and move the cable well away. The negative cable can also be disconnected.
- Remove the radiator grille.
- Remove the front end of the vehicle together with the bonnet lock.
- Disconnect the cable from the signal horn.

Fig. 1.2 – Disconnecting the lower radiator hose inside the cooling fan shroud.

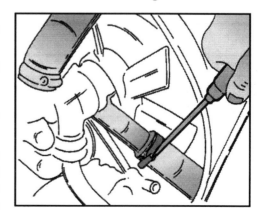

- From below the vehicle remove the protective panel for the radiator. Fig. 1.1 shows the operation.
- Drain the cooling system as described later on for the 616 and 617 engines.
- Remove the upper and lower radiator hose at both ends and withdraw the hoses from the radiator and the engine. Access to one of the hoses is carried out inside the

ventilator shroud, near the cooling fan, as shown in Fig. 1.2.

• Remove the radiator.

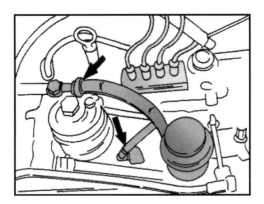

Fig. 1.3 – Slacken the union nuts shown by the arrows to disconnect the vacuum line from the vacuum pump.

• Disconnect the fuel feed and return pipes. Take care as fuel may run out.

• Disconnect the vacuum hose leading to the brake servo unit at the vacuum pump. Figs. 1.3 shows with the arrows where two union nuts must be removed. Also disconnect a vacuum line from the vacuum unit on the injection pump.

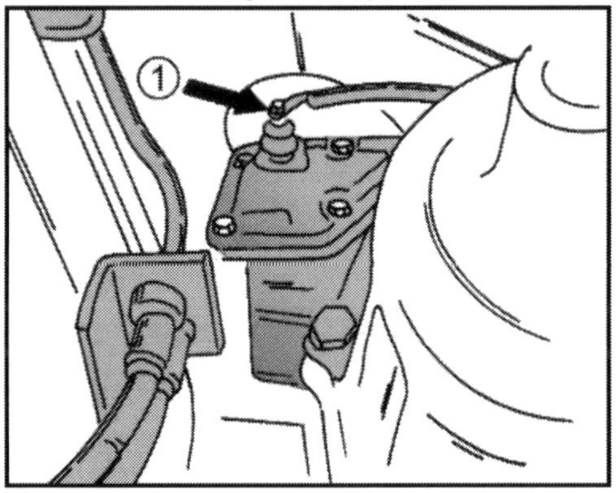

Fig. 1.4 – The oil pressure switch cable (1) must be disconnected from the top of the oil filter housing.

• Disconnect the cable connections from the 4 or 5 glow plugs and the cables from the two temperature sensors.

• Disconnect the cable from the oil pressure switch from the oil filter housing. This is fairly hidden, but you should be able to find it by referring to Fig. 1.4.

• Disconnect all regulating linkages. Refer to Fig. 1.5. Remove the retaining clip marked with the arrow and push the longitudinal linkage towards the rear. Unscrew the bracket (1) and unclip the idle control cable (2) together with the plastic sleeve. (3).

Fig. 1.5 – Removal of the regulating linkages. The numbers are referred to in the text.

• Remove the alternator and the starter motor.

• Slacken the clamps securing the heater hoses and withdraw the hoses from their connections.

• Disconnect the exhaust pipe from the exhaust manifold.

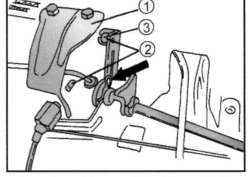

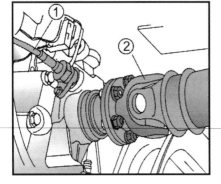

Fig. 1.6 – The speedometer drive cable (1) and the propeller shaft (2) connections.

• Disconnect the propeller shaft from the transmission drive flange, push it to one side and use a piece of wire to secure it to the underside of the vehicle. Also disconnect the speedometer drive cable. Fig. 1.6 shows the connections.

• Disconnect the gear selector rods from the levers on the transmission. Retaining clips must be removed. Push the rods to one side, out of the way.

• Remove the bracket securing the slave cylinder fluid pipe to the transmission and unscrew the slave cylinder together with the hose and the pipe (Fig. 1.7). Push the cylinder to one side and tie it up. Remove a plastic washer underneath the cylinder, as it must be refitted.

Fig. 1.7 – Removal of the clutch slave cylinder.

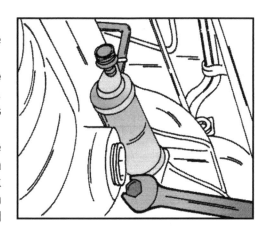

- Remove the exhaust pipe bracket and the earth cable from the gearbox.
- From underneath the vehicle remove the bolts securing the gearbox mounting. Fig. 1.8 shows the two mountings on the sides of the gearbox.
- Attach suitable ropes or chains to the engine lifting eyes and attach the ends to a hoist or crane. Also place a trolley jack underneath the power unit to support it from below. Operate the lifting equipment until the ropes/chains are just tight.

Fig. 1.8 – The arrows show the bolts to remove to free the gearbox mountings.

- Carefully lift the engine and transmission from the engine compartment and lift it out towards the front. Continuously check that none of the cables, leads, etc. can get caught in the engine. Stop the lifting operation immediately as soon as problems can be seen. Under no circumstances force the assembly out of the engine compartment.

Installation of the engine

The installation is carried out in reverse order to the removal, but the following points should be noted during the installation:

- Do not connect or refit any of the disconnected parts until the engine and transmission are refitted to their mountings and the engine is free from the ropes or chains.
- Remove the engine mounts if their condition requires it. Keep oil or grease away from the rubber parts.
- If work has been carried out on engine or transmission make sure that the oil drain plug(s) have been tightened and check the oil level after installation.
- Connect the propeller shaft in accordance with the instructions in section 4.
- Tighten the nuts and bolts to the correct tightening torque values. The following values should be noted:

M10 engine mountings: ....3.5 – 4.0 kgm
Engine to gearbox: ....5.5 kgm
Radiator drain plug: ....0.6 – 1.0 kgm
Exhaust pipe to exhaust manifold flange: ....2.0 kgm

- Refill the cooling system with anti-freeze of the correct strength for the temperatures to be expected. If the original anti-freeze is re-used, check its strength before filling it in.
- Check the air cleaner element before re-use. Dirty elements should be replaced, mainly if overhaul work has been undertaken on the engine.
- After starting the engine and allowing it to warm up, check the cooling system for leaks. Drive the vehicle a few miles to check, for example, for exhaust rattle.

1.2.   Engine - Dismantling

The engines are sensitive to dirt or other contamination. It is therefore essential to make sure that no foreign matter can enter the pipes, connections, etc. during the dismantling operations.

Dismantling of the engine will be made much easier, if a swivelling engine stand is available. Otherwise place the engine/transmission on a work bench, supporting is adequately to prevent if from falling over.

Before commencing dismantling, block up the inlet and exhaust openings and give the exterior of the engine a thorough cleaning to remove all loose dirt and oil. Pay particular attention to all joint surfaces, brushing these to remove loose debris which might otherwise find its way into the interior of the engine.

Many of the parts are made of aluminium alloy and must be treated accordingly. Only use plastic or rubber mallets to separate parts, if necessary.

As a complete strip-down of the engine is in most cases not necessary, and many of the operations can be carried out with the engine fitted, you will find in the following text a description of individual operations which can be carried out with the engine fitted and removed. Combining these, will give you the complete dismantling of the engine.

1.3.   Engine - Overhaul

1.3.0.   Cylinder Head and Valves – Technical Data

Cylinder Head:

Cylinder head height:	84.8 – 85.0 mm (min. 84.0 mm)
Max. Distortion of Cylinder Head Faces:	
- Longitudinal direction:	0.08 mm
- Across the face:	0.00 mm
Max. deviation of faces between upper and lower sealing faces (parallel to each other):	0.10 mm
Depth of valve head faces and cylinder head sealing face:	- 0.5 mm
- With re-cut valve seats:	1.5 mm – all valves

Valves

Valve Head Diameter:	
- Inlet valves:	39.90 – 38.70 mm
- Exhaust valves:	34.30 – 34.10 mm
Valve seat angle:	30°
Valve Stem Diameter:	
- Inlet valves:	9.940 – 9.925 mm
- Exhaust valves:	9.940 – 9.9185 mm
Valve Length:	
- Inlet valves:	131.30 – 131.70 mm
- Exhaust valves:	130.8 – 131.20 mm
Valve Seat Width:	
- Inlet valves:	1.3 to 1.6 mm
- Exhaust valves:	2.5 – 2.9 mm
Valve Identification:	
- Inlet valves:	E 616 02
- Exhaust valves:	A 616 05

Valve Seats

Valve seat width:
- Inlet valves: 1.3 to 1.6 mm
- Exhaust valves: 2.5 – 2.9 mm

Valve seat angles: 30°
Upper correction angle: 60°

Valve Springs

Outer diameter: 30.20 mm
Wire diameter: 3.80 mm
Free length: 50.50 mm
Length under load of 46.3 to 53 kg: 29.90 mm, min.

Valve Guides

Inlet Valve/Exhaust Valve Guides:
- Length:
  Inlet valves: 61.00 mm
  Exhaust valves: 49.50 mm
- Outer diameter – Std., all guides: 14.03 – 14.04 mm
- Outer diameter – Repair size, all guides: 14.23 – 14.24 mm
- Inner diameter, all guides: 10.00 – 10.015 mm
- Max. inner diameter: 10.025 mm
- Basic bore in cylinder head:
  Std.:   14.000 – 14.020 mm
  Repair size: 14.200 – 14.220 mm
- Interference fit of valve guides – All guides:
  Std.:   0.01 – 0.04 mm

Camshaft

Camshaft bearing running clearance: 0.025 – 0.066 mm (max. 0.11 mm)
Camshaft end float: 0.05 – 0.128 mm (max. 0.18 mm)

1.3.0.1.   Cylinder Head – Removal and Installation

The following information should be noted when work is carried out on a cylinder head:
- The cylinder head is made of light-alloy. Engine coolant, engine oil, the air required to ignite the fuel and the exhaust gases are directed through the cylinder head. Glow plugs, injectors, pre-combustion chambers and valve tappets are fitted to the cylinder head. Also in the cylinder heads you will find the camshaft.
- The exhaust manifold and the inlet manifold are bolted to the outside of the head. The fuel enters the head on one side and exits on the other side, i.e. the head is of the well-known "crossflow" type.
- The cylinder head is fitted with various sender units, sensors and switching valves, responsible for certain functions of the temperature control.
- As the cylinder head is made of light alloy, it is prone to distortion if, for example, the order of slackening or tightening of the cylinder head bolts is not observed. For the same reason never remove the cylinder head from a hot engine.
- A cylinder head cannot be checked in fitted position. Sometimes the cylinder head gasket will "blow", allowing air into the cooling system. A quick check is possible after opening the coolant reservoir cap (engine fairly cold). Allow the engine to warm-up and observe the coolant. Visible air bubbles point in most cases to a

"blown" gasket. Further evidence is white exhaust smoke, oil in the coolant or coolant in the engine oil. The latter can be checked at the oil dipstick. A white, grey emulsion on the dipstick is more or less a confirmation of a damaged cylinder gasket.

- If you are convinced that water has entered the engine and you want to get home or to the nearest garage, unscrew the injectors and crank the engine with the starter motor for a while to eject the water. Refit the injectors, start the engine and drive to your destination without switching off the engine. This is the only method to avoid serious engine damage (bent connecting rods for example).

The cylinder head must only be removed when the engine is cold. The head is removed together with the exhaust manifold, but the inlet manifold must be separated from the cylinder head before the head can be lifted off. New cylinder head gaskets are wrapped in plastic and must only be unwrapped just before the gasket is fitted. The cylinder head can be removed with the engine fitted and these operations are described below, but note that operations may vary, depending on the equipment fitted:

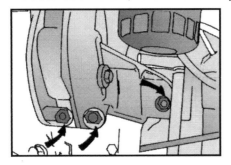

Fig. 1.9 – After removal of the three bolts remove the parts mentioned below. Shown is the lower attachment.

- Disconnect the battery earth cable and remove the engine bonnet.
- Drain the cooling system (Section 1.8.1.).
- Remove the air cleaner.
- If a power-assisted steering is fitted remove the steering pump together with the mounting bracket and the fuel filter. Refer to Fig. 1.9 and remove the bolts indicated by the arrows. This is the lower attachment. At the upper end remove the bolts shown in Fig. 1.10. The complete assembly can now be lifted out.

Fig. 1.10 – Remove the single bolt in the upper view and the two bolts in the lower view and remove the steering/mounting bracket and the fuel filter assembly.

- Remove the oil dipstick guide tube bracket.
- On a vehicle without power-assisted steering remove the fuel filter together with the attached hoses and the hose leading to the first injector.
- Disconnect all coolant, fuel and vacuum hoses and the electrical cables connected to the cylinder head or any other unit on the cylinder head which cannot be removed together with the cylinder head (also see below).
- Separate the throttle control linkage at the ball joint connection.
- Disconnect the vacuum pipes from the exhauster (vacuum) pump. One hose and one union nut must be removed.
- Separate the exhaust pipe flange from the exhaust manifold.

- In the case of a 616 engine unscrew the inlet manifold support from the position shown in Fig. 1.11.
- Remove the regulating linkages as described during the removal of the engine (see also Fig. 1.5).

Fig. 1.11 – The support bracket for the inlet manifold of a 616 engine.

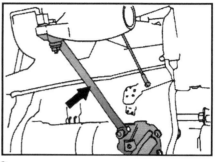

- Disconnect the injection pipes. Close off the hose end in suitable manner (a bolt of suitable diameter can be pushed into the hose end.

- Disconnect the three coolant hoses from the thermostat housing and the breather pipe between the cylinder head and the water pump housing.

- Disconnect the electrical leads from the glow plugs.

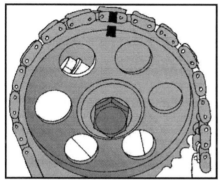

Fig. 1.12 – Mark the chain and sprocket with a spot of paint before removal of the sprocket.

- Remove the cylinder head cover. Six screws must be removed. Two are located on each long side of the cover and two on the timing side of the engine. If an automatic transmission is fitted, there is a regulating rod fitted across the cylinder head cover, which must be separated on one side at the ball joint. A sticking cylinder head cover must not be freed by tapping it with a hammer. If difficult to remove, try to unstick it by pushing it by hand to one side. Use a plastic mallet, if necessary.

- Rotate the engine until the piston of No. 1 cylinder is at top dead centre in the firing position, i.e. the "0" mark must be opposite the adjusting pin. A 27 mm socket can be applied to the crankshaft pulley to rotate the crankshaft. Never attempt to rotate the crankshaft by applying a socket to the camshaft timing wheel bolt. The crankshaft must be rotated in the direction of rotation.

- Remove the chain tensioner as described under a separate heading. The chain tensioner plug must be unscrewed by applying a spanner to the hexagon. The plug is located above the water pump and the thermostat cover, next to the large tube.

- Mark the camshaft sprocket and the timing chain at opposite points, as shown in Fig. 1.12, using a spot of paint.

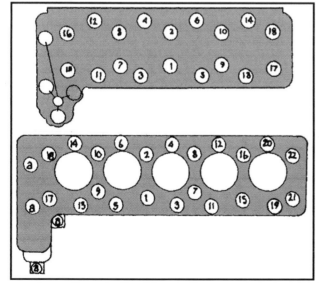

Fig. 1.13 – Tightening sequence for the cylinder head. In the upper view for the 616 engine, in the lower view for the 617 engine. Bolts "a" show the M8 bolts.

- Unscrew the camshaft sprocket bolt. To counterhold the camshaft against rotation, insert a strong screwdriver blade or steel bolt into one of the holes of the camshaft sprocket.

- Remove both rocker shafts. The camshaft must be rotated until none of the valve rockers are under tension. Mark the shafts before removal.

- Remove the camshaft sprocket from the shaft without disengaging the timing chain from the crankshaft sprocket. Pull the chain tight and use a piece of wire to tie chain and sprocket together.

- Remove the camshaft as described under the relevant section.

616 and 617 Diesel Engines

- Remove the slide rail from the cylinder head as described later on.
- In the inside of the chain case remove two 8 mm socket head bolts with an Allen key (6 mm). An extension and a socket is required to reach the bolts.

Fig. 1.14 – Removal of an injector.

- Unscrew the cylinder head bolts in reverse order to the one shown in Fig. 1.13 on the previous page. A multi-spline bit must be used to slacken the bolts (MB Part No. 601 589 00 10 00). A normal Allen key is not suitable as it will damage the bolt heads. In order to remove the bolts "4" and "5" it will be necessary to remove the injectors. A socket, as shown in Fig. 1.14 is used. Immediately after removal of the bolts measure their length if the bolts have an internal multi-tooth socket. If the dimension from the end of the bolt to the underside of the bolt head is more than 105.6, 120.5 or 145.0 mm, depending where the bolts are located, replace the bolts. New bolts have a length of 104.0, 119 mm or 144.0 mm. i.e. bolts which nearly approach the max. length should also be replaced.

Note: Certain bolts are fitted through the camshaft bearings. As the cylinder head bolts are of different length, mark them before removal to assure refitting in the original positions.

- Lift off the cylinder head. If a hoist or other lifting equipment is available, hook a rope to the two lifting eyes and lift off the head. Remove the cylinder head gasket.
- Immediately after removal, clean the cylinder head and block surfaces of old gasket material.
- If necessary, overhaul the cylinder head as described in Section 1.3.0.2. after dismantling.

Install the cylinder head in the following manner:
- Place a new cylinder head gasket in position.
- Place the cylinder head carefully in position, taking care to engage the dowel sleeves. Use a soft-faced mallet to tap the head in position.
- Coat the threads of the cylinder head bolts and the underside of the bolt heads with oil. It is assumed that original bolts have been measured for their re-use, if bolts with internal multi-spline heads are used.
- Insert the cylinder head bolts as originally fitted (and hopefully marked) and tighten them in the sequence shown in Figs. 1.13 in several stages. The tightening is carried out in stages as follows:

Bolts with internal hexagons (Allen head bolts) (make sure the bolts are inserted into their correct bores – different length):
- Tighten all bolts in the correct order to 7 kgm (50 ft.lb.).
- Tighten all bolts in the correct order to 9 kgm (65 ft.lb.).
- Wait 10 minutes.
- Tighten all bolts in the correct order to 10 kgm (72 ft.lb.).

Bolts with internal multi-spline (12-point) heads
- Tighten all bolts in the correct order to 4 kgm (29 ft.lb.).
- Tighten all bolts in the correct order to 7 kgm (50 ft.lb.).
- Wait 10 minutes.
- Angle-tighten all bolts in their correct tightening order. To do this, insert the multi-spline bit with the socket into each bolt and fit the tommy bar so that it is in line with the longitudinal axis of the engine. Tighten the bolt until the tommy bar is at

right angle to the engine, i.e. the bolt has been tightened by 90° (1/4 of a turn). Do not use the torque wrench for this operation.

- Re-tighten each bolt in the order given by a further 90° in the manner described above.
- Fit the two M8 socket head screws to the inside of the timing chain chamber and tighten them to 2.5 kgm (18 ft.lb.).
- Refit the slide rail to the head as described later on (Section 1.3.5.3.).

Fig. 1.15 – Locking the camshaft timing sprocket.

- Fit the camshaft sprocket together with the timing chain to the end of the camshaft, making sure that the paint marks made during removal are in line (Fig. 1.12). The sprocket must engage with its bore over the dowel pin in the camshaft.
- Fit the camshaft sprocket bolt and tighten the bolt to 8.0 kgm (58 ft.lb.). Counterhold the camshaft by inserting a strong screwdriver blade or drift through one of the openings in the sprocket, as shown in Fig. 1.15.
- Refit the timing chain tensioner and tighten the plug to 8.0 kgm (58.5 ft.lb.) and fit the two rocker shaft assemblies.

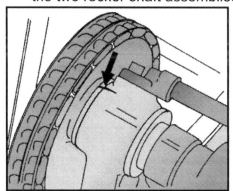

Fig. 1.16 – Alignment of the notch in the camshaft flange and the lug on the No. 1 camshaft bearing cap assures the T.D.C. position of the engine.

- Check the marking for top dead centre for the No. 1 cylinder in the camshaft (see Fig. 1.16). A notch is machined into the camshaft which should be in line with a mark machined into the cylinder head. The alignment can be seen by looking from above and comparing it with Fig. 1.16.
- Re-connect the glow plug cables.
- Check and adjust the valve clearances as described later on.
- Refit the inlet manifold and the injectors and re-connect the injection pipes.
- Fit the exhaust pipe to the exhaust manifold.
- The remaining operations are carried out in reverse order to the removal procedure. Check and, if necessary adjust, the throttle cable operation.

NOTE: Multi-spline head socket bolts require no re-tightening after they have been fitted as described above. Socket head bolts must be tightened after 300 to 600 miles, as described above. To do this, slacken each bolt in the order shown in Fig. 1.13 and immediately re-tighten it to 10.0 kgm (72 ft.lb.).

1.3.0.2.   Cylinder Head - Dismantling

The following description assumes that the cylinder head is to be replaced. If only a top overhaul is asked for, ignore the additional instructions. The cylinder head must be removed.

It should be noted that special tools are required to remove the valves. A spanner is required to counterhold the valve spring cups (No. 615 589 00 01 00) and two valve adjusting spanners with 14 mm across the flats (No. 615 589 00 01 00) are used to slacken the dome nuts and locknuts of the valves. Proceed as follows during dismantling:

Fig. 1.17 – Counterhold the valve spring cup as shown when removing the valves.

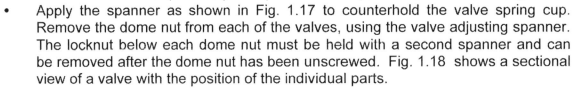

- Remove all auxiliary parts from the cylinder head, including the inlet and exhaust manifolds.
- Valves are not held in position by the usual valve cotter halves, but by means of a dome nut with locknut. Dome nuts have been changed during production and only the later version is supplied. Valve spring cups have also been modified (February 1981). The new cups are suitable for all engines.
- Apply the spanner as shown in Fig. 1.17 to counterhold the valve spring cup. Remove the dome nut from each of the valves, using the valve adjusting spanner. The locknut below each dome nut must be held with a second spanner and can be removed after the dome nut has been unscrewed. Fig. 1.18 shows a sectional view of a valve with the position of the individual parts.

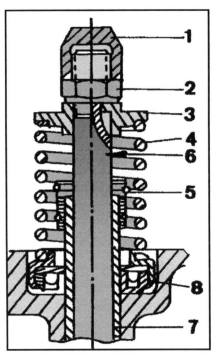

Fig. 1.18 – Valve stem and valve spring in a sectional view.
1 Dome nut
2 Locknut
3 Valve spring seat
4 Valve spring
5 Valve stem seal
6 Valve
7 Valve guide
8 "Rotocap"

- Remove the spring cup, valve spring, valve stem oil seal and the "rotocap" (prevents valves from rotating). Valve springs (one per valve) are with paint spots. Only use springs with the same colour identification of springs being replaced. Remove valve stem oil seals carefully with a screwdriver or a pair of pliers.
- Remove the valves one after the other out of the valve guides and pierce them in their fitted order through a piece of cardboard. Write the cylinder number against each valve if they are to be re-used.

- A few words should be said about the camshaft. The camshaft has three bearings (616 engine) or four bearings (617 engine), all having the same diameter. The camshaft is located in axial direction by the No. 1 bearing cap. Excessive end float is due to a worn bearing cap thrust face.
- Camshafts are marked with identification numbers. If a shaft is replaced, only fit a shaft with the same number.

1.3.0.3   Cylinder Head – Overhaul

The cylinder head must be thoroughly cleaned and remains of old gasket material removed. The checks and inspections are to be carried out as required.

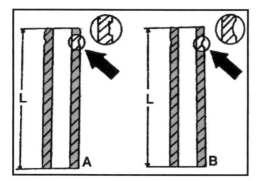

Fig. 1.19 – View of the earlier valve guides (A) and the later guides (B).

Valve Springs: If the engine has a high mileage, always replace the valve springs as a set. To check a valve spring, place the old spring and a new spring end to end over a long bolt (with washer under bolt head) and fit a nut (again with a washer). Tighten the nut until the springs are under tension and measure the length of the two springs. If the old spring is shorter by more than 10%, replace the complete spring set. When a spring tester is available, check the spring length when the loads given in Section 1.3.0.0. are applied.

The springs must not be distorted. A spring placed with its flat coil on a surface must not deviate at the top by more than 2 mm (0.08 in.).

Valve Guides: Valve guides for inlet and exhaust valves are made of cast iron and have the same diameter. Guides for exhaust valves are shorter. Valve guides have been modified in their length during production and only the shorter guides are available as replacement parts. These guides are marked as shown in Fig. 1.19 and only the guides shown in the R.H. view must be fitted to engines covered in this manual.

Clean the inside of the guides by pulling a petrol-soaked cloth through the guides. Valve stems can be cleaned best by means of a rotating wire brush. Measure the inside diameter of the guides. As an inside micrometer is necessary for this operation, which is not always available, you can insert the valve into its guide and withdraw it until the valve head is approx. level with the cylinder head face. Rock the valve to and fro and check for play. Although no exact values are available, it can be assumed that the play should not exceed 1.0 - 1.2 mm (0.04 -0.047 in.). Mercedes workshops use gauges to check the guides for wear.

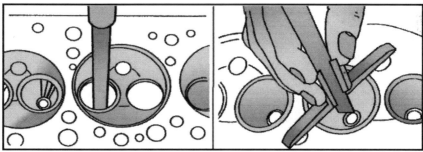

Fig. 1.20 – Pressing out a valve guide on the left and measuring the installation height of a guide on the right.

Guides are removed with a shouldered mandrel from the combustion chamber side of the cylinder head, as shown in Fig. 1.20. If guides with nominal dimensions can be used, drive them in position, until the dimension between the cylinder head face and the bottom end of the guide is 32.0 mm in the case of inlet valves or 43.5 mm in the case of exhaust valves. A tolerance of 0.5 mm is permissible. Measurement takes place as shown in Fig. 1.20 on the R.H. side. If repair guides are fitted, the locating bores in the cylinder head must be reamed out to take the new guides. As dry ice is required to fit the new valve guides, we recommend to have the work carried out in a workshop.

Before a valve guide is replaced, check the general condition of the cylinder head. The guides must be reamed after installation, and after the cylinder head has cooled down,

616 and 617 Diesel Engines

if applicable, to their correct internal diameter, given in Section 1.3.0.0 noting the different diameters for inlet and exhaust valves.

Valves must always be replaced if new valve guides are fitted. The valve seats must be re-cut when a guide has been replaced. If it is obvious that seats cannot be re-ground in the present condition, new valve seats inserts must be fitted and the work should be carried out in a workshop.

Valve Seats: If the camshaft bearings are excessively worn, fit a new or exchange cylinder head. In this case there is no need to renovate the valve seats.

Check all valve seats for signs of pitting or wear. Slight indentations can be removed with a cutter. If this operation is carried out properly, there should be no need to grind-in the valves. Use correction cutters to bring the valve seating area into the centre of the valve seat. Make sure that the valve seat width, given in Section 1.3.0.0. is obtained. This again is achieved by using cutters of different angles (15° and 60°). Valve seat inserts can be fitted to the cylinder head (workshop).

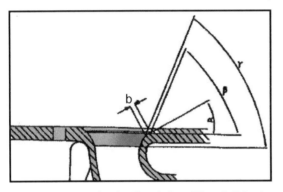

Fig. 1.21 – The important valve seat dimensions (Refer to Section 1.3.0.).

b   Valve seat width

Replacement of valve seat inserts will require that the old seat insert is removed by machining. The machining must not damage the bottom face of the head recess. As this is a critical operation, we advise you to bring the cylinder head to your Mercedes Dealer who has the necessary equipment and experience to do the job. Fig. 1.21 shows a valve seat. It may be possible to obtain a reconditioned cylinder head in exchange for the old one to avoid time delay. In this case remove all ancillary parts from the old head and refit them to the new head.

Fig. 1.22 – The dimension "a" must not exceed 1.5 mm for re-used and new valves.

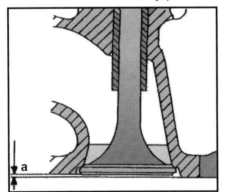

If the valve seats have been re-cut, use the valve and measure the dimension "a" in Fig. 1.22. To do this, insert the valve into the respective bore and, using a depth gauge, measure the gap between the cylinder head face and the valve face, as shown in Fig. 1.23.

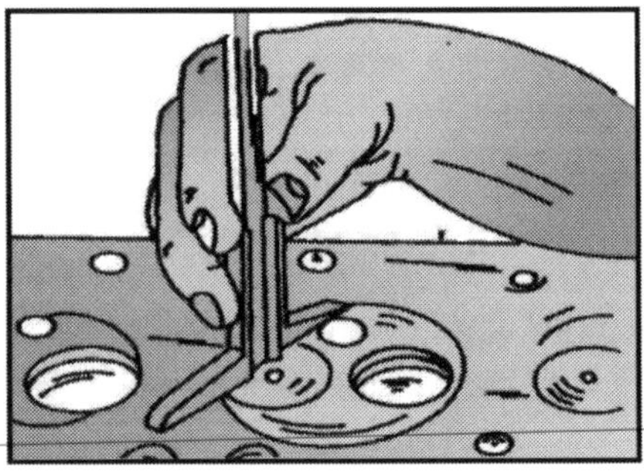

Fig. 1.23 – Measuring the distance between the valve head face and the cylinder head surface.

Valves can be ground into their seats in the conventional manner.

Valves: Valves can be cleaned best with a rotating wire brush. Check the valve faces for wear or grooving. If the wear is only slight, valves can be reground to their original angle in a valve grinding machine, but make sure that there is enough material left to have an edge on the valve head (min. 1.5 mm/0.06 in.), as shown by "h" in Fig. 1.24.

Measure the valves in accordance with the values given in Section 1.3.0.0. and replace any valve which is outside the limits given. Note the following when valves are replaced. Note that these valves are not filled with sodium, as is the case with other Mercedes engines.

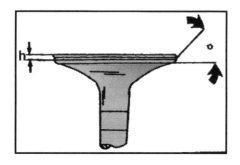

Fig. 1.24 – The valve head edge must be measured before a valve is refitted. The minimum permissible dimension is 1.5 mm.

Always quote the model year and the engine number when ordering new valves, as different valves are used. These are marked by means of a number in the end of the valve stem. The valves are marked as follows:

Inlet Valves: E 616 02

Exhaust Valves: A 616 05

Sometimes it is only required to replace the exhaust valves, if these for example are burnt out at their valve head edges.

Cylinder Head: Thoroughly clean the cylinder head and cylinder block surfaces of old gasket material and check the faces for distortion. To do this, place a steel ruler with a sharp edge over the cylinder head face and measure the gap between ruler and face with feeler gauges. Checks must be carried out in longitudinal and diagonal direction and across the face. If a feeler gauge of more than 0.10 mm (0.004 in.) can be inserted, when the ruler is placed along the cylinder head, have the cylinder head face re-ground. If the measurement is carried out across the cylinder head, there should be no gap. The min. height of the cylinder head must not be less than 84.0 mm (3.31 in.). If the cylinder head is reground, correct the fitting dimension of the valves ("a", Fig. 1.22) accordingly. This will, however, be a job for the workshop.

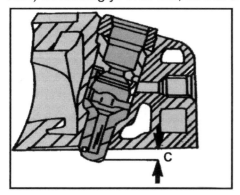

Fig. 1.25 – Dimension "C" shows the protrusion of a pre-combustion chamber above the cylinder head face.

A further check must be carried out on the pre-combustion chambers for the fuel injection as shown in Fig. 1.25. These must protrude by 7.6 - 8.3 mm (616 engine) or 5.5 – 5.9 mm (617 engine). Mercedes workshops correct this dimension by fitting sealing washers of different thicknesses, to correct the protrusion.

A further check must be carried out on the pre-combustion chambers for the fuel injection. These must protrude by 5.5 - 5.9 mm (0.21 - 0.23 in.), as shown by "C" in Fig. 1.25. Mercedes workshops correct this dimension by fitting sealing washers of different thicknesses, to correct the protrusion.

Camshaft: Place the camshaft with both end journals into "V" blocks or clamp the shaft between the centres of a lathe and apply a dial gauge to the centre journal. Slowly rotate the shaft to check for run-out. If the run-out exceeds 0.01 mm, fit a new shaft. The following points must be observed when replacing the camshaft:

*   The rocker arms must be replaced if a new camshaft is fitted.

*   Make sure to fit the correct shaft if the shaft is to be replaced. Check the identification in the shaft.

1.3.0.4.   Cylinder Head - Assembly

The assembly of the cylinder head is a reversal of the dismantling procedure, but the following points should be noted:

- Lubricate the valve stems with engine oil and insert the valves into the correct valve guides.

- Valve stem seals are different for different engines. Make sure to order the correct seals. The repair kit contains fitting sleeves and these must be used to fit the seals. The sleeves are fitted over the valve stem before the seal is pushed in position.

- Fit the valve spring and valve spring collar over the valve and use the valve lifter to compress the spring. Fit the locknut and the dome nut in reverse order to the removal procedure. The valves must be adjusted as described later on.

1.3.0.5.   Cylinder Head Cover – Removal and Installation

- Disconnect the crankcase ventilation hose from the side of the cylinder head cover. If an automatic transmission is fitted disconnect a vacuum hose from the switch-over valve on the cover. The connectors and the vacuum hoses are coloured and must not be interchanged.

Fig. 1.26 – Removal of the cylinder head cover.

- Disconnect all regulating linkages as described during the removal of the engine (see Fig. 1.5).

- Remove the cylinder head cover securing nuts and lift the cover off the cylinder head as shown in Fig. 1.26.

Check the gasket for damage and replace if necessary. Place the gasket over the cylinder head cover (use grease to keep it in position) and place the cover carefully over the cylinder head. Tighten the nuts evenly to 1.5 kgm.

The remaining operations are carried out in reverse order.

1.4.1.   PISTON AND CONNECTING RODS

1.4.1.0.   Technical Data

All dimensions are given in metric units.

Pistons (both engines)
Piston Diameter
- Standard:..90.98 mm
- Oversize 1:...90.99 mm
- Oversize 2:...91.009 mm
Piston Running Clearance:
- New:...0.02 – 0.03 mm
- Wear limit: ....0.12 mm

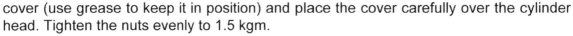

Max. weight difference within engine:
- New:...4 grams
- Wear limit: ....10 grams

Piston Pins:
Pin diameter:...25.995 – 26.000 mm
Piston pin running clearance:
- In small end bush:...0.012 – 0.023 mm

- In piston..0.000 – 0.001 mm

Piston Rings:
Piston Ring Gaps:
- Upper rings:...0.30 - 0.45 mm
  - Wear limit: ....1.5 mm
- Centre rings:..0.30 - 0.45 mm
  - Wear limit: ....1.0 mm
- Lower rings:.. 0.20 - 0.44 mm
  - Wear limit: ....1.0 mm
Side Clearance in Grooves:
- Upper rings:... 0.10 - 0.13 mm
  - Wear limit: ....0.20 mm
- Centre rings:... 0.07 - 0.102 mm
  - Wear limit: ....0.15 mm
- Lower rings:.. 0.030 - 0.062 mm
  - Wear limit: ....0.10 mm

Connecting Rods
Distance from centre small end bore to
    centre big end bore:...149.05 – 148.95 mm
Width of con rod at big end bore: ....32.10 – 32.08 mm
Basic bore diameter of big end bore: ....55.60 – 55.62 mm
Basic bore diameter of small end bore: ....29.000 – 29.02 mm
Small End Bush:
- Outer diameter:...29.096 – 29.058 mm
- Inner diameter:..26.012 – 26.018 mm
Max. twist of connecting rods:... 0.10 mm per 100 mm
Max. bend of connecting rods: .... 0.03 mm per 100 mm
Max. weight difference in same engine:.. 5 grams (per set)
Connecting Rod Bolts:
- Thread:.. M10 x 1
- Diameter of stretch neck: .... 8.4 mm
- Min. diameter of stretch neck: .... 8.0 mm
- Tightening torque of bolts:.............. 4.0 – 5.0 kgm, then 90° – 100° angle-tightening

Connecting rod bearing details:... See under "Crankshaft"

1.3.1.1.   Piston and Connecting Rods – Removal

The pistons are made of light-alloy. Each piston has a star-shaped cavity, a pre-combustion chamber and two round recesses for the valve heads. The exit of the pre-combustion chamber is connected with the combustion cavity.

Three piston rings are fitted to each piston. The two upper rings are the compression rings, i.e. they prevent the pressure above the piston crown to return to the crankcase. The lower ring is the oil scraper ring. Its function is to remove excessive oil from the cylinder bore, thereby preventing the entry of oil into the combustion chamber. The three rings are not the same in shape. The upper ring has a rectangular section, the centre ring has a chamfer on the inside and the lower ring is chrome-plated on its outside. Only the correct fitting of the piston rings will assure the proper operation of the piston sealing.

Pistons and connecting rods are pushed out towards the top of the cylinder bores, using a hammer handle alter connecting rod bearing caps and shells have been removed. Before removal of the assemblies note the following points:

- Pistons and cylinder bores are graded in three diameter classes within specified tolerance groups and marked with the numbers 0, 1 and 2. The class number is stamped into the upper face of the cylinder block, next to the particular cylinder bore. The class number of the piston must always be identical with the letter stamped next to the cylinder bore. This rule does, however, not apply to cylinder No. 1, as the piston running clearance is 0.01 mm more, i.e. for example if the cylinder bore is marked with "1" a piston marked with "0" can be fitted. A bore marked with "2" can be fitted with a piston marked "1" – Rather complicated.

- Since model year 1979 pistons with a smaller diameter are fitted (90.9 instead of 91.0 mm). If pistons are replaced you will have to note the difference (quote the model year, engine number, etc.). The combustion chambers have also be changed to adapt to the new pistons.

- The second piston ring has been changed during March 1981. The new piston rings can be fitted to earlier engines.

- Mark each piston and the connecting rod before removal with the cylinder number. This can be carried out by writing the cylinder number with paint onto the piston crown. Also mark an arrow, facing towards the front of the engine (the arrow in the piston crown will be covered by the carbon deposits). When removing the connecting rod, note the correct installation of the big end bearing cap. Immediately after removal mark the connecting rod and the big end bearing cap on the same side. This is best done with a centre punch (cylinder No. 1 one punch mark, etc.

- Mark the big end bearing shells with the cylinder number. The upper shells have an oil drilling (to lubricate the piston pin).

Fig. 1.27 – Removal of the securing clip for the piston pins. Apply the screwdriver blade at the ring gap.

- Big end bearing journals can be re-ground to four undersizes (in steps of 0.25 mm between sizes). Corresponding bearing shells are available.

- Remove the bearing caps and the shells and push the assemblies out of the cylinder bore. Any carbon deposits on the upper edge of the bores can be carefully removed with a scraper.

- Remove the piston pin snap rings. A notch in the piston pin bore enables a pointed drift to be inserted, as shown in Fig. 1.27, to remove the rings. Press the piston pins out of the pistons. If necessary heat the piston in boiling water.

- Remove the piston rings one after the other from the pistons, using a piston ring plier if possible. If the rings are to be re-used, mark them in accordance with their pistons and position.

1.3.1.2. Measuring the Cylinder Bores

An inside caliper is necessary to measure the diameter of the cylinder bores. The following operations are not possible if none is available or cannot be hired.

Cylinder bores must be measured in longitudinal and transverse direction and at three positions down the bore, i.e. 10 mm (0.4 in.) from the upper bore edge, 10 mm from the lower bore edge and once in the centre, totalling 6 measurements. The worst measurement must be taken when deciding on the size for the pistons to be fitted (Fig. 1.28).

Note that all cylinder bores must be re-bored, even if only one of the bores is outside the diameter limit. A tolerance of 0.20 mm is permissible. If the wear is outside the limits, it is possible to have new cylinder liners fitted to the block. Your dealer will advise you what can be done.

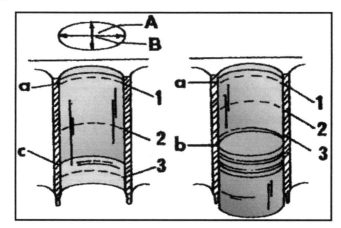

Fig. 1.28. - Measuring diagram for the cylinder bores. Numbers 1, 2 and 3 indicate the three levels where measurements should take place.

A = Measurement parallel to bore
B = Measurement across bore
a = Upper return point of
    upper piston ring

b = Bottom dead centre of piston
c = Lower return point of oil
    control ring
1-3 = Measuring points

The final cylinder bore diameter is determined after measuring the piston diameter. To measure the diameter, apply an outside micrometer 10 mm (0.4 in.) from the bottom edge and at right angle to the piston pin bore. Add the piston running clearance to this dimension and 0.03 mm for the honing of the cylinders. The piston running clearance must not exceed 0.12 mm.

To measure the running clearance, determine the piston and cylinder bore diameters as described above and calculate the difference between the dimensions.

If the difference is more than 0.12 mm, have the cylinder bores re-bored to fit oversize pistons.

1.3.1.3.   Checking Pistons and Connecting Rods

All parts should be thoroughly inspected. Signs of seizure, grooves or excessive wear require the part to be replaced. Check the pistons and connecting rods as follows:

- Check the side clearance of each piston ring in its groove by inserting the ring together with a feeler gauge. The grooves must be thoroughly cleaned before the check. If the wear limit exceed the values in the technical data is reached, either the rings or the piston are worn.

- Check the piston ring gap by inserting the ring from the bottom into the cylinder bore. Use a piston and carefully push the piston ring approx. 1 in. further into the bore. This will square it up. Insert a feeler gauge between the two piston ring ends to check the ring gap. Refer to Section 1.3.1.0. for the wear limits. Rings must be replaced, if these are exceeded. New rings should also be checked in the manner described.

- Piston pins and small end bushes must be checked for wear or seizure. One individual connecting rod can be replaced, provided that a rod of the same weight group is fitted. Connecting rods are marked with either one or two punch marks and only a rod with the same mark must be fitted.

- Before re-using the connecting rod bolts check their diameter at the position shown in Fig. 1.29. If this is smaller than given, replace the bolt. A second check is carried out by placing the connecting rod bearing on one of the connecting rod bolts, as shown in the R.H. view of Fig. 1.29. If the bearing cap is moving under its own weight, renew bolt.

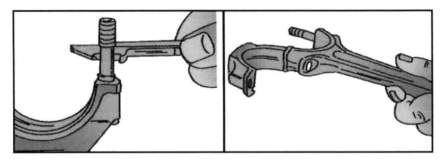

Fig. 1.29 – Measuring the diameter of the stretch bolts on the left. The R.H. view shows how the bolts can be checked for free movement.

• Connecting rods should be checked for bend or twist, particularly when the engine has covered a high mileage. A special jig is necessary for this operation and the job should be carried out by an engine shop. The max. values are given in Section 1.3.1.0.

Fig. 1.30 – When fitting a new small end bush make sure to align the oil drillings.

The following information concern the connecting rods:

• Connecting rods which were over-heated due to bearing failure (bluefish colour) must not be refitted.

• Connecting and bearing caps are matched to each other and must be fitted accordingly.

• New connecting rods are supplied together with the small end bearing bush and can be fitted as supplied.

• Fit the bearing cap with the inserted bearing shells, tighten the nuts to 4.0 – 5.0 kgm and a further one quarter of a turn and clamp the connecting rod into a vice. Using an internal micrometer, measure the big end bore diameter at various points. If the value of 55.62 mm is exceeded, or the bore is out of round, replace the complete connecting rod.

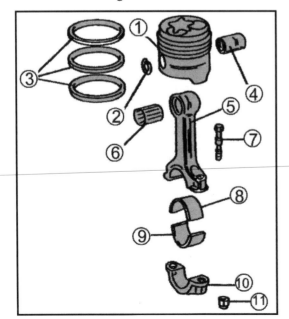

Fig. 1.31 – Component parts of a piston and a connecting rod.

2	Piston
3	Piston pin retaining ring
4	Piston rings
5	Piston pin
6	Connecting rod
7	Small end bush
8	Connecting rod bolt
9	Upper bearing shell
10	Lower bearing shell
11	Big end bearing cap
12	Bearing cap nuts

If the piston pin has excessive clearance in the small end bush, fit a new bush. When pressing in the new bush, align the oil bore in the bush with the oil bore in the connecting rod, as shown in Fig. 1.30. The small end bush must be reamed to a diameter of

26.012 – 26.018 mm to obtain the correct piston pin running clearance and again we recommend to have the job carried out by an engine shop.

1.3.1.4.   Checking the Big End Bearing Clearance

These operations are described in connection with the crankshaft.

1.3.1.5.   Piston and Connecting Rods - Assembly

If new pistons are fitted, check the piston crown markings to ensure the correct pistons are fitted. If the original pistons are fitted, arrange them in accordance with the cylinder number markings.

• Insert the connecting rod into the piston and align the two bores. Make sure that the arrow in the piston crown and locating lugs for the bearing shell location are facing the L.H. side of the engine.

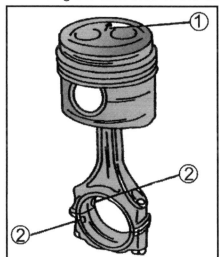

Fig. 1.32 – The arrow in the piston crown (1) must face the front end of the engine when the locating lugs for the bearing shells (2) are on the L.H. side of the cylinder block.

• Generously lubricate the piston pin with engine oil and insert it into the piston and connecting rod, using thumb pressure only. Never heat the piston to fit the piston pin. Fit the circlips to both sides of the piston, making sure of their engagement around the groove. Move the piston up and down to check for free movement.

• Using a pair of piston ring pliers, fit the piston rings from the top of the piston, starting with the bottom ring. The two compression rings could be mixed up corresponding care must be taken. Under no circumstances mix-up the upper and lower compression rings.

1.3.1.6.   Pistons and Connecting Rods - Installation

Generously lubricate the cylinder bores with oil. Markings on connecting rods and bearing caps must be opposite each other. The arrows in the piston crowns must face towards the front of the engine.

Fig. 1.33 – Fitting a piston with a piston ring compressor.

Arrange the piston rings at equal spacings of 120° around the circumference of the piston skirt and use a piston ring compressor to push the rings into their grooves. Check that all rings are fully pushed in (Fig. 1.33).

Insert the second bearing shell into the connecting rod bearing cap, with the locating tab on the L.H. side and fit the assembly over the connecting rod. Check that connecting rod/cap marks are facing each other.

Coat the contact areas for the cap bolts with engine oil and fit and tighten the bolts to 4.0 - 5.0 kgm in several stages. From this position tighten each bolt by a further 90° –

100° (approx. 1/4 of a turn) without using the torque wrench. It is assumed that the stretch bolts have been measured as previously described.

Rotate the crankshaft until the two remaining crankpins are at bottom dead centre and fit the two other piston/connecting rod assemblies in the same manner.

Check the pistons and connecting rods once more for correct installation and that each piston is fitted to its original bore, if the same parts are refitted.

With a feeler gauge measure the side clearance of each big end bearing cap on the crankpin. The wear limit is 0.50 mm.

Rotate the crankshaft until the pistons are at top dead centre and with a caliper measure the protruding end of each piston above the cylinder block face. The correct dimension is 0.65 – 1.05 mm in the case of a 616 engine or 0.50 – 0.90 mm in the case of a 617 engine.

1.3.2.2. CYLINDER BLOCK
1.3.2.0. Technical Data

Cylinder Bore Diameter (both engines): ....91.000 – 91.022 mm
Max. wear, longitudinal and across: ....0.20 mm
Max. out-of-round or taper of bores:
- New condition:..0.013 mm
- Wear limit: ....0.05 mm
Measuring point for bores: ....Upper edge, centre and lower edge,
in longitudinal and transverse

Note: Repair sizes are not available for this engine, as cylinder liners are supplied with nominal diameter.

Crankcase
Cylinder block height, new: ....242.80 – 242.90 mm
Cylinder block height, minimum: ....242.50 mm
Permissible unevenness of:
  Upper crankcase face: ....0.10 mm
  Lower crankcase face: ....0.05 mm
Difference between upper and lower sealing face: .... 0.10 mm (0.004 in.)

1.3.2.1. Servicing

Special attention should be given to the cylinder block each time the crankshaft has been removed, irrespective whether the bores are to be re-machined or not.

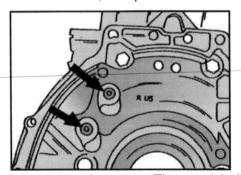

Fig. 1.34 – View of the rear end of the cylinder block, showing the steel ball for the main oil gallery.

Thoroughly clean all cavities and passages and remove all traces of foreign matter from the joint faces. If any machining or honing of the bores takes place, it is essential that all swarf is removed before assembly of the engine takes place. The main oil gallery is closed off by steel balls of 17 mm diameter at the front and 15 mm diameter at the rear. The steel balls must be removed in order to clean the main oil gallery. The steel balls can be refitted unless they show deep grooves. Figs. 1.34 shows where these steel balls are located. We must point out that the special drift 601

589 06 15 00 is used to drive the steel balls in position to ensure their correct seating. If possible always clean oil galleries with compressed air.

The following instructions apply to the advanced engineer:

If oil leaks can be detected at the front or rear of the cylinder block and the mentioned special drift cannot be obtained, it will be possible to close off the bores with threaded plugs.   At the front an M18 x 15 mm plug (Part No. 000906 0 18 000), at the rear an M16 x 15 mm plug (Part No. 000906 0 16 002) is used. Corresponding threads must be cut into the cylinder block. The thread depth at the front is 10 mm, at the rear 14 mm. Remove all metal chips and fit the plugs with "Loctite" thread locking agent before installation.

If the special drift can be obtained, replace the steel balls as follows (it is assumed that the engine is fitted):

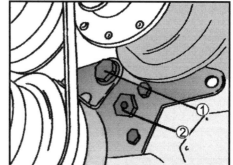

Fig. 1.35 – Remove the two plugs (Allen head bolt "2" and hexagonal head bolt "1" to remove the steel balls.

Steel ball in upper main oil gallery

- Remove the transmission and the flywheel and the radiator.
- Remove a plug and the Allen head bolt in Fig. 1.35.
- Use a steel rod of 13 mm diameter and 850 mm in length and drive out the steel balls from the rear towards the front. Thoroughly clean the main oil gallery.

Steel ball in upper main oil gallery

- Remove the transmission and the flywheel and the radiator.
- In the case of a 617 engine remove the accelerator shaft and the vibration damper.
- Remove the screw plug (2) in Fig. 1.35 near the crankshaft pulley. The plug (1) must be removed to replace the upper steel ball.
- Remove the oil sump and the oil pump.
- Remove the inner glide rail for the timing chain.
- Use a steel rod of 13 mm diameter and 850 mm in length and drive out the steel balls from the rear towards the front. Thoroughly clean the main oil gallery.

Fitting the steel balls

- Coat the ball-shaped recess of the special drift with grease and insert the ball.
- Insert the steel ball into the corresponding bore and drive it into position to its stop.
- Refit the all removed parts, i.e. oil pump, oil sump, flywheel, etc., as applicable and run the engine. Check the area of the steel ball for leaks.

Measurement of the cylinder bores should be made in accordance with the data given in Section 1.3.2.0. and the instructions in Section 1.3.1.2. The difference between the upper and the lower measurements gives the taper, the difference between the longitudinal and transverse measurements gives the out-of-round.

The cylinder block upper face and the crankcase lower face must be checked for distortion in a similar manner as described for the cylinder head. Section 1.3.2.0. gives the distortion values.

Replacing the Welsh Plugs: Welsh plugs are fitted into the side of the cylinder block. These plugs will be "pushed" out if the coolant has been allowed to freeze and can be replaced with the engine fitted, provided the special tool 102 589 07 15 00 can be obtained. On the side where the cylinder block drain plug is located you will find a plug of 34 mm diameter, on the opposite side, i.e. the side with the oil filter there are two more plugs with the same diameter. A further welsh plug of 17 mm diameter is fitted into the front end of the block. A plug of 34 mm diameter is also fitted to the rear end.

Welsh plugs can be replaced as follows:

- Drain the cooling system and remove all parts obstructing the welsh plug in question, i.e. transmission, intermediate flange, injection pump, etc.
- Place a small chisel or strong screwdriver blade below the lip of the welsh plug and drive the plug towards the inside until it has swivelled by 90° Then grip the plug with a pair of pliers, as shown in Fig. 1.36 and remove it.

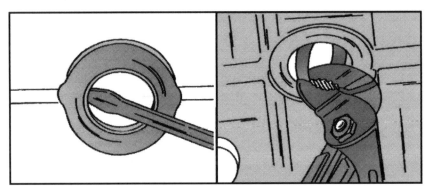

Fig. 1.36 – Removal of a welsh plug.

Thoroughly clean the opening in the cylinder head from grease and coat the locating bore with "Loctite 241". Fit the large new welsh plug with the special tool mentioned above. Drift No. 602 589 07 15 00 is required for the 17 mm plug.

- Refit all removed parts and allow the vehicle to stand for at least 45 minutes before the cooling system is filled and the engine is started. Then start the engine and check for coolant leaks.

Note: Replacement cylinder liners are available for the engine. Check with your dealer before considering replacement of the cylinder block.

1.3.3. CRANKSHAFT AND BEARINGS

1.3.3.0. Technical Data

All dimensions in metric units.
Machining tolerances:

Max. out-of-round of journals:	0.010 mm
Max. taper of main journals:	0.010 mm
Max. taper of crankpins:	0.015 mm
Max. run-out of main journals*:	
Journals Nos. II and IV (II and V 617 engine):	0.07 mm
Journal No. II I (III and IV 617 engine):	0.10 mm

     * Crankshaft placed with outer journals in "V" blocks.

Main Bearing Journal Diameter:
Nominal:	69.98 – 69.95 mm
1st repair size:	69.71 – 69.70 mm
2nd repair size:	69.46 – 69.45 mm
3rd repair size:	69.21 – 69.20 mm
4th repair size:	68.96 – 69.95 mm

Width of Journal on fitted Bearing:
Nominal dimension:	34.00 – 34.03 mm
Repair size:	to 34.63 mm

Crankpin Diameter:
 Nominal dimension:... 51.95 - 51.96 mm
 1st repair size:... 51.70 - 51.71 mm
 2nd repair size:... 51.45 - 51.46 mm
 3rd repair size: .... 51.20 - 51.21 mm
 4th repair size:.. 50.95 - 50.96 mm

Width of Crankpins:
 Nominal Dimension :... 32.00 - 31.10 mm
 Repair sizes: ....Up to 32.20 mm

Bearing Running Clearances:
 Main bearings:..0.03 - 0.07 mm (best 0.055 mm)
 Big end bearings: ....0.03 - 0.07 mm (best 0.50 mm)
 Wear limit: .... 0.080 mm
Bearing End Float:
 Main bearings:... 0.10 - 0.24 mm
 Big end bearings: .... 0.12 - 0.25 mm
 Wear limit - Main bearings: .... 0.30 mm
 Wear limit - Big end bearings: .... 0.50 mm

Bearing Shells:

	Main Bearings	Big End Bearings
Nominal Dimension:	2.25 mm	1.80 mm
1st repair size:	2.37 mm	1.92 mm
2nd repair size:	2.50 mm	2.05 mm
3rd repair size:	2.62 mm	2.17 mm
4th repair size:	2.75 mm	2.30 mm

Connecting Rod Bolts:
 Thread: . . . . M10 x 1
 Diameter of stretch neck: . . . . 8.4 mm
 Min. diameter of stretch neck: . . . . 8.0 mm
Tightening torque: . . . . 4.0 – 5.0 kgm (29 – 36 ft.lb.) + 90° – 100°

1.3.3.1.   Crankshaft - Removal and Installation

The engine must be removed to take out the crankshaft. The operations are similar on all engines.

* Remove the transmission from the engine. Take care not to distort the clutch shaft.
* Counterhold the flywheel in suitable manner and evenly slacken the clutch securing bolts. Use a centre punch and mark the clutch and flywheel at opposite points. Lift off the clutch plate and the driven plate. Immediately clean the inside of the flywheel and unscrew the flywheel.
* Remove the drive plate for a torque converter of an automatic transmission in the same manner.
* With the flywheel still locked, remove the crankshaft pulley bolt and remove the crankshaft pulley/damper as described later on.
* Remove the cylinder head as described in Section 1.2.1. and the timing cover as described in Section 1.3.4. Remove the oil sump and oil pump.
* Remove the pistons and connecting rods as described in Section 1.3.1.

Fig. 1.37 – Checking the crankshaft end float.

- The crankshaft end float should be checked before the crankshaft is removed. To do this, place a dial gauge with a suitable holder in front of the cylinder block and place the gauge stylus against the end flange of the crankshaft, as shown in Fig. 1.37. Use a screwdriver to push the crankshaft all the way to one end and set the gauge to "0". Push the shaft to the other side and note the dial gauge reading. The resulting value is the end float. If it exceeds 0.50 mm replace the thrust washers during assembly, but make sure to fit washers of the correct width. These are located left and right at the centre bearing. Note that only two washers of the same thickness must be fitted.

- Unscrew the oil seal flange from the rear of the cylinder block.

- Unscrew the main bearing bolts evenly across. The bearings caps are marked with the numbers 1 to 5 or 1 to 6, depending on the engine. The numbers are stamped into the centre of the caps, as shown in Fig. 1.38. No. 1 cap is located at the crankshaft pulley side.

Fig. 1.38 – The arrows show the numbering of the main bearing caps. Caps must be fitted in their original order.

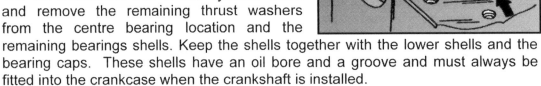

- Remove the bearing shells from the bearing journals (they could also stick to the caps) and immediately mark them on their back faces with the bearing number.

- Lift the crankshaft out of the cylinder block and remove the remaining thrust washers from the centre bearing location and the remaining bearings shells. Keep the shells together with the lower shells and the bearing caps. These shells have an oil bore and a groove and must always be fitted into the crankcase when the crankshaft is installed.

1.3.3.2.   Inspection of Crankshaft and Bearings

Main and crankpin journals must be measured with precision instruments to find their diameters. All journals can be re-ground four times and the necessary bearing shells are available, i.e. undersize shells can be fitted.

Place the crankshaft with the two end journals into "V" blocks and apply a dial gauge to the centre main journal. Rotate the crankshaft by one turn and read off the dial gauge. If the reading exceeds 0.06 mm, replace the crankshaft.

Check the main bearing and big end bearing running clearance as follows:

- Bolt the main bearing caps without shells to the crankcase, oil the bolt threads and fit each cap. Tighten the bolts to 9.0 kgm (65 ft.lb.). Bearing caps are offset and can only be fitted in one position.

- Referring to Fig. 1.39 measure the bearing bores in directions A, B and C and write down the results. If the basic diameter is exceeded (see Section 1.3.3.0.), the bearing cap and/or the cylinder block must be replaced.

- Remove the bearing caps and refit them, this time with the well cleaned bearing shells. Re-tighten the bolts as specified.

- Measure the diameter of each bearing in accordance as shown in Fig. 1.39 and write down the results. Deduct the journal diameter from the bearing diameter.

The resulting difference is the bearing running clearance, which should be between 0.031 - 0.073 mm, with a wear limit of 0.080 mm.

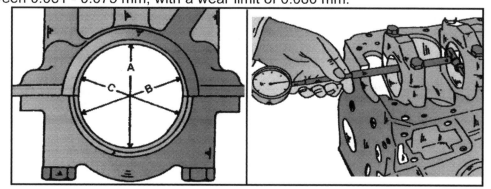

Fig. 1.39 – Measuring the inside diameter of the fitted bearing shells and the inner diameter of the fitted bearings.

• Check the big end bearing clearances in a similar manner, but bolt the bearing caps to the connecting rods. Tighten the nuts to the value given in the technical data. The bearing clearance should be between 0.031 - 0.073 mm, with the same wear limit.

Selection of bearing shells is rather complicated, and we advise you to take the cylinder block to an engine shop, if the above measurements have revealed that new bearing shells are necessary.

1.3.3.3. Crankshaft - Installation

Thoroughly clean the bearing bores in the crankcase and insert the shells with the drillings into the bearing bores, with the tabs engaging the notches. Fit the thrust washers to the centre bearing, with the oil grooves towards the outside. Use the two forefingers to hold the thrust washers against the bearing cap and fit the cap in position.

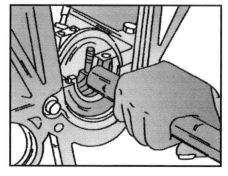

Fig. 1.40 – Fitting the oil seal into the crankcase. Use a hammer handle to push the seal in position.

Fit a new oil seal into the crankcase. Use a hammer handle to work the seal into the bore, as shown in Fig. 1.40. The protruding end of the seal must be cut to leave 0.6 mm above the crankcase face, as can be seen in Fig. 1.41.

Fig. 1.41 – After cutting the ends of the fitted oil seal make sure that the ends protrude as shown.

Lift the crankshaft in position and fit the bearing caps with the inserted shells (again shells well oiled and locating tabs in notches). Fit the two thrust washers to the centre bearing cap, as shown in Fig. 1.42, again with the oil groove towards the outside. Place this cap in position, guiding the two thrust washers in order not to dislodge them. Use the forefingers, as shown in Fig. 1.42, to hold the

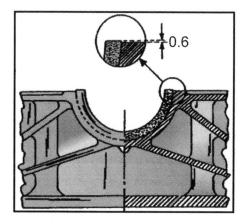

washers. Note that the thrust washers have been changed. Quote the engine number when new washers are ordered.

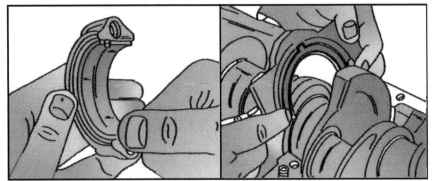

Fig. 1.42 – Fitting a bearing shell and a thrust washer into the bearing cap.

Check the numbering of the bearing caps and fit the well oiled bolts. Tighten the bolts from the centre towards the outside in several steps to a torque reading of 9.0 kgm (65 ft.lb.) if bolts with hexagonal heads are used. If the bolts have a double-hexagonal head and a shoulder, tighten them to 5.5 kgm (39.5 ft.lb.) and from this position a further 90° – 100°.

Rotate the crankshaft a few times to check for binding (hard spots).

Re-check the crankshaft end float as described during removal. Attach the dial gauge to the crankcase as shown in Fig. 1.37. The remaining operations are carried out in reverse order to the removal procedure. The various sections give detailed description of the relevant operations, i.e. piston and connecting rods, rear oil seal flange, timing mechanism, flywheel and clutch or drive plate, oil pump, oil sump and cylinder head.

1.3.3.4.   Flywheel or Drive Plate (Automatic)

Figs. 1.43 shows the end of the crankshaft together with the flywheel and the driven plate respectively. Always check the height of the old flywheel before fitting a new one. Both flywheel and drive plate can be replaced with the engine fitted, but the help of a workshop is required when the flywheel is replaced. You will have to take the old flywheel and the new flywheel to the workshop to have them re-balanced. Proceed as described:

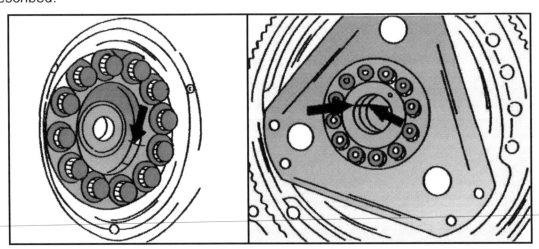

Fig. 1.43 – The arrow points to the alignment bore in flywheel and crankshaft flange (left). Drive plates are drilled in the same manner (right).

- Remove the transmission (Section 3.1.).
- Counterhold the flywheel in suitable manner and remove the clutch after having marked its relationship to the flywheel. Remove the drive plate in a similar manner. 8 bolts are used to secure the flywheel. A hole has been drilled between two of the bores and a similar hole is drilled into the crankshaft. These two bolts

must be aligned when the flywheel or the drive plate is fitted. Fig. 1.43 shows the alignment bore in the case of the flywheel. The drive plate has a similar hole.

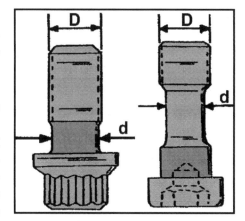

Fig. 1.44 – Stretch bolts must be measured between the arrows "d". "D" indicates the thread diameter. On the L.H. side for a flywheel, on the R.H. side for the driven plate.

*   Remove the flywheel or the drive plate. Distance washers are used in the case of the drive plate, which can also be removed. Measure the diameter of the mounting bolts at their smallest section (stretch neck). If less than 8.1 mm in the case of the flywheel or 7.3 mm in the case of the drive plate, replace the bolts. The measurement is carried out as shown in Fig. 1.44 and explained earlier on for the connecting rod bolts.

*   If the flywheel or the starter ring looks worn, take the wheel to your dealer to have the flywheel re-machined and/or the ring gear replaced.

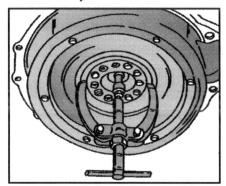

Fig. 1.45 – Removal of the ball bearing inside the crankshaft. The flywheel must be fitted.

To replace the ring gear of a drive plate, unscrew the ring gear with the steel ring from the drive plate. When refitting the new ring gear, align the bores for the ring gear mounting and the converter and on the drive plate.

Fit the flywheel or the drive plate with the alignment bores in line. Fit a distance washer underneath and on top of the drive plate. Tighten the bolts evenly across to 3.0 - 4.0 kgm (22 - 29 ft.lb.) and from this position a further 90° – 100°. The angle is important to give the stretch bolts their correct tension.

Engines for manual transmissions are fitted with a ball bearing in the end of the crankshaft. A retaining ring is used to hold the bearing in position and must be removed to withdraw the ball bearing with a suitable puller, as shown in Fig. 1.45. Grease the new bearing with heat-resistant grease and drive it into the crankshaft bore. Fit the retaining ring after installation.

1.3.3.5. Crankshaft Pulley, Vibration Damper and Pulley Hub

The engine is fitted with a crankshaft pulley and a vibration damper. The mounting bolts for the crankshaft pulley are automatically aligned if a dowel pin in inserted into the corresponding bore.

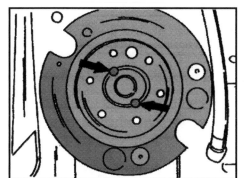

Fig. 1.46 – The arrows show the dowel pins to locate the hub on the crankshaft.

Remove the parts as follows, noting that a puller may be necessary to withdraw the hub:

*   Remove the radiator and the cooling fan.
*   Release the tension of the drive belt, as described under a different heading.
*   Engage a gear and apply the handbrake to lock the engine against rotation. In the case of a vehicle with automatic transmission remove the starter motor and lock the starter motor ring gear in suitable manner.

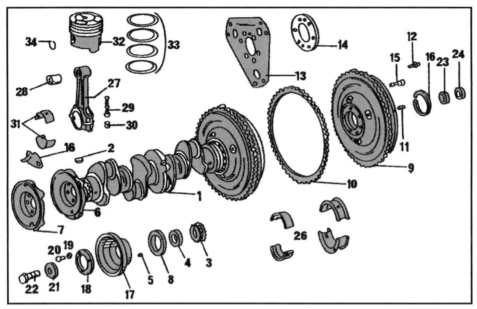

Fig. 1.47 – Exploded view of crankshaft together with main bearings, piston and connecting rods and other parts.

1 Crankshaft	13 Plate, A/T	25 Tensioning ring
2 Woodruff key	14 Washer	26 Main bearing shells
3 Crankshaft timing sprocket	15 Flywheel bolt	27 Connecting rod
4 Spacer ring	16 Rear oil seal	28 Small end bush
5 Dowel pin	17 Crankshaft puller	29 Connecting rod bolt
6 Balancing disc	18 Intermediate spacer	30 Nut
7 Vibration damper	19 Plain washer	31 Big end bearing shells
8 Front crankshaft oil seal	20 Bolt	32 Piston
9 Flywheel	21 Washer	33 Piston rings
10 Flywheel ring gear	22 Crankshaft pulley bolt	34 Piston pin circlip
11 Dowel pin	23 Ball bearing in flywheel	
12 Stretch bolt	24 Washer	

• Unscrew the crankshaft pulley, together with the vibration damper in the case of a 617 engine.

• Remove the centre bolt from the crankshaft pulley hub and withdraw the hub with a suitable puller. Make a note of the fitting position of the three spring discs, as they must face the same way during installation. The hub is located on the crankshaft by means of two dowel pins, as shown in Fig. 1.46.

The crankshaft pulley has a certain diameter. If replaced, quote the engine type and number.

The installation of the crankshaft pulley and the hub or the vibration damper proceed as follows:

• Rotate the crankshaft until the Woodruff key is visible and slide the hub with the key way over the key and the shaft end. Make sure that the dowel pins are in position. Place the three spring discs correctly over the centre bolt, coat the bolt threads with engine oil and fit the bolt. Tighten the bolt to 27.0 to 33.0 kgm. The crankshaft must still be locked against rotation.

• Fit the vibration damper (616 engine) and the crankshaft pulley.

• The remaining operations are carried out in reverse order.

1.3.3.6.   Rear Crankshaft Oil Seal and Oil Seal Carrier

The rear crankshaft oil seal is located in the rear crankshaft bearing and the engine and crankshaft must be removed to replace the sealing ring. Apply two screwdrivers and carefully lever the oil seal out of the groove in the crankcase.

Insert the new oil seal into the crankcase (well lubricated with engine oil) and work it in position as already shown in Fig. 1.40. To obtain the protrusion of the seal ends cut off the ends to obtain the dimension shown in Fig. 1.41.

1.3.3.7.   Front Crankshaft Oil Seal

The front crankshaft oil seal is located in the timing cover, but different types of oil seal are used in production, depending on the type of spacer washer fitted below the oil seal. When replacing the oil seal is therefore necessary to check the type of spacer washer fitted. Take it to your parts supplier to obtain the correct seal. Oil leaks at this position can also be caused by a leaking timing cover gasket. Check before replacing the oil seal.

The radiator and cooling fan, the hub or the vibration damper (617 engine) and the crankshaft pulley must be removed as already described before the oil seal can be replaced. The seal can be carefully removed with a screwdriver. Screw a self-tapping screw into the outside of the seal and apply the screwdriver plate under the screw head. If the spacer ring on the crankshaft shows signs of wear, remove it with a suitable puller.

Thoroughly clean the surrounding parts. Burrs on the timing cover bore can be removed with a scraper. Fill the space between sealing lip and dust protection lip with grease and carefully drive a new oil seal into the timing cover and over the crankshaft until the ring outer face is flush. Refit the vibration damper or hub as described in Section 1.3.3.5. and refit the radiator and the cooling fan. Fig. 1.47 shows the crankshaft together with the associated parts.

1.4.   Timing Mechanism and Rocker Shafts

The component parts covered in this section can all be removed with the engine fitted to the vehicle. The endless timing chain is fitted over the camshaft sprocket, the injection pump sprocket and the crankshaft sprocket. The chain is guided by two slide rails and is held under tension by means of a hydraulic chain tensioner, which is fitted to the crankcase and pushes against a light alloy tensioning rail.

The camshaft sprocket is secured to the camshaft by means of a bolt and is located by a Woodruff key.

1.4.0.   Removal and Installation of Rocker Mechanism

The following points must be noted when the rocker arms are replaced:

Fig. 1.48 – The arrows show the location of the rocker arm securing screws.

- Rocker arms must be refitted to their original location if re-used.
- The camshaft must be replaced if any of the rocker arms require renewal. The removal of a rocker arm, with the engine fitted, is carried out as follows:
- Remove the cylinder head cover. If an automatic transmission is fitted, disconnect the vacuum lines from their connections. Connections and hoses are colour-coded and must be re-connected accordingly.
- Disconnect the throttle operating linkage as described during the removal of the engine.

- Rotate the camshaft until all rocker arms are without tension, i.e. the cam tips must be free of the rocker arms. To rotate the engine apply a socket and a ratchet to the crankshaft pulley bolt.
- Use a suitable Allen key and remove the rocker arm pedestal bolts, shown in Fig. 1.48 by the arrows.
- Remove the rocker arm pedestals after marking their fitted position. Sticking pedestals can be freed with a plastic or rubber mallet.

Rocker arms and camshaft have been modified during production of these engines. Quote the engine type and number when new parts are required. To replace a rocker arm, proceed as follows:

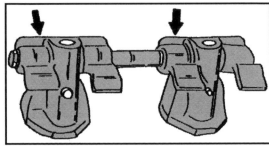

Fig. 1.49 – The position of the wire clip on the rocker arm pedestal.

- Remove the wire clips, shown in Fig. 1.49, from the rocker arms. Referring to Fig. 1.50, remove the tension spring, i.e. the wire clip (6), the pedestals (2) and the rocker arms from the rocker arm shaft (4). Generously oil the new parts and refit in reverse order to the rocker arm shaft.

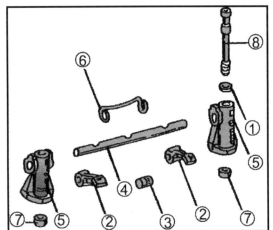

Fig. 1.50 – The component parts of the rocker shaft mounting.

1	Washer
2	Rocker arm
3	Bush in rocker arm
4	Rocker arm shaft
5	Rocker shaft pedestal
6	Wire clip
7	Dowel sleeve
8	Stretch bolt

- Fit one of the wire clip loops over the rocker arm shaft and insert the wire clip into the notch of the rocker arm shaft pedestal. Fig. 1.51 shows the fitted wire clip.

Fig. 1.51 – The arrow shows where the wire clip is fitted to the rocker arm pedestal.

Fit the rocker shafts as follows:

- Place the assembled rocker shaft assembly in position. Rocker shaft pedestals are located by dowel sleeves at the bottom faces.
- Tighten all bolts to 3.8 kgm (27.5 ft.lb.) in several stages. Check that none of the rocker arms are under tension whilst the bolts are tightened, i.e. the cams must be in a similar position as shown in Fig. 1.52.
- Adjust the valve clearances as described later on and refit the cylinder head cover. Tighten the nuts to 0.5 kgm (3.5 ft.lb.).

1.4.1.   Camshaft – Removal and Installation

Note the following points if a camshaft is to be replaced:

- If a new camshaft is fitted, also replace the rocker arms.
- Worn camshaft bearing journals can be re-ground. Camshaft bearing shells are available in two undersizes.

Fig. 1.52 – The cam tips must be facing away from the rocker lever before the bearing caps are tightened.

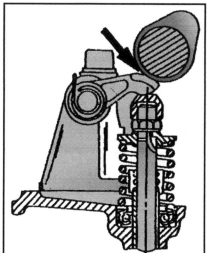

- All camshafts are marked with a number in their end face. Most engines have camshafts with camshaft identification "06", but always check with your parts supplier if a camshaft is purchased.

Remove the camshaft with the engine fitted as follows:

- Drain the cooling system.
- Remove the cylinder head cover.
- Remove the rocker shaft mechanism as described in the last section and the slide rail as described later on.
- Rotate the crankshaft by applying a socket and a ratchet to the crankshaft pulley bolt until the piston of No. 1 cylinder is at top dead centre firing point.
- Remove the chain tensioner. Section 1.4.2 gives further details of these operations.
- Using paint, mark the timing chain and the camshaft sprocket at opposite points, as shown during the removal of the cylinder head.
- Insert a strong steel rod into one of the openings in the sprocket, rest the rod against the cylinder head and remove the bolt securing the camshaft sprocket to the shaft. Remove the shim.
- Remove the camshaft bearing cap bolts with a 10 mm Allen key one after the other. Also remove the M8 nuts.
- Remove the camshaft together with the bearing caps and the oil lubrication pipe. The bearing caps are located by means of dowel sleeves and a rubber mallet may be required to free them from the cylinder head.
- Withdraw the camshaft towards the rear out of the camshaft bearing caps.

Fit the camshaft as follows:

- Coat the bearing journals, bearings and cams with engine oil and insert the camshaft from the rear into the camshaft bearings.
- Place the camshaft with the bearings and the oil lubrication pipe over the cylinder head, taking care to engage the dowel pins.
- Tighten the camshaft bearing caps. Tighten the M8 nuts to 2.5 kgm (18 ft.lb.). Turn the camshaft by hand to check for binding. If heavy spots can be found, slacken each bearing cap one after the other, every time rotating the camshaft. The "heavy" bearing can be found in this manner. Remove the camshaft and "level" the respective bearing on a surface plate with fine sandpaper.
- Fit the shim over the end of the camshaft and fit the camshaft sprocket and timing chain over the camshaft, aligning the paint marks accordingly. Insert a strong steel rod into one of the openings of the sprocket and tighten the bolt to 8.0 kgm (58 ft.lb.).
- Refit the remaining parts as described in the relevant sections, adjust the valve clearances and fit the cylinder head cover.

1.4.2.   Removal and Installation of Chain Tensioner

Note the following points before removal of the chain tensioner:
- The chain tensioner must be filled with oil before installation. A faulty tensioner must always be replaced.

616 and 617 Diesel Engines

Remove the chain tensioner as follows:
- Drain the cooling system.
- Remove the thermostat housing (disconnect the coolant hoses).
- Unscrew the chain tensioner and remove. Check the "O" sealing rings, one on the shaft and the other one inside the bore (if fitted) and if necessary replace.

Refit the chain tensioner as follows. Fig. 1.53 shows where the tensioner is located, together with other parts of the timing mechanism:

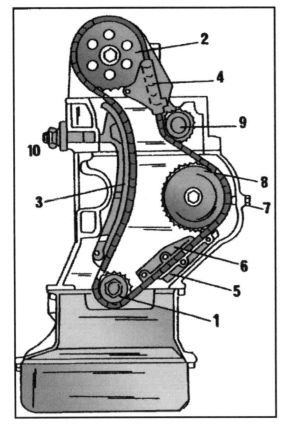

Fig. 1.53 – View of the timing mechanism.
1   Crankshaft timing sprocket
2   Camshaft timing sprocket
3   Tensioning rail
4   Slide rail
5   Outer slide rail
6   Inner slide rail
7   Chain arrester
8   Injection pump sprocket
9   Intermediate sprocket
10   Chain tensioner

- Fill the chain tensioner with oil. This requires the use of a hand press and a glass jar, filled with SAE 10 engine oil. Hold the tensioner on the thrust bolt and insert up to the flange into the oil. Using the hand press, push the thrust bolt about 7 to 10 times into the tensioner. As the tensioner is filled with oil, the pressure required to compress the tensioner will increase.
- Fit a new gasket or "O" seals and fit the chain tensioner. Tighten the bolts evenly.
- Refit all other parts in reverse order and fill the cooling system.

1.4.3. Removal and Installation of Timing Chain

Fig. 1.53 shows the arrangement of the timing chain. The following operations can be carried out by referring to this illustration. Note the following points before commencing any operation:
- A hand-held grinding machine must be available to replace the timing chain with the engine fitted. The new timing chain has a chain lock to connect the two chain ends.
- When an engine has been dismantled, always fit an endless timing chain.
- Before a new timing chain is fitted, check all sprockets. Worn sprocket teeth will very soon wear the new chain.
- Timing chains have been modified during the production of the engine. Always quote the engine type, engine number and model year of the vehicle.

Replace the timing chain with the engine fitted as follows:
- Unscrew the glow plugs. A special wrench of 20.8 mm across the flats is used for this operation. A 21 mm ring spanner can be used in emergency.
- Remove the cylinder head cover.
- Remove the chain tensioner (Section 1.4.2).

- Cover the chain chamber with rags to prevent grinding particles from falling inside and cut both chain bolts by grinding down one link of the timing chain. Do not remove the chain at this stage.
- Connect the new timing chain with the connecting link to the old chain, at the same time pushing out the old link.
- Slowly rotate the crankshaft in direction of rotation, using a 27 mm socket applied to the crankshaft pulley bolt. The timing chain must remain in engagement with the camshaft sprocket whilst the crankshaft is rotated. Do not turn the camshaft by applying a spanner to the sprocket bolt.

Fig. 1.54 – Marking of the camshaft.

- Disconnect the old timing chain from the new chain and push the new connecting link from the inside towards the outside through the two chain ends. Secure the link with the lock washers from the front. Temporarily attach the timing chain to the camshaft sprocket (on both sides), to prevent the chain from falling into the timing chamber.
- Rotate the crankshaft until the piston of No. 1 cylinder is at TDC firing point and check that the timing marks on the camshaft sprocket are aligned as shown in Fig. 1.54. The chain is correctly fitted if this is the case. Otherwise the chain has moved by one tooth.
- Carry out all other operations in reverse order.

1.4.4 Tensioning Rail - Replacement

The location of the tensioning rail can be taken from Fig. 1.53. A slide hammer and a threaded adapter, to be screwed into the bearing bolt, are required to remove the tensioning rail. The tensioning rail is marked for 4- and 5-cylinder engines. The tensioning rail for a 4-cylinder engine has no hole at the upper end and is also wider. Remove the tensioning rail as follows:

- Remove the radiator and the cooling fan.
- Remove cylinder head cover
- Remove the crankshaft pulley in the case of a 616 engine or the pulley and the vibration damper in the case of a 617 engine. Description. See earlier on.

Fig. 1.55 – Removal of the bearing bolt for the tensioning rail, using an impact hammer and a threaded adapter.

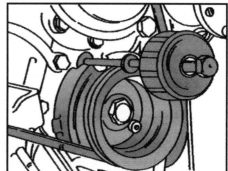

- Rotate the crankshaft in the direction of rotation using a 27 mm socket and ratchet, applied to the crankshaft pulley bolt (fit the bolt back in place), until the opening in the balance disc appears opposite the bearing bolt for the tensioning rail.
- Using paint, mark the relationship between the timing chain and the crankshaft sprocket, similar, as shown in Fig. 1.12 for the camshaft sprocket and mark the camshaft sprocket and chain as shown in this illustration.
- Remove the slide rail or slide rails from the cylinder head (refer to next section).
- Push back the thrust bolt of the chain tensioner.

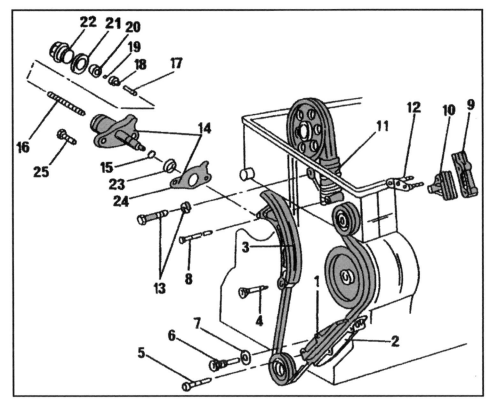

Fig. 1.56 – Exploded view of the timing mechanism.

1 Slide rail	10 Slide rail	19 Steel ball
2 Slide rail	11 Slide rail	20 Ball bearing
3 Slide rail	12 Bracket	21 Sealing ring
4 Bolt	13 Bolt/washer	22 Screw plug
5 Bolt	14 Chain tensioner	23 Sealing ring
6 Bolt	15 Retaining ring	24 Sealing washer
7 Sealing ring	16 Spring	25 Bolt
8 Bearing bolt	17 Bolt	
9 Slide rail	18 Ball bearing	

- Counterhold the camshaft by inserting a strong steel rod into one of the openings of the camshaft sprocket and remove the sprocket bolt. Remove the camshaft sprocket.
- Fit the slide hammer with a suitable threaded adapter into the end of the bearing bolt and withdraw the bearing bolt by hitting the weight of the slide hammer against its stop (Fig. 1.55). Remove the tensioning rail towards the top.

The installation of the tensioning rail is a reversal of the removal procedure. Coat the outside of the bearing bolt with sealing compound, arrange the tensioning rail in the correct position and fit the bearing bolt, again using the slide hammer. Fit the camshaft sprocket, counterhold the camshaft and tighten the camshaft sprocket bolt to 8.0 kgm (58 ft.lb.). When fitting the timing chain to the camshaft sprocket make sure that the paint marks are in line, as shown in Fig. 1.12.

1.4.5. Slide Rails - Removal and Installation

The position of the slide rails is shown in Fig. 1.53. To remove a slide rail, a slide hammer with a suitable, threaded adapter is required, to remove the bearing bolts. The bolt is screwed into the end of the bearing bolt and the impact hammer (slide hammer) attached to the end of the bolt (Fig. 1.55). Provided that these tools can be obtained, the rails can be removed as described below. Remove the slide rail (4) in Fig. 1.53 as follows:

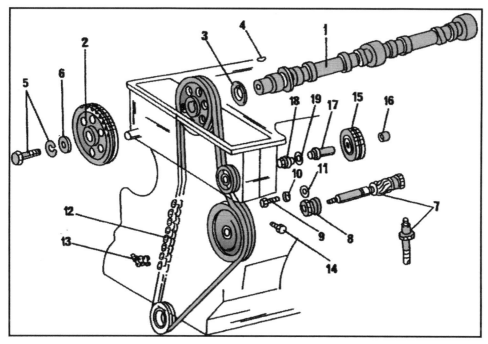

Fig. 1.57 – Exploded view of camshaft and timing chain parts.

1 Camshaft	8 Bearing	15 Tensioning sprocket
2 Camshaft sprocket	9 Bolt	16 Bush
3 Spacer washer	10 Spring washer	17 Bearing spigot
4 Woodruff key	11 Washer	18 Screw plug
5 Bolt/washer	12 Roller chain	19 Sealing ring
6 Washer	13 Chain link	
7 Intermediate shaft	14 Bolt	

- Remove cylinder head cover.
- Remove the bolt shown in Fig. 1.55 and remove the bracket from the slide rail. Remove the slide rail bearing bolt with the slide hammer and the threaded adapter and remove the outer slide rail towards the top.
- Coat the new or original bearing bolt on the flange with sealing compound, position the slide rail in the correct position and drive in the bearing bolt. Counterhold the slide rail during the bearing bolt installation with a screwdriver to prevent distortion.
- The remaining installation is a reversal of the removal procedure.

Replace the slide rail (6) in Fig. 1.53 as follows:
- Remove the radiator and the cooling fen and the vacuum pump for the operation of the brake servo unit.
- Remove the crankshaft pulley or the crankshaft pulley and the vibration damper, depending on the engine.
- Remove the cylinder head cover and the injection pump timing advancer.
- Remove the screw plug with the upper bearing bolt and remove the lower bearing bolt by means of the impact hammer and a threaded adapter.
- Remove the slide rail towards the top.
- Coat the new or the original bearing bolt with sealing compound, position the slide rail and drive in the bearing bolt with the impact hammer. The guide lug of the slide rail must engage with the location groove in the bearing bolt.
- Carry out the remaining operations in reverse order to the removal procedures.

Replace the slide rail (5) in Fig. 1.53 as follows:
- Remove the radiator, cooling fan and the vacuum pump for the brake servo unit.
- Remove the cylinder head cover and the injection timing advancer.

- Remove both bearing bolts for the slide rail by means of the impact hammer and a threaded adapter and withdraw the slide rail towards the top.
- The installation of the slide rail is a reversal of the removal procedure. Coat the bearing bolts with sealing compound. Again engage the guide lug of the slide rail with the locating groove of the bearing bolt.

1.4.6. Valve Clearance - Checking and Adjusting

Mercedes workshops use special spanners to adjust the valve clearance. The clearance is adjusted on a cold engine (0.10 mm inlet valves, 0.30 mm exhaust valve). Different values apply if the clearance check is carried out on a warm engine (0.15 mm inlet valves, 0.35 mm exhaust valves).

The valve clearance is checked between the rocker arm face and the cam for the respective valve, using a feeler gauge. The feeler gauge must have a tight fit. To obtain the correct valve position for the check, rotate the camshaft until the point of the cam is facing downwards, i.e. the round section of the cam must face towards the rocker arm, as shown in Fig. 1.52. The following text describes the checking and adjusting with the engine fitted. The valves should be checked, and if necessary adjusted, at intervals of 12,000 miles. Proceed as follows:

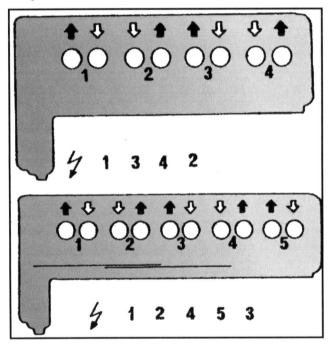

Fig. 1.58 – The location of inlet and exhaust valves. In the upper view for the four-cylinder, in the lower view for the five-cylinder.

- Remove the air cleaner and the cylinder head cover.
- Use a 27 mm socket and a ratchet, place it over the crankshaft pulley bolt and rotate the engine until both valves of No. 1 cylinder are closed. Fig. 1.58 shows the position of the inlet and exhaust valves on the two engine types. The white arrows indicate the inlet valves, the black ones the exhaust valves.
- Apply the special wrench, shown in Fig. 1.59 to the valve spring cup. Two flats in the cup enable the wrench to be applied.

Fig. 1.59 – Using the special wrench to counterhold the valve spring cup is shown.

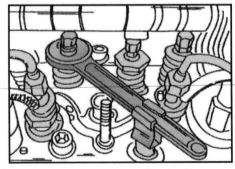

- Apply the two valve adjusting spanners to the valve in question, one to the locknut and the other one to the dome nut, as shown in Fig. 1.60, and slacken the dome nut.
- Alter the valve clearance by adjusting the dome nut. In the case of a cold engine, adjust the inlet valves to 0.100 mm (0.004 in.) and the exhaust valves to 0.30 mm (0.012 in.). If the clearances are adjusted on a warm engine, adjust the inlet valves to 0.15 mm (0.006 in.) and the exhaust valves to 0.35 mm (0.014 in.). As already mentioned, the clearance is checked by inserting a feeler gauge into the gap shown by the arrow in Fig. 1.52. A good

indication for a correct clearance is if the feeler gauge will enter without binding, then bends slightly and "jumps" into the gap.

Fig. 1.60 – Using the two special wrenches to adjust the valve clearances.

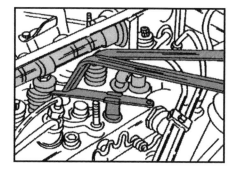

- When the correct clearance is obtained, hold the dome nut in its position and tighten the locknut, without moving the dome nut.
- Rotate the engine until the next set of valves are fully closed and check and/or adjust as described above, following the diagram shown in Fig. 1.58.
- Carry out all other operations in reverse order to the removal procedure.

1.5. Tightening Torque Values

Cylinder Head Bolts (internal hexagon head):
- 1st stage:..7.0 kgm (50.5 ft.lb.)
- 2nd stage: ....9.0 kgm (65 ft.lb.)
- 3rd stage: ....Wait 10 minutes
- 4th stage: ....10.0 kgm (72 ft.lb.)
Cylinder head bolts (in timing case): .... 2.5 kgm (18 ft.lb.)
Cylinder Head Bolts (Polygon heads):
- 1st stage:..4.0 kgm (29 ft.lb.)
- 2nd stage: ....7.0 kgm (50.5 ft.lb.)
- 3rd stage: ....90° angle-tightening
- 4th stage: ....90° angle-tightening
Cylinder head bolts (in timing case): .... 2.5 kgm (18 ft.lb.)
Rocker levers to cylinder head: ....4.0 kgm (29 ft.lb.)
Cylinder head cover nuts:... 1.5 kgm (11 ft.lb.)
Camshaft sprocket bolt:..8.0 kgm (58 ft.lb.)
Injectors to cylinder head: .... 7.0 – 8.0 kgm (50.5 - 58 ft.lb.)
Injection pipe union nuts:...2.5 kgm (18 ft.lb.)
Threaded ring for combustion chamber in head:....... 15.0 – 18.0 kgm (110 - 130 ft.lb.)
Drain plug in oil sump:
- M26 thread:..5.0 kgm (35 ft.lb.)
- M12 thread: ....4.0 kgm (29 ft.lb.)
Centre bolt and nuts of oil filter cover:.......................... 2.0 – 2.5 kgm (14.5 - 18 ft.lb.)
Oil filter to crankcase:...3.0 kgm (22 ft.lb.)
Oil pressure valve:..4.0 kgm (29 ft.lb.)
Coolant drain plug (radiator):......................................2.0 kgm (14.5 ft.lb.)
Connecting Rod Bearing Caps:
- 1st stage:... 4.0 – 5.0 kgm (29 - 35 ft.lb.)
- 2nd stage: ....Angle-tighten 90° – 100°
Main Bearing Cap Bolts:
- Without stretch bolts: ....9.0 kgm (65 ft.lb.)
- With stretch bolts – 1st stage: ....5.5 kgm (40 ft.lb.)
                    – 2nd stage: ....Angle-tighten 90° – 100°
Chain tensioner: ....8.0 kgm (58 ft.lb.)
Cylinder head cover bolts:...1.0 kgm (7.2 ft.lb.)
Camshaft bearing caps (M8 bolts): ....2.5 kgm (18 ft.lb.)
Vacuum pump to head: ....1.0 kgm (7.2 ft.lb.)
Vacuum pump housing:..1.0 kgm (7.2 ft.lb.)

Lubrication System

Crankshaft pulley hub to crankshaft (M18):.............. 27.0 – 33.0 kgm (194 - 238 ft.lb.)
Crankshaft pulley to hub (M8): ....3.5 kgm (25 ft.lb.)
Flywheel or driven plate:
- 1st stage:...3.0 – 4.0 kgm (22 – 30 ft.lb.)
- 2nd stage: .... Angle-tighten by 90° – 100°
Inlet manifold to cylinder head:...3.0 kgm (22 ft.lb.)
Alternator to mounting bracket: ....4.5 kgm (32.5 ft.lb.)
Plug in injection pump: ....3.0 – 3.5 kgm (22 – 25 ft.lb.)
Injection pump flange: ....2.0 – 2.5 kgm (14.5 – 18 ft.lb.)
Bolt for rear support bracket:...................................2.0 – 2.5 kgm (14.5 – 18 ft.lb.)
Banjo bolts for fuel pipes: ....2.5 kgm (18 ft.lb.)
Upper oil sump part to cylinder block: ....1.0 kgm (7.2 ft.lb.)
Lower oil sump part to upper part: ....1.0 kgm (7.2 ft.lb.)
Exhaust manifold to cylinder head: ....3.0 kgm (22 ft.lb.)
Centre bolt, fan to water pump: ....2.5 kgm (18 ft.lb.)
Water pump bolts: ....0.9 kgm (7 ft.lb.)
Timing Cover:
- M6 bolts:...1.0 kgm (7.2 ft.lb.)
- M8 bolts:...2.5 kgm (18 ft.lb.)
Exhaust manifold to exhaust pipe flange:....................................3.0 kgm (22 ft.lb.)
Exhaust pipe to transmission bracket:......................................2.0 kgm (14.5 ft.lb.)
Oil pipes to automatic transmission:..2.5 kgm (18 ft.lb.)
Earth strap to chassis:...2.3 kgm (17.0 ft.lb.)
Bolt for injection timing advancer: ....4.0 kgm (30 ft.lb.)
Nut for injection timing advancer: ....7.0 kgm (50.5 ft.lb.)
Rubber mount to engine/transmission mounting bracket: ....8.0 kgm (58 ft.lb.)
Engine and transmission mounting bracket to frame: ....5.0 kgm (36 ft.lb.)
Propeller shaft flange to transmission flange: ....4.0 kgm (29 ft.lb.)

1.6.   Lubrication System

The lubrication system used in all engines is a pressure-feed system. A gear-type oil pump is driven via the crankshaft by means of a separate chain. The pump is not the same for all engine types and capacities. The oil pump is located in the crankcase (for example as shown in Fig. 1.61), but the drive is not the same on all engines covered.

The following description refers to the major parts of the lubrication system of all engines. Overhaul or other repairs of the pump are not possible.

Fig. 1.61 – The location of the oil pump at the bottom of the crankcase of a 616/617 engine.

A warning light in the instrument panel will light up, when the oil level is approaching the lower limit of the oil dipstick. At least 1 litre of oil should be filled in as soon as possible.

Oil pressure indication is electrical by means of a contact switch, fitted to the lower part of the oil filter. Increased oil pressure increases the resistance in the switch and changes the reading in the instrument accordingly. The oil filter is fitted in upright position to the cylinder block. The oil flows through the filter element from the outside to the inside. A return shut-off valve prevents oil from flowing back through the oil pump into the oil sump when the engine is switched off. A by-pass valve opens when the pressure differential between the dirty and the clean end of the filter exceeds a certain value. The oil is then directed to the oil gallery without being cleaned. It should be noted that the oil filter element must be changed after 600 - 1,000 miles if the engine has been overhauled.

1.6.1.   OIL PUMP - REMOVAL AND INSTALLATION

616/617 Diesel Engines
•   Remove the oil sump as described in Section 1.6.2.
•   Unscrew the oil pump. Fig. 1.61 shows where the pump is located.
The installation is a reversal of the removal procedure. Fill the engine with the correct amount of engine oil.

Fig. 1.62 – The centre bolt of the pump drive sprocket must be removed and the sprocket together with the timing chain taken off in the case of a 602/502 engine.

602/603 Diesel Engines
•   Remove the oil sump as described in Section 1.6.2.
•   Remove the bolt in the centre of the oil pump drive sprocket (Fig. 1.62) and remove the sprocket together with the drive chain from the pump drive shaft.

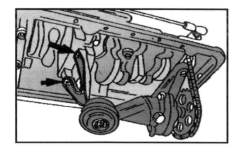

Fig. 1.63 – Remove the support bridge at the points shown by the arrows when removing the oil pump (5-cyl).

•   Remove the socket head bolts and take off the pump. Three bolts are used. Two on one side and one on the other side. In the case of the five-cylinder engine a support bridge is fitted to the pump and the bottom of the crankcase, as can be seen in Fig. 1.63, which must also be removed. Also on this engine remove the inlet manifold support bracket.
•   If necessary remove the plug for the oil relief valve. The plug is under spring tension and must be pushed towards the inside, before it is fully unscrewed. Remove the internal parts from the bore and check them for wear.

The installation is a reversal of the removal procedure. Tighten the pump securing bolts to 25 kgm (18 ft.lb.). When fitting the pump drive sprocket over the shaft, take care to align the flats shown in one of the illustrations in the section covering these engines (see under removal and installation of the crankshaft timing gear).

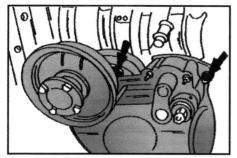

Fig. 1.64 – The oil pump of an M110 engine. Similar on an M115 engine. The arrows show where the bolts are located.

M115 and M110 Petrol Engines
•   Drain the engine oil and remove the lower part of the oil sump (M110 engine) or the complete oil sump (M115 engine).
•   Remove the bolts securing the oil pump to the crankcase and the crankshaft main bearing cap. Fig. 1.64 shows the fitted pump on the example of an M115 engine. The pump of an M115 engine is attached in a similar manner. Remove the pump.
•   In the case of the six-cylinder engine unscrew the suction strainer and remove the strainer after removal of the retaining ring.

Lubrication System

The installation is a reversal of the removal procedure. Fit the suction strainer with a new gasket. Fit and tighten the pump. Refit the lower part of the oil sump or the complete sump, depending on the engine and fill the engine with the correct amount of engine oil.

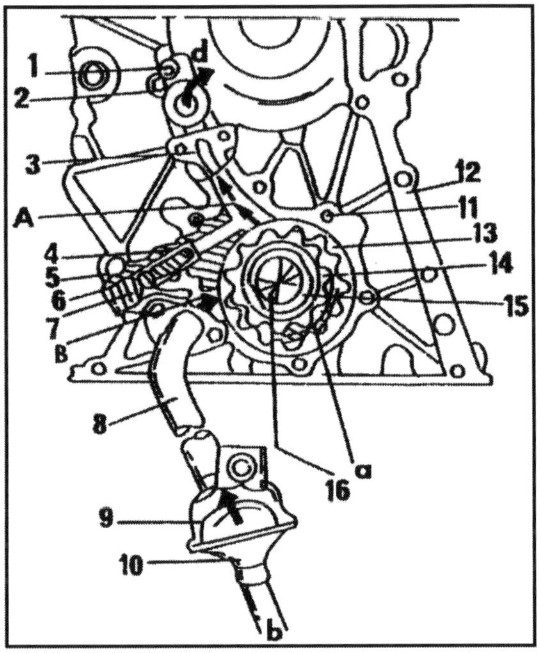

Fig. 1.65 – Sectional view of the M102 engine.

 1 M8 x 30 mm bolt
 2 Dowel pin
 3 Oil pump cover
 4 Plunger, relieve valve
 5 Compression spring
 6 Sealing ring
 7 Plug
 8 Oil suction tube
 9 Oil suction strainer
10 Oil suction funnel
11 M6 x 15 bolt
12 Timing case cover
13 Outer pump gearwheel
14 Inner pump gearwheel
15 Drive sleeve
16 Crankshaft
 A Delivery chamber
 B Suction chamber
 a Pump gearwheel section
 b From oil sump
 d To oil filter

M102 Petrol Engine

The pump is driven by a driver in front of the crankshaft timing gear. Fig. 1.65 shows a view of the engine front with the location of the oil pump. Remove the pump as follows:

• Remove the timing cover as described for this engine and remove the oil sump.

• Remove the oil suction tube and the pump cover from the timing cover.

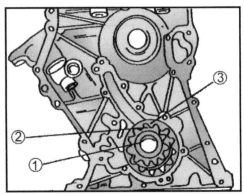

Fig. 1.66 – View of the fitted oil pump in the timing cover (M102 engine).
1   Drive sleeve
2   Pump gearwheel
3   Pump gearwheel

• The oil pump is now visible as shown in Fig. 1.66. Remove the two pump gears (2) and (3) out of the pump housing. Check the drive sleeve (1) on the crankshaft for wear or damage. If the two flats are worn round, replace the sleeve.

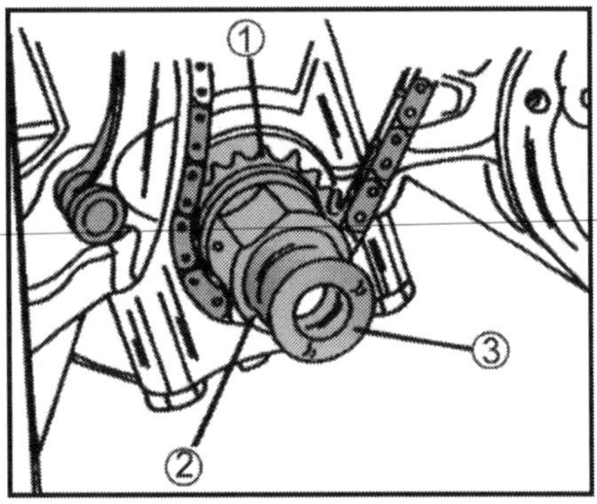

Fig. 1.67 – Marking the crankshaft sprocket (1) and the timing chain before removal of sprocket and drive sleeve (3) from the crankshaft (3).

• To do this mark the crankshaft sprocket and the timing chain at opposite points with a spot of paint (Fig. 1.67), remove the timing chain tensioner plug and the camshaft sprocket (refer to the section dealing with the M102 engine) and remove the crankshaft sprocket and the driving sleeve with a suitable puller.

Clean all exposed parts. If the gearwheels show excessive wear, replace them as a pair. Worn tooth flanks can be identified by a dull colour. Lubricate the gearwheels with oil and insert them into the timing cover as shown in Fig. 1.66. Replace the "O" sealing ring at the upper end of the timing cover.

Fit the oil pump cover and the oil suction tube with a new gasket. Quote the engine number of a new suction pipe is required (modified during production). The gasket can be fitted the wrong way and care should be taken. Wrong fitting will cover the oil bores. Check that the pump gears can be rotated freely.

If the crankshaft sprocket and the drive sleeve have been removed, insert the sprocket into the chain in accordance with the paint marks and use a suitable piece of tube to drive the sprocket over the crankshaft end. Fit the drive sleeve in the same manner, but make sure the dowel pin is engaged.

All operations are carried out in reverse order. Refer to the section dealing with the M102 engine to refit the parts of the timing mechanism.

1.6.2. OIL SUMP - REMOVAL AND INSTALLATION

NOTE: The engines have different oil capacities. Refer to Page 9.

In general it can be said that the removal of the oil sump is straight forward. To reach the oil sump bolts a 5 mm Allen key and an extension is required, not in the case of all engines, but definitely necessary in the case of an M115 engine. The sealing faces of oil sump and crankcase must be thoroughly cleaned before the sump is fitted. Use a new gasket during installation and fill the engine with the correct amount of oil. The following instructions are given for the removal and installation of the sump when an **M115 or M110 engine** is dealt with:

* Place a suitable container underneath the oil drain plug. Remove the oil drain plug and allow the oil to drain into the container. Remove the oil filler cap to speed up the draining of the oil. It also helps, if the engine oil is warm, i.e. drive the vehicle a few miles before the oil is drained.
* Unscrew the upper part of the oil sump until it is held in position by two of the bolts and then remove the lower oil sump part (M110 engine).
* Remove the bracket for the oil dipstick guide tube (M115 engine).
* Remove the oil sump with the Allen key mentioned above.
* Remove the oil dipstick guide tube out of the bracket and from below knock it out of the upper oil sump part (M110).
* Immediately remove the oil seal out of the groove at the rear of the oil sump as it must be replaced.

The installation of the oil sump is carried out in reverse. Note the following points:

* When installing the rear seal follow the instructions as given earlier on for the diesel engines (also see Figs. 1.40 and 1.41), making sure to obtain the seal protrusion as described.
* Coat the oil sump sealing face with sealing compound and position the sump against the cylinder block. Inset two bolts at the front and two at the rear to retain the sump in position. First secure the sump to the intermediate flange and then tighten the bolts evenly around the circumference to the crankcase.
* Refit all detached or removed parts in reverse order and fill the sump with the correct amount of engine oil. Start the engine and check the oil sump sealing faces for leaks.

1.6.3. OIL FILTER

616/617/602/603 Engines

The oil filter is located on the starter motor side of the engine. The component parts of the filter are shown in Fig. 1.68. If the engine has been overhauled a different oil filter is fitted, which must, however, be replaced after approx. 1,000 miles. Refer to your parts supplied for details.

Lubrication System

Fig. 1.68 – The component parts of an oil filter (616/617 engine).
1 Filter cover
2 Sealing ring
3 Filter insert
4 Filter element
5 Compression spring and spring seat
6 Filter housing
7 Sealing ring
8 Centre bolt

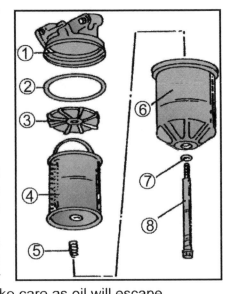

Different oil filters have been fitted during the model years covered in the manual. The differences can be obtained from Figs. 1.68 and 1.69. The filter can be replaced as follows:

- In the case of the oil filter shown in Fig. 1.68 remove the centre bolt (8) of the filter housing (next to the oil sump) and remove the filter housing (6) together with the sealing ring (7). Take care as oil will escape.

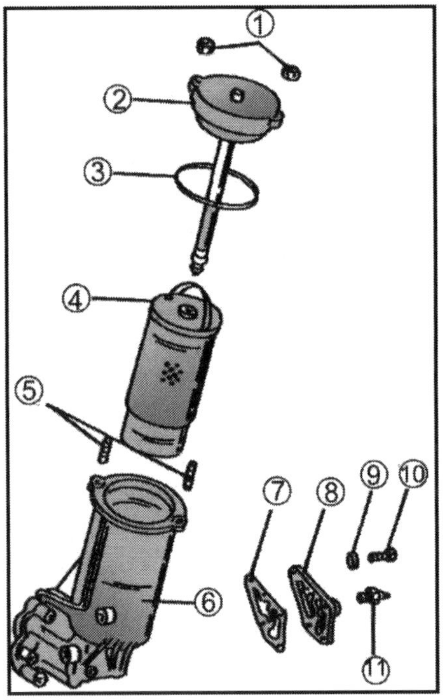

Fig. 1.69 – Component parts of an oil filter with combined filter element (diesel engines).
1 Nut
2 Filter housing cover
3 Sealing ring
4 Filter element
5 Threaded stud
6 Filter housing
7 Gasket
8 Intermediate plate
9 Spring washer
10 Bolt
11 Oil pressure switch

- In the case of the filter shown in Fig. 1.69, place a suitable container underneath the oil filter and slacken the nuts (1) securing the filter housing cover (2) without removing them fully.
- Separate the cover from the filter housing, allowing the oil to drain. Completely remove the nuts and lift off the cover.
- Remove the filter element and the sealing rings.

Fit the new filter element with the new sealing rings and refit the filter cover. Make sure that the oil seals are properly fitted. Tighten the nuts equally to 2.3 kgm (16 ft.lb.).

- Check the oil level in the sump and correct if necessary. Start the engine and check for oil leaks in the immediate surrounding of the filter.
- In the case of the filter shown in Fig. 1.69 fit the new filter element with the new sealing rings and refit the filter cover. Make sure that the oil seals are properly fitted. Tighten the nuts equally to 2.3 kgm (16 ft.lb.).
- In the case of the filter shown in Fig. 1.68 assemble the filter with the two elements and new gaskets.
- Check the oil level in the sump and correct if necessary. Start the engine and check for oil leaks in the immediate surrounding of the filter.

M110 Petrol Engine (six-cylinder)

The oil filter is fitted on the L.H. side of the engine. Fig. 1.70 shows a sectional view of this filter. If the engine has been overhauled a different oil filter is fitted, which must, however, be replaced after approx. 1,000 miles. Refer to your parts supplier for details. The filter element can be replaced without removing the complete filter.

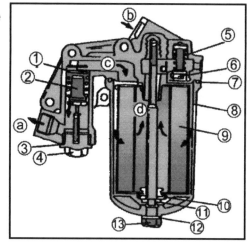

Fig. 1.70 – Sectional view of the oil filter fitted to the M110 petrol engine.
1 Pressure spring
2 Thermostat
3 Sealing ring
4 Closing plug
5 Upper filter housing
6 Thrust spring
7 Check valve
8 Lower filter housing
9 Filter element
10 Spring seat
11 Pressure spring
12 Centre bolt
a Outlet
b Inlet   c Filter bore   d Filter bore

• Remove the centre bolt at the bottom of the filter and withdraw it downwards. Remove the sealing ring.

• Thoroughly clean the sealing faces and fit the new filter with a new oil seal to the cylinder block. Fill the engine with the correct amount of oil, start the engine and check the filter area for leaks.

M115 petrol engine

• Remove the bolt at the bottom of the filter and withdraw the filter downwards. Oil will escape.

• Remove a plug from the top of the upper filter part and remove the compression spring and the pressure relief valve. Remove all sealing rings and replace if necessary.

• Unscrew the upper filter part from the crankcase.

• Fit the relief valve and the compression spring, the closing plug with the sealing ring and tighten the plug to 4.0 kgm (29 ft.lb.).

Fig. 1.71 – Oil filter details – M102 petrol engine. The oil filter screw cap (1) is removed with the wrench shown in the R.H. view. The L.H. arrow shows the oil pressure sensor.

• Fit the upper filter part with a new gasket to the crankcase. Tighten the M8 bolts to 2.3 kgm (16.5 ft.lb.) and the M10 bolts to 4.5 kgm (32.5 ft.lb.). Then insert the filter element from below into the lower filter part.

• Fit the lower filter part with a new sealing ring to the upper filter part and fit and tighten the bolt at the bottom to 4.0 kgm (29 ft.lb.).

Cooling System

- Fill the engine with the correct amount of oil, start the engine and check the filter area for leaks.

M102 petrol engine

The oil filter is fitted as shown in Fig. 1.71. The filter is a throw-away, cartridge type filter. An oil pressure indicator is fitted to the bottom of the filter (arrow, L.H. view).

A different filter element is fitted if the engine has been overhauled or a new exchange engine has been fitted. Remember to change the filter element after 600 to 1,000 miles. The filter element can be replaced without removing the filter housing. A strap type filter wrench is required to remove and install the filter cartridge. Mercedes workshops use a special tool to unscrew the filter cartridge, as can be seen in Fig. 1.71. If neither is available, remove the air cleaner and release the filter by tapping with a screwdriver or similar against the filter ridges. While unscrewing some oil may run out until the return flow locking valves in the cartridge are closing. Hold a rag underneath the engine.

After removal of the filter, clean the sealing face of the filter bracket. Lubricate the seal on the new cartridge with engine oil and screw the cartridge in position until finger-tight. From this position tighten the filter a further quarter of a turn, either using the tool or the hands.

Check the oil level in the sump and top up if necessary.

1.6.4.   ENGINE OIL CHANGE

The engine oil should be changed every 10,000 miles. Remember that there are a few litres of engine oil to handle and the necessary container to catch the oil must be large enough to receive the oil. Dispose of the old oil in accordance with the local laws. You may be able to bring it to a petrol station. **Never discharge the engine oil into a drain.** Drain the oil as follows, when the engine is fairly warm:

- Jack up the front end of the vehicle and place the container underneath the oil sump. Unscrew the oil drain plug (ring spanner or socket). Take care, as the oil will "shoot" out immediately. Remove the oil filler cap to speed-up the draining.
- Check the plug sealing ring and replace if necessary. Clean the plug and fit and tighten to 3.0 kgm (22 ft.lb.).
- Fill the engine with the necessary amount of oil. Make sure that the oil is suitable for diesel engines or petrol engines, depending on the type.
- Refit the oil filler cap and drive the vehicle until the engine operating temperature is reached. Jack up the vehicle once more and check the drain plug area for oil leaks.

1.6.5.   ENGINE OIL PRESSURE

The oil pressure can only be checked with an oil pressure gauge, which is fitted with a suitable adapter in place of the oil pressure switch. We recommend to leave the oil pressure check to a workshop. Low oil pressure can also be caused through a low oil level in the sump.

1.7.   Cooling System

The cooling system operates with an expansion tank (except for example 616 and 617 engines), fitted on the R.H. side of the engine compartment. The system will take the quantity given on Page 9. Operations covered in this section are not the same on all engine and must be carried out as applicable. Fig. 1.72 shows a sectional view of the cooling system parts in the case of a four-cylinder 616 engine. The difference in the case of a five-cylinder engine (617) is practically only the additional cylinder.

The water pump is fitted to the front at the bottom of the cylinder block and contains the thermostat with an opening temperature of 87° C.

A fluid coupling with cooling fan is fitted to the engine (not all engines) and operates independently of the engine coolant temperature. The clutch is operated by means of a bi-metal strip, which responds to temperature changes. The clutch is filled with silicone and drives the fan when cooling is required. When the engine is fairly cold, the clutch is disengaged and the fan spins with approx. 1000 rpm. As soon as the temperature reaches approx. 85° C, the bi-metal strip expands and the clutch is engaged. The fan turns now with the same speed as the engine. The heavier drive clutch for the fan required the reinforcement of the water pump housing and the bearing. Fig. 1.73 shows sectional view of the fluid clutch for reference.

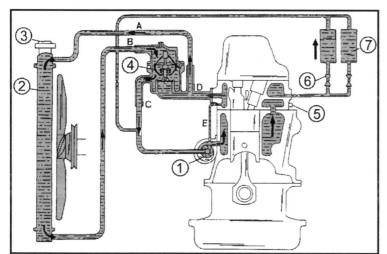

Fig. 1.72 – Sectional view of the cooling system (616/617 engines).

1   Water pump
2   Radiator
3   Radiator cap
4   Thermostat
5   Temperature sensor
6   Heater pipe
7   Heat exchanger
A   to radiator
B   from radiator
C   to water pump
D   from engine
E   Ventilation pipe

Fig. 1.73 – Sectional view of the fluid coupling for the cooling fan.

1.   Clutch body
2.   Cover
3.   Drive disc
4.   Engagement pin
5.   Ball bearing
6.   Bearing bush
7.   Bi-metal strip
8.   Sealing ring
9.   Valve
A   Fluid chamber
B   Working chamber

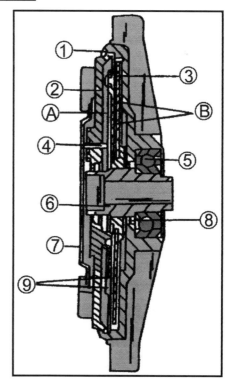

A coolant level indicator is fitted into the expansion tank (generally from model year 1985). If the level drops below the "Min" mark for any reason, the switch contacts will close and light up a warning light in the instrument panel. A check of the coolant level is therefore redundant.

1.7.0.   TECHNICAL DATA

Type: ....Water pump-assisted thermo-siphon system with
.... impeller-type water pump
Filling Capacity: ....See Page 9

Cooling System

Anti-freeze amount: .... See Section 1.7.1.0
Thermostat:
- Opens at:..87° C
- Fully opens at:...102° C

1.7.1 COOLANT - DRAINING AND REFILLING

- If the engine is hot open the expansion tank cap or the radiator cap, depending on the model, to the first notch and allow the pressure to escape. The coolant must have a temperature of less than 90° C.
- If fitted, remove the noise dampening panel from underneath the vehicle.
- Unscrew the coolant drain plugs. One is located at the bottom of the radiator. A second plug is fitted to the cylinder block, but rather hidden. Immediately refit the plug and tighten it to 3.0 kgm (22 ft.lb.).

To ensure that the cooling system is filled without air lock, proceed as follows when filling in the coolant. Refer to Section 1.7.1.0 for the correct anti-freeze amount to be added. Anti-freeze marketed by Mercedes-Benz should be used, as this has been specially developed for the engine.

- Set both heater switches to the max. heating capacity, by moving the controls.
- Fill the pre-mixed anti-freeze solution into the expansion tank filler neck until the level reaches the "Max" mark on the outside of the tank or on the mark on the radiator filler elbow. Do not fit the expansion tank cap or tank cap at this stage.
- Start the engine and run it until the operating temperature has been reached, i.e. the thermostat must have opened. Fit the cap when the coolant has a temperature between 60° to 70° C. A thermometer can be inserted into the radiator filler neck or the expansion tank to check the temperature.
- Check the coolant level after the engine has cooled down and correct if necessary.
- Refit the noise dampening panel underneath the vehicle, if removed.

1.7.1.0. Anti-freeze Solution

The cooling system is filled with anti-freeze when the vehicle leaves the factory and the solution should be left in the system throughout the year. When preparing the anti-freeze mixture, note the following ratio between water and anti-freeze solution. We recommend to use the anti-freeze supplied by Mercedes-Benz. It may cost you a little more, but your engine will thank you for it. The following ratios should be observed for the various engines:

616 Engine
To – 20° C:
  3.5 litres anti-freeze, 6.5 litres water
To – 30° C:
  4.5 litres anti-freeze, 5.5 litres water
To – 40° C:
  5.25 litres anti-freeze, 4.75 litres water

616 Engine
To – 20° C:
  3.75 litres anti-freeze, 7.25 litres water
To – 30° C:
  5.0 litres anti-freeze, 6.0 litres water

  5.75 litres anti-freeze, 5.25 litres water

602/603 Engine
To – 30° C:
  3.75 litres anti-freeze, 4.25 litres water
To – 45° C:
  4.5 litres anti-freeze, 3.5 litres water

M102 Engine
To –30° C:
  3.75 litres anti-freeze, 4.75 litres water
To – 45° C:
  4.5 litres anti-freeze, 4.0 litres water

M115/M110 Engine
To – 20° C:
 3.5 litres anti-freeze, 6.5 litres water
To – 30° C:
 4.5 litres anti-freeze, 5.5 litres water
To – 40° C:
 5.25 litres anti-freeze, 6.75 litres water

1.7.2. RADIATOR AND COOLING FAN

1.7.2.0. Checking Radiator Cap and Radiator

The cooling system operates under pressure. The expansion tank cap or the radiator cap is fitted with a spring, which is selected to open the cap gasket when the pressure has risen to 1.2 kg/sq.cm. If the cap is replaced, always fit one with the same marking, suitable for the models covered.

To check the cap for correct opening, a radiator test pump is required. Fit the pump to the cap and operate the pump until the valve opens, which should take place near the given pressure (1.2 kg/sq.cm. = 17 psi.). If this is not the case, replace the cap.

The same pump can also be used to check the cooling system for leaks. Fit the pump to the expansion tank or the radiator filler neck and operate the plunger until a pressure of 1.5 kg/sq.cm. is indicated. Allow the pressure in the system for at least 5 minutes. If the pressure drops, there is a leak in the system.

Fig. 1.74 – Dimensions to adjust the radiator air baffle. The letters are referred to in the text.

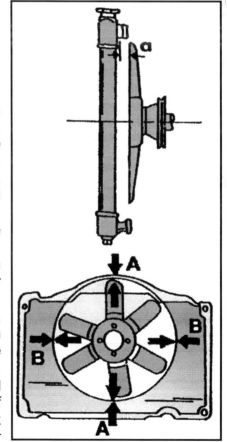

1.7.2.1. Radiator – Removal and Installation

The radiator can be removed as follows:
*   Drain the cooling system as described in Section 1.7.1. On a model with automatic transmission, use clamps and clamp off the two hoses for the oil cooler. Disconnect the hoses from the R.H. side of the radiator. Some fluid will drip out. Immediately plug the hose ends and connections in a suitable manner.
*   At the lower end of the radiator remove the locking clips on both sides of the radiator and pull them upwards, out of the radiator fan shroud. Lift the shroud out of the lower attachment and place it over the cooling fan.
*   Disconnect all coolant hoses from the radiator, unclip the spring clips on the outside on both sides and raise the radiator upwards to remove it.

The installation is a reversal of the removal procedure. Moisten the rubber mountings on top of the radiator. After installation of the radiator check that the gap between the fan blades and the radiator air baffle is the same on all sides, as shown in Fig. 1.74. Dimension "A" must be 25 mm, dimension "B" 20 mm and dimension "a" 60 mm.

If an automatic transmission is fitted, re-connect the hose connections. Check the fluid level in the automatic transmission, if you think some fluid has drained. Finally refill the cooling system as described in Section 1.7.1.

Cooling System

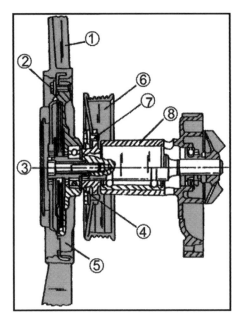

Fig. 1.75 – Sectional view of the fluid coupling.
1. Cooling fan
2. Bolt (3), M6 x 14
3. Bolt, M10 x 40
4. Ball bearing
5. Fluid coupling
6. Belt pulley
7. Bolts (4), M6 x 12
8. Water pump body

1.7.2.2 Fluid Coupling (602 and 603)

The removal and installation of the fluid coupling is carried out in a similar manner as described above, with the difference that there is no need to carry out some of the operations. It is important to remove all parts located in front of the engine. The coupling is secured with an M10 socket-head bolt. The bolt is tightened to 4.5 kgm (32.5 ft.lb.) during installation. Fig. 1.73 shows a sectional view of the coupling.

After installation run the engine and check the fan for correct operation.

1.7.3.   WATER PUMP

602/603 Engines

The water pump is fastened to a light-alloy housing which is bolted to the lower front of the crankcase. The thermostat is located inside the housing. The fan is attached directly to the pump shaft. Fig. 1.75 shows a sectional view of the water pump with fluid coupling for the fan. Note that the housing and the bearing of this pump have been strengthened to allow for the additional load of the fluid coupling.

The removal of the water pump is a straight-forward operation as it can be unscrewed from the engine after the fluid coupling has been removed as already described. The cooling system must be drained. The light-alloy housing and the hoses remain on the engine.

If the water pump housing is to be removed, proceed as follows after removal of the pump:

- Disconnect the battery earth cable.
- Remove the alternator and place it to one side. Remove the alternator mounting bracket (4 bolts in the centre).
- Disconnect the hoses from the pump housing.
- Disconnect the cable connector plug from the temperature sensor and unscrew the thermostat housing.
- Unscrew the water pump housing from the cylinder block. Immediately clean the mating faces on the cylinder block (and the pump housing, if re-used).

The water pump cannot be overhauled and must be replaced in case of damage or wear.

The installation is a reversal of the removal procedure. If a gasket is used, attach it with two or three spots of sealing compound to the water pump housing. If no gasket is used, coat the water pump thinly, but evenly with sealing compound (Loctite) and fit it to the water pump housing. Tighten the bolts to 1.0 kgm (7.2 ft.lb.). Fit the fluid coupling. Tighten the centre bolt to 4.5 kgm (32.5 ft.lb.).

If the water pump housing has been removed, fit a new "O" sealing ring to the return pipe and push the pipe carefully into the housing. Fit the housing with a new gasket to the cylinder block and tighten the bolts to 1.0 kgm (7.2 ft.lb.). Then refit the return pipe to the cylinder block. The following tightening torques should be observed:

Alternator mounting bracket   2.5 kgm (18 ft.lb.)

Alternator to mounting bracket   4.5 kgm (32.5 ft.lb.)

Finally adjust the tension of the single belt as described below and refill the cooling system. Check the cooling system for leaks.

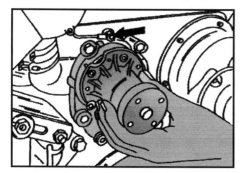

Fig. 1.76 – Removal of the water pump.

616/617 Engines

Water pumps should not be overhauled and must be replaced in case of damage or wear. The pump is fitted to the cylinder block. Fig. 1.76 shows the water pump and associated parts. Remove the pump as follows:

- Disconnect the battery and drain the cooling system.
- Remove the cooling fan after removing the four bolts in the centre.
- Slacken the alternator tensioning link, push the alternator downwards and remove the drive belt.
- Unscrew the pump securing bolts and remove the pump from the engine. Immediately clean the pump and timing cover faces.

The installation is a reversal of the removal procedure. Place a new seal on the water pump. Install the pump so that the bleed hole points diagonally up and the drain hole vertically down. Secure the pump with new self-locking bolts and tighten the bolts to 1.0 kgm (7.2 ft.lb.).

Refit the cooling fan and adjust the water pump drive belt tension as described in the next section.

M102 Engine

The water pump cannot be repaired and must be replaced in case of damage or wear. The pump is fitted to the timing cover and can be removed as follows:

Drain the cooling system and remove the air cleaner and the radiator. Slacken the hose clamps and disconnect the heater return pipe and the coolant hose from the water pump.

Remove the cooling fan and the magnetic body for the fan coupling as described later on. Slacken the adjuster bolt for the single belt drive and remove the drive belt.

Unscrew the alternator together with the mounting bracket and place the assembly to one side.

Remove the lower clamp of the by-pass hose, unscrew the pump securing bolts and remove the pump from the engine, at the same time disengaging it from the hose. Immediately clean the pump and timing cover faces.

The installation is a reversal of the removal procedure. If a gasket is used, attach it with two of three spots of sealing compound to the timing cover. If no gasket is used, coat the water pump face thinly but evenly with sealing compound (Loctite) and fit it to the timing cover. Tighten the bolts evenly to 1.0 kgm (7.2 ft.lb.). Refit the radiator as already described and fit and adjust the drive belt as described on next page.

M115 and M110 Engine

Drain the cooling system and remove the radiator if a magnetic fan coupling is fitted. Unscrew the fan together with the clutch.

Release the drive belt and in the case of an engine with magnetic fan clutch remove the drive pulley. The pulley must be prevented from rotating as shown in Fig. 1.77.

Cooling System

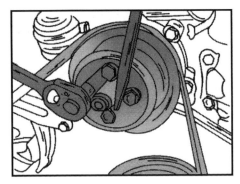

Fig. 1.77 – The water pump pulley bolts can be removed in the manner shown.

Unscrew the water pump securing bolts and remove the pump. Immediately clean the pump and cylinder block faces.

The installation is a reversal of the removal procedure. Use a new gasket and a new sealing ring in the pump. Finally adjust the drive belt tension as described for these engines below.

1.7.4.   DRIVE BELTS AND DRIVE BELT TENSION

602/603 Engines

New on these 602 and 603 diesel engines is the arrangement and construction of the drive belt for the water pump and the alternator and any other belt-driven unit. A single belt, so-called poly V-belt is used to drive the units. The belt has small teeth which engage into similar teeth in the drive pulleys. Fig. 1.78 shows how the engagement of the belt takes place in one of the pulleys.

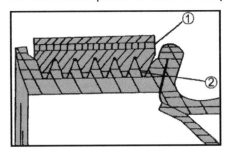

Fig. 1.78 – The arrangement of the poly V-belt in a belt pulley.
1   Belt pulley
2   Poly V-belt

The tensioner roller of the system is held under constant tension by means of a tension spring. A fitted shock absorber prevents vibration in the belt system. Fig. 1.79 shows the component parts of the system in detail. The tensioning rollers are not the same on all engines. Basic models without additional belt-driven units have a tensioning roller of similar construction as the remaining pulleys. All other models have a roller with a plain running face.

Fig. 1.79. – The component parts of the belt tensioning system.
1   Tensioning lever
2   Flanged nut
3   Tensioning spring
4   Tensioning roller
5   Cover
6   Tensioning roller lever
7   Damper
8   Upper damper mounting

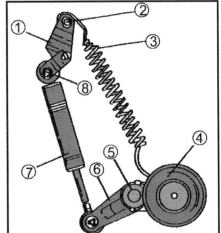

Figs. 1.80 and 1.81 show the belt layout on some of the engines. If an A/C system is fitted, you will find an additional pulley below the pulley for the steering pump. The belt drive should be checked every 12,000 miles. To do this, mark an easily accessible part of the belt with chalk and crank the engine by at least one turn with the starter motor. To prevent the firing of the cylinders, push the stop lever on the injection pump towards the bottom. Ask a helper to operate the starter motor and check the whole length of the belt, i.e. until the chalk mark can be seen once more. From the condition of the belt you will be able to judge if a new belt is required.

A belt can be replaced as follows:

•   Refer to Fig. 1.82 and slacken the flanged nut (4) for the tensioning lever (1).

•   Insert a suitable drift into the spring tensioning lever (1). The drift should have a diameter of 12 - 13 mm and must be 300 mm long.

Fig. 1.80 – Layout of the drive belt for basic models without power-assisted steering.

1   Crankshaft pulley
2   Alternator pulley
3   Water pump pulley
4   Steering pump pulley
5   Tensioning roller

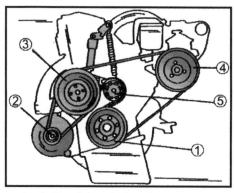

- Push the drift slightly towards the left until the bolt (6) can be pushed back.

- Move the drift slightly to the right to slacken the tensioning spring.

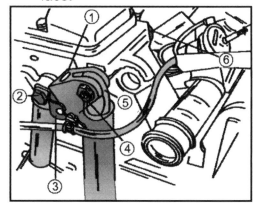

Fig. 1.81 – Layout of the drive belt when a power-assisted steering and an A/C system are fitted.

1   Crankshaft pulley
2   Alternator pulley
3   Water pump pulley
4   Steering pump pulley
5   Compressor pulley
6   Tensioning roller

- Push the tensioning pulley downwards until the belt is slack enough to be taken off. Immediately check the belt profile and the tensioning device for damage. Cracked, burnt or worn out belts must always be replaced. Remember that the tensioning pulley on basic engines without power steering or air conditioning has grooves; other pulleys have a smooth running face.

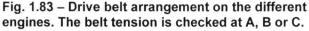

Fig. 1.82 – Removal and installation of the drive belt in the case of a 602 or 603 engine. The numbers are referred to in the text.

Always make sure to fit the correct belt. The installation is a reversal of the removal procedure. Place the belt first over the tensioning pulley, ending up at the water pump pulley. Check the belt alignment after the belt has been refitted.

Fig. 1.83 – Drive belt arrangement on the different engines. The belt tension is checked at A, B or C.

1   Crankshaft pulley
2   Water pump pulley
3   Alternator pulley
4   Compressor (A/C)
5   Tensioning roller
6   Steering pump

616/617 Engines

The belt must always be tensioned when water pump, alternator or crankshaft pulley have been removed. Squealing noises during acceleration also suggest that the belt must be re-tensioned. Fig. 1.83 shows the belts which may be fitted to the engine.

The tension is checked at the centre of the belt between the pulleys for the water pump and the alternator, etc. at the point shown by A, B or C.

Cooling System

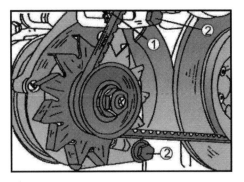

Fig. 1.84 – Details for the tensioning of the drive belt (616/617 engines). Bolts (1) and (2) must be tightened as described.

A belt can be removed as follows:

*   Refer to Fig. 1.84 and slacken the nut (1) and the bolt (2), push the alternator towards the inside and take off the belt.
*   Fit the new belt into all pulley grooves and push the alternator towards the outside.
*   To adjust the tension, tighten the tensioning bolt (1) in Fig. 1.84. The bolt engages into the toothed adjusting link and moves the alternator towards the outside. The belt is correctly tensioned when it can be deflected by approx. 6 mm (1/4 in) with firm thumb pressure.
*   Tighten the two bolts (2) when the correct tension is obtained.

M102 Engine

The accessories are driven by a single poly V-belt. An automatic tensioning device provides the correct belt tension at all times, but must be pre-tensioned if a new belt has been fitted or an original belt has been re-fitted. Fig. 1.85 shows the layout of the belt drives for engines with different accessories. The following text describes the replacement of the single belt.

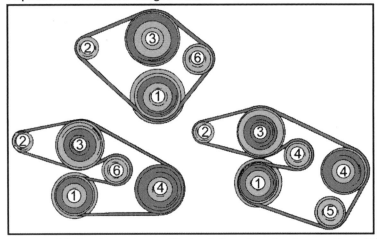

Fig. 1.85 – Layout of the single drive belt with different accessories. In the upper view without power-assisted steering, in the lower view with power-assisted steering and A/C system.

1   Crankshaft pulley
2   Alternator pulley
3   Water pump pulley
4   Steering pump pulley
5   Compressor pulley
6   Tensioning roller

*   Refer to Fig. 1.86 and slacken the bolt (2) by a ¼ to ½ a turn. Swivel the tensioning roller (3) back by turning the nut (1) counter-clockwise. The belt can now be removed.

Fig. 1.86 – Details for the adjustment of the drive belt of an M102 engine.

*   Turn the adjustment pointer (arrow in the illustration) towards the left until it is in line with the first graduation mark.
*   Check the pulley profiles and/or the tensioning device for damage or contamination and replace the part(s) in question.
*   Fit the new belt over the tensioning roller (3) and place it around the remaining pulleys, finishing always at the water pump pulley.
*   The belt must now be tensioned. To do this, turn the nut (1) towards the right until the adjustment pointer is above the following long graduation mark: If no power-assisted steering is fitted, this is the **third** graduation, if a power-assisted steering

or a power-assisted steering and an A/C system is fitted, this is the **fourth** long graduation mark.

- Tighten the bolt (2) after the adjustment has been completed.

1.7.5.   MAGNETIC FAN COUPLING – REMOVAL AND INSTALLATION (M102)

The engine is provided with a temperature-controlled electro-magnetic fan coupling. The coupling switches on and off by means of a sensor fitted to the cylinder head. The coupling is maintenance-free. Remove the coupling as follows:

- Remove the air cleaner and the radiator.

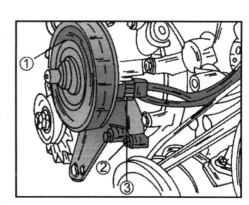

Fig.1.87 – Removal and installation of the magnetic body for the fan coupling.
1   Fan coupling
2   Securing bolts
3   Plug connector

- Unscrew the cooling fan (unscrew the bolt in the centre of the fan). Remove the single drive belt for the alternator, water pump, etc.

- Remove the water pump pulley. To do this, unscrew the four socket head bolts in the centre of the pulley and withdraw the pulley.

- Referring to Fig. 1.87, disconnect the plug (3) of the electrical cable from the magnetic body, unscrew the securing bolts (2) and remove the magnetic body (1).

The installation is a reversal of the removal procedure. Tighten the belt pulley and the magnetic body to 1.0 kgm (7.2 ft.lb.). Tighten the centre bolt of the cooling fan to 2.5 kgm (18 ft.lb.).

1.7.6.   THERMOSTAT

616/617 Engines

The thermostat is located in a separate housing which is connected with a short hose to the water pump and closed off with a cover (connecting elbow).

The thermostat can be removed after removal of the hose at the end of the housing cover and removal of the cover. Remove the cover sealing ring. The cooling system should be drained, at least below the level of the thermostat location. Remove the sealing ring from the thermostat.

Fig. 1.88 – Checking a thermostat.

A thermostat cannot be repaired, but can be tested by immersing it in a container of cool water and gradually raising the temperature to check the opening temperature.

- Suspend the thermostat on a piece of wire so that it does not touch the sides or the bottom of the container. Suspend a thermometer in a similar manner. Fig. 1.88 shows details.

- Gradually heat the water and observe the thermometer. The thermostat should begin to open at 80° C and should be fully open at 94° C. The thermostat pin must emerge at least 7 mm from the thermostat. Otherwise replace the thermostat. Allow the thermostat to cool down and check if it closes properly.

When fitting the thermostat use a new gasket. Fit the thermostat so that the arrow in the thermostat faces upwards or towards the rear. This is important. Tighten the cover

Cooling System

bolts to 1.0 kgm (7.2 ft.lb.). Check the hose clamp before re-using it. Refill the cooling system.

NOTE: To remove the thermostat housing, proceed as above, and disconnect the hose between the thermostat housing and the water pump housing. The thermostat housing can then be unscrewed.

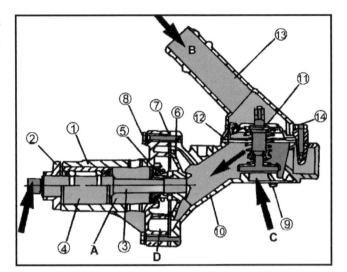

Fig. 1.89 – Sectional view of the water pump and the location of the thermostat (602/603 engines).

1 Pump body
2 Water pump flange
3 Water pump shaft
4 Water pump bearing
5 Housing gasket
6 Impeller
7 Gasket
8 Bolt, M8 x 35 mm
9 Guide pin
10 Light alloy housing
11 Thermostat
12 Sealing ring
13 Thermostat housing cover
14 Bolt, M6 x 35 m
A Pump chamber   B from radiator   C from engine   D to engine

602/603 Engines

The thermostat is fitted in the upper face of the water pump, as shown in Fig. 1.89. A self-bleeding line is inserted between cylinder head outlet and the cooling system expansion tank. The pipe takes care of the air bleeding during the filling of the cooling system.

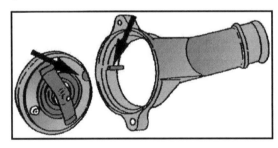

Fig. 1.90 – Correct fitting of the thermostat. The points shown by the arrows must be aligned.

A thermostat is removed as follows:

- Drain the cooling system. Always wait until the temperature is below 90° C. Even then remove the expansion tank cap very slowly. Use a thick rag to protect your fingers and hands. Only turn the cap to its first stop to allow all vapour to escape. It is enough to drain the cooling system to the level of the thermostat.

- Unscrew and remove the thermostat cover from the water pump housing. The hose can remain on the cover. Remove the gasket from the thermostat housing and the thermostat.

- A thermostat cannot be repaired, but can be tested as described above and shown in Fig. 1.88. The thermostat should begin to open at 87° C and should be fully open at 105° C. Otherwise replace the thermostat. Allow the thermostat to cool down and check if it closes properly.

When fitting the thermostat use a new gasket. Fit the thermostat so that the recess in the thermostat is in line with the lug in the inside of the thermostat housing cover. This is shown in Fig. 1.90. Tighten the cover screws to 1.0 kgm (7.2 ft.lb.). All other operations are carried out in reverse order to the removal procedure. Finally fill the cooling system and check the whole system for leaks.

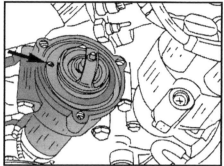

Fig. 1.91 – The thermostat of a petrol engine. The arrow shows the ball valve.

Petrol Engines

The thermostat is located in a housing at the end of the cylinder head as shown in Fig. 1. 91. The arrow shows the ball valve in the thermostat, which performs the automatic venting when coolant is filled in.

The thermostat can be removed after removal of the hose at the end of the housing cover, disconnecting the vent pipe between the thermostat housing cover and water pump and removal of the cover. Remove the cover sealing ring.

Test the thermostat as described above. The thermostat should begin to open at 87° C and should be fully open at 105°C.

When fitting the thermostat use a new gasket. Fit the thermostat so that the ball valve is at the highest position, as shown in Fig. 1.91.

2 CLUTCH

2.0. Technical Data

Type:...Single dry plate diaphragm clutch
Operation: .... Hydraulic system
Diameter of clutch master cylinder: ....19.05 mm
Diameter of clutch slave cylinder: ....23.81 mm
Clutch diameter: ....Refer to parts lists
Thickness of clutch linings:
- With Valeo F 201 linings: 3.6 – 3.8 mm
- With Thermoid 856 FT linings: 3.8 – 4.0 mm

2.1. Removal and Installation

To remove the clutch unit, it will be necessary to separate the transmission from the engine, with the assembly fitted to the vehicle.
• Remove the transmission (Section 3.1).
• Mark the clutch in its fitted position on the flywheel if there is a possibility that the clutch unit is re-used. To remove the clutch, unscrew the six bolts securing the pressure plate to the flywheel plate and lift off the flywheel and then the driven plate, now free. Before removing the driven plate, note the position of the longer part of the driven plate hub, as the driven plate must be refitted in the same way.
Install in the reverse sequence to removal, noting the following points:
• If the old clutch unit is fitted, align the marks made before removal. A new clutch can be fitted in any position.
• A centering mandrel is required to centre the clutch driven plate inside the flywheel. Tool hire companies normally have sets of mandrels for this purpose. An old transmission (clutch) shaft, which you may be able to obtain from a Mercedes workshop, can also be used. Experienced D.I.Y. mechanics will also be able to align the clutch plate without the help of a mandrel.
• Fit and tighten the six clutch to flywheel bolts to a torque reading of 2.0 kgm (14.5 ft.lb.). The flywheel must be locked against rotation when the clutch bolts are tightened.

Clutch

2.2. Servicing

The cover assembly - pressure plate and diaphragm spring- must not be dismantled. Replace, if necessary with a complete assembly from your dealer or distributor.

Fig. 2.1. – To check the driven plate for run-out, clamp it between the centres of a lathe and check with a dial gauge.

Inspect the driven plate and the linings, replacing the complete plate if the linings are worn down close to the rivets. A driven plate with the linings contaminated with grease or oil cannot be cleaned successfully and should also be replaced. All rivets should be tight and the torsion springs should be sound and unbroken. Check the condition of the driven plate splines. Clamp the driven plate between the centres of a lathe and apply a dial gauge to the outside of the plate as shown in Fig. 2.1, at a diameter of approx. 175.0 mm (6.4 in.). The max. run/out of the driven plate should be no more than 0.5 mm (0.02 in.).

Check the rivet fastening of the clutch pressure plate and replace the plate, if loose rivets can be detected.

Fig. 2.2 – Checking the clutch pressure plate for distortion. The gap should not be more than given below.

Place a straight edge (steel ruler) over the friction face of the pressure plate and insert feeler gauges between the ruler and the surface. If the gap at the innermost spot of the friction face is no more than 0.03 mm (0.012 in.), the plate can be re-used. Fig. 2.2 shows this check.

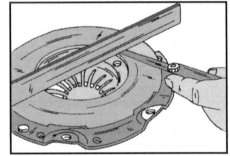

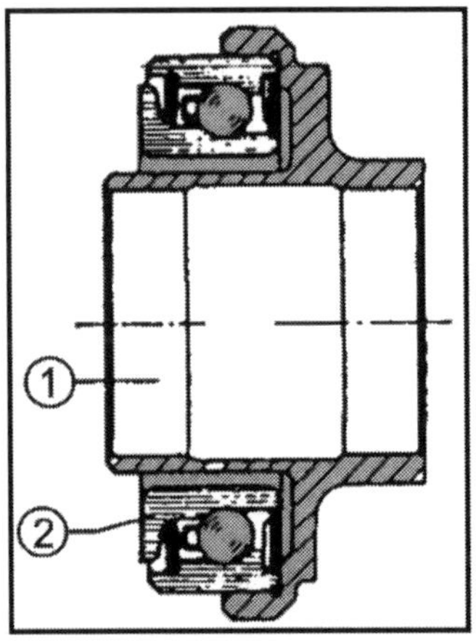

Fig. 2.3 – Sectional view of the clutch release bearing.
1   Bearing sleeve
2   Release bearing

2.2. Clutch Release Mechanism

Engagement and disengagement of the clutch is by means of the slave cylinder push rod, acting on the clutch release lever and sliding the ball bearing-type release bearing along a guide tube on the clutch shaft of the transmission. The fitting of the bearing can be seen in Fig. 2.3. The release system is free of play, as the wear of the clutch linings is compensated automatically.

2.2.0.   REMOVAL AND INSTALLATION

The transmission must be removed to replace the release bearing. Remove the bearing from the bearing sleeve on the front transmission housing cover, as shown in Fig. 2.4. To remove the release fork, refer to Fig. 2.5 and move it in direction of arrow (a) and then pull it from the ball pin in the clutch housing in direction of arrow (b).

Thoroughly grease the guide sleeve on the front transmission cover, the ball pin and all of the parts of the release mechanism in contact with the release bearing with long term grease. Push the release lever in reverse direction of arrow (b) over the ball pin until the spring clip of the release lever engages with the ball pin. Check for secure fitting. Then move the lever in reverse direction of arrow (a) until the slave cylinder push rod is engaged with the ball-shaped cut-out in the release lever.

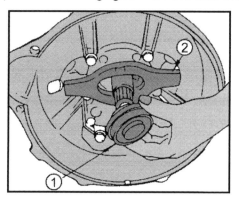

Fig. 2.4. – Removal of the clutch release bearing (1) from the release lever (2).

Fig. 2.5. – Removal and installation of the clutch release lever (see text).
1 Ball pin
2 Release lever

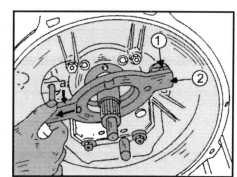

Grease the release bearing on the inside and on both sides at the rear, where it rests against the release lever and slip the bearing over the guide sleeve. Rotate the bearing until it snaps in position into the release lever. Check that the bearing is properly fitted and refit the transmission.

2.2.1. CHECKING CLUTCH LININGS FOR WEAR (clutch fitted)

As the clutch is fully enclosed it is not possible to check the clutch linings on the driven plate for wear. Your dealer has, however, a special gauge which can be used to check the lining wear on the push rod of the clutch slave cylinder. If in doubt about the condition of the clutch, see your dealer. Excessive clutch lining wear can lead to damage to the flywheel friction face (if the rivets of the driven plate rub against the flywheel).

2.3. Clutch Slave Cylinder
2.3.0. REMOVAL AND INSTALLATION

Cylinders for all models are the same. Unscrew the fluid pipe from the slave cylinder, using an open-ended spanner. Close the end of the pipe in suitable manner to prevent fluid leakage (rubber cap for bleeder screw). Remove the two cylinder securing screws and take off the cylinder. Observe the fitted shim. When fitting, insert the shim with the grooved side against the clutch housing and hold in position. Fit the slave cylinder, engaging the push rod into the ball-shaped cut-out of the clutch release lever, and insert the two screws. Tighten the screws. Finally bleed the clutch system as described in the next section.

2.4. Bleeding the Clutch System

A pressure bleeder is used by Mercedes workshops. The following description involves the brake system and is therefore to be treated with caution. Make absolutely sure that the brakes have correct operating pressure after the clutch has been bled. A transparent hose of approx. 1 meter (3 ft.) in length is required. Proceed as follows:

• Fill the brake/clutch fluid reservoir.

• Remove the dust cap of the bleeder screw on the R.H. front brake caliper, push the hose over the bleeder screw and open the bleeder screw.

• Ask a second person to operate the brake pedal until the hose is completely filled with brake fluid and no more air bubbles can be seen. Place a finger over the hose end to prevent fluid from running out.

Manual Transmission

- Push the free end of the hose over the bleeder screw on the slave cylinder and open the bleeder screw. Remove the dust cap first.
- The following operations must now be carried out in exactly the given order: Depress the brake pedal, close the bleeder screw on the wheel brake cylinder, allow the brake pedal to return and open the bleeder screw on the wheel brake cylinder. Repeat this operation until no more air bubbles can be seen in the fluid reservoir. During the pumping, keep an eye on the reservoir to make sure it has enough fluid.
- Close the bleed screws on caliper and slave cylinder and remove the hose. Refit the dust caps (easily forgotten).
- Check the fluid level in the reservoir and, if necessary, top it up to the "Max." mark. Start the engine, depress the clutch pedal and engage reverse. No grating noises should be heard.

3   MANUAL TRANSMISSION

The vehicles covered in this manual are either fitted with a four-speed transmission or a five-speed transmission. Depending on the vehicle type either a gearbox of type 711.101 or 711.200 (four-speed) or a five-speed transmission is used, but both transmissions are of the same basic construction.

The overhaul of the transmission is not described in this manual. The description in the overhaul section is limited to some minor repair operations, not involving the gear train or the gear shafts. If the transmission appears to be damaged or faulty, try to obtain an exchange unit. Transmission overhaul is now limited to specialised workshops which are equipped with the necessary special tools.

3.0.   Technical Data

Fitted Transmission:
- Four-speed transmission 711.101
- Five-speed transmission 711.200

Transmission Ratios:	Four-Speed (711.101)	Four-Speed (711.200)
- First gear	4.043 : 1	4.628 : 1
- Second speed	2.206 : 1	2.460 : 1
- Third speed	1.381 : 1	1.473 : 1
- Fourth speed	1.000 : 1	1.000 : 1
- Reverse speed	3.787 : 1	4.348 : 1

Transmission Ratios:	Five-Speed (for example 300 GD)
- First gear	3.822 : 1
- Second speed	2.199 : 1
- Third speed	1.398 : 1
- Fourth speed	1.000 : 1
- Reverse speed	3.705 : 1

Oil capacity	1.6 litres

Lubrication Oil:

ATF (as in A/T): Some transmissions are fitted with SEA 80 oil. Always check with the gearbox type.

3.1   Removal and Installation

The following text describes the general removal and installation operations of both transmission types. The transmission is heavy and the necessary precautions must be taken when it is lifted out.

* Disconnect the battery earth cable from the battery.
* To prevent damage of the insulation when the transmission is lowered later on, insert a piece of hardboard between the engine and the bulkhead.
* Place the front end of the vehicle on chassis stands and jack up the transmission until under tension. A wooden block must be inserted between jack head and transmission casing.

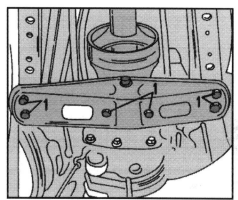

Fig. 3.1 – The bolts (1) secure the rear transmission crossmember to the transmission and the vehicle floor.

* Remove the mounting on the rear transmission cover. This is the bolt immediately below the propeller shaft coupling. Remove the two bolts, shown by the arrows in Fig. 3.1. Remove the crossmember from the vehicle floor panel and the transmission. Make sure that the transmission is adequately supported. To prevent excessive tilting of the power unit we suggest to suspend the engine and transmission on a hoist, using ropes or chains, attached to the lifting eyes.

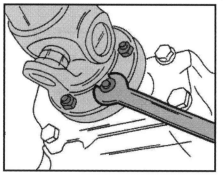

Fig. 3.2 – Removal of the propeller shaft flange from the transmission drive flange.

* Unscrew the propeller shaft flange from the transmission flange (Fig. 3.2), move the shaft to one side and tie it to the vehicle floor with a piece of wire.
* Remove the retaining clips securing the gearchange rods and push the rods away from the levers on the transmission.
* Unscrew the bracket for the clutch hydraulic line from the clutch housing. Unscrew the clutch slave cylinder from the clutch housing and pull towards the rear until the push rod is clear of the clutch housing. Note the plastic washer on the cylinder flange. There is no need to disconnect the hydraulic line.
* Disconnect the starter motor cables, remove the mounting bolts and lift out the starter motor.
* Remove the bolts connecting the transmission to the intermediate flange. The two upper bolts are removed last. Check under which bolt the earth strap is fitted.
* Pull the transmission, still resting on the jack, towards the rear until it is clear of the dowel pins and the clutch shaft before it is lowered to the ground. Never allow the weight of the transmission to rest on the clutch shaft as this may bend the shaft or damage the clutch driven plate or the clutch pressure plate (depending where the weight is placed).

Manual Transmission

The installation is a reversal of the removal procedure, but the following points must be noted:

• Lightly grease the centering lug and the clutch shaft splines with long term grease. Place the transmission onto the jack and lift it into the approximate fitting position. Place the clutch slave cylinder and the hydraulic line over the transmission.

• Engage a gear (not reverse), align the engine with the transmission and push the transmission against the engine. Rotate the drive flange at the end of the transmission to and fro until the clutch shaft has engaged with the driven plate. Fully push the transmission against the engine.

• Insert the bolts into the transmission, not forgetting the earth strap and tighten them evenly. Also fit the starter motor and tighten the two bolts. Re-connect the cables.

• Refit the clutch slave cylinder and secure. Pay attention to the correct fitting of the plastic shim. Secure the hydraulic line with the clamp and screw.

• Re-connect the gear selector rods to the levers, securing them with the spring locks. Make sure that the spring discs are fitted to the intermediate levers.

• Re-connect the speedometer drive cable and attach it with the securing clamp.

• Re-connect the propeller shaft flange to the transmission flange. Use new self-locking nuts and tighten them to 3.5 kgm (18 ft.lb.).

• Refit the rear engine mounting with the crossmember to the transmission and the vehicle floor and tighten the bolts to 3.5 kgm (18 ft.lb.). Fig. 3.1 shows where the bolts are located.

• Carry out all operations in reverse order to the removal procedure. Check the correct operation of the gear change after installation.

3.2   Transmission Repairs

Many repairs can be carried out without dismantling the transmission completely. The following sections describe some of the jobs which do not need special tools.

3.2.0.   FRONT TRANSMISSION COVER

A suitable drift must be available to replace the clutch shaft oil seal in the front cover. The transmission must be removed from the vehicle.

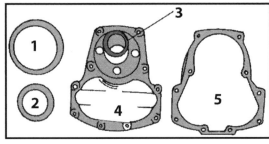

Fig. 3.3 – Shims and gasket of the front transmission cover.
1   Shim, output shaft
2   Shim, main shaft
3   Bearing tube
4   Front cover
5   Gasket

• Remove the clutch release bearing and the clutch release lever from the inside of the transmission case as described in the "Clutch" section.

• Separate the clutch bell housing from the gearbox as described below.

• Unscrew the cover screws on the outside of the transmission case and carefully withdraw the cover over the clutch shaft. Shims are fitted in the cover openings They could either stick to the cover or remain on the bearing. These shims must be refitted. The parts removed are shown in Fig. 3.3.

• Carefully clamp the cover into a vice, with the inside towards the top, and lever the oil seal out of the cover, using a screwdriver. Place a thick rag underneath the pivot point for the screwdriver.

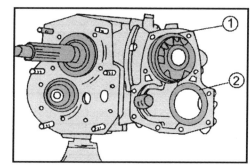

Fig. 3.4 – The removed front cover. The two shims (1) and (2) must be fitted as shown.

- Thoroughly clean the cover and fit a new oil seal with a piece of tube. The seal is fitted from the inside of the cover.

- Fit the shims to the cover as shown in Fig. 3.4 (attach them with a little grease). Also using grease, stick a new gasket to the cover.

- Coat the oil seal of the sealing lip and the running area for the seal on the clutch shaft with a little grease and carefully slide the cover over the clutch shaft and against the transmission case face. Clean the cover screws and coat their threads with "Loctite 573" sealing compound. Tighten the screws evenly to a torque of 1.5 kgm (11 ft.lb.). Refit the clutch housing.

3.2.1.   REAR TRANSMISSION COVER

Again oil leaks may be the reason for the removal of the rear transmission cover. The cover can also be removed with the transmission fitted. In this case remove the propeller shaft from the transmission flange as described in Section 3.1. It should be noted that the drive flange is fitted with a grooved nut. The grooved nut is removed with a peg spanner (115 589 07 00). If this spanner is nit available it may be possible to use a drift to slacken the nut which must, of course, be replaced during installation.

Remove the cover as follows:
- Drain the transmission oil.
- Unlock the grooved nut and slacken it. The flange must be prevented from rotation. To do this, insert a round metal bar into one of the flange holes and rest the bar against the transmission.

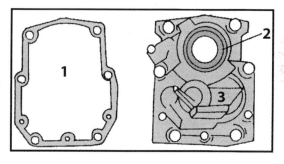

Fig. 3.5 – Removed rear cover.
1   Gasket
2   Oil sealing ring
3   Rear cover

- Remove the drive flange from the end of the shaft. A two or three-arm puller may be required.
- Unscrew the cover screws and remove the cover.

- Place the cover with the sealing face downwards over a bench and drive out the oil seal with a piece of tube of 52 mm diameter. The new oil seal is fitted from the same side until the outer face is flush with the cover. Fig. 3.5 shows the cover with the gasket.

- Using grease, stick the new gasket to the transmission case and fit the cover. Coat the cover screws with sealing compound and fit them into the cover and the transmission. Tighten the screws evenly to 1.5 kgm (11 ft.lb.).

- Fit the drive flange over the transmission shaft and fit and tighten the grooved nut finger-tight. Prevent the flange from rotating as suggested above and tighten the nut with the special wrench to 15.0 kgm (108 ft.lb.). Two different grooved nuts are used. When purchasing a new one take the old one to your parts supplied to ensure that you obtain the correct one. Secure the nut into the groove of the transmission shaft.

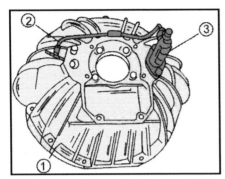

Fig. 3.6 – View of the removed clutch housing.
1   Clutch housing
2   Hydraulic line
3   Clutch slave cylinder

3.2.2.   CLUTCH HOUSING

• Remove the clutch release bearing and the clutch release lever as described in section "Clutch".

• Slacken and remove the bolts securing the clutch housing to the gearbox case evenly and remove the bolts and spring washers.

• Separate the clutch housing from the gearbox case, tapping it off with the help of a plastic or copper mallet and lift it off together with the clutch slave cylinder and the hydraulic lines from the studs. Fig. 3.6 shows the removed clutch housing.

The installation is a reversal of the removal procedure. Again the housing must be tapped in position over the guide shoulder on the gearbox case. Tighten the bolts evenly.

3.3   Gearbox Oil Level

The gearbox is filled with 1.6 litres of automatic transmission fluid or gearbox oil, as specified in Section 3.0 (depending on the gearbox number). Fluid or oil can only be lost if a leak has developed. To check the oil level, remove the oil filler plug from the side of the transmission and check that the fluid/oil is up to the lower edge of the plug bore. If necessary top-up with the specified oil. A grease gun (thoroughly cleaned) can be used to fill in the required fluid/oil. Refit and tighten the filler plug (6.0 kgm/43 ft.lb.).

Drain the transmission fluid/oil in the usual manner. The drain plug is tightened to 6.0 kgm (43 ft.lb.).

3.5   Gearbox - Tightening Torques

Front gearbox cover . . . . 1.5 kgm (11 ft.lb.)
Drive flange nut . . . . 15.0 kgm (108 ft.lb.)
Bolt for speedometer drive . . . . 2.5 kgm (18 ft.lb.)
Oil level/filler plug . . . . 6.0 kgm (43 ft.lb.)
Oil drain plug . . . . 6.0 kgm (43 ft.lb.)

4   Front Axle and Front Suspension

4.1.   Front Shock Absorbers – Removal and Installation

As there is enough room, a shock absorber can be removed without placing the front end of the vehicle on chassis stands.

At the lower end of the shock absorber, using a socket and a tommy bar, as shown in Fig. 4.1, remove the securing nut and take off the mounting parts. The upper end of the shock absorber is secured by means of a bolt and a nut to the mounting bracket. Prevent the bolt from rotating by applying an open-ended spanner to the bolt head and undo the nut with a ring spanner. Drive out the bolt and remove the shock absorber towards the top.

The installation is a reversal of the removal procedure. Note the different tightening torques. The upper mounting is tightened to 12.0 kgm (86.5 ft.lb.), the lower mounting to 7.0 kgm (50.5 ft.lb.).

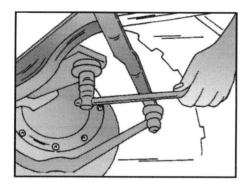

Fig. 4.1 – Removal of the lower shock absorber mounting.

If the shock absorber is replaced with the front of the vehicle on chassis stands you will have to place a jack underneath the area of the shock absorber mounting to compress the damper before the mountings are removed.

4.2. Front Springs – Removal and Installation

• Place the front end of the vehicle on chassis stands. Chock the rear wheels to prevent the vehicle from "rolling" off the chassis stands.

• Disconnect the propeller shaft flange from the flange on the transmission (see Fig. 3.2).

Fig. 4.2 – Removal of a front coil spring. The front axle must be lowered until the spring is free to be lifted out.

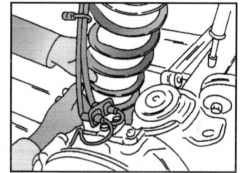

• Remove the shock absorber from its lower mounting as explained in section 4.1.

• Place a jack underneath the front axle until the axle is just under tension and remove both front wheels.

• Remove the split pin from the castle nut on the steering lever, remove the nut and separate the steering linkage connection ball joint with a suitable puller.

• Follow the routing of the two brake pipes and free the spring plates by tapping against them with a screwdriver and then withdrawing them with a pair of pliers. This enables the axle to be lowered without bringing the brake lines under tension.

• Ask a helper to lower the jack until the coil spring is free and can be removed (Fig. 4.2). Observe the brake pipes and the operational lines of the differential lock to prevent them from damage.

During installation place the spring onto the front axle with the end of the coil against the stop in the spring seat. Now lift the front axle, at the same time engaging the lower shock absorber end with the mounting. Fit the mounting parts and the nut and tighten the nut to 7.0 kgm (50.5 ft.lb.).

Fit the steering linkage to the steering lever. Fit the castle nut, tighten it to 9.0 – 10.0 kgm (65 – 72 ft.lb.) and fit a new split pin.

Re-connect the propeller shaft. Fit the front wheels and tighten them to 18.0 kgm (130 ft.lb.).

Note: The wheel bolts should be re-tightened to the specified torque after approx. 50 miles have been driven.

4.3. Oil Change in Front Axle

The front axle has a capacity of 2.6 litres. To remove the oil drain plug and the oil level/oil filler plug an Allen key of 14 mm A/F is required. Hypoid oil SAE 90 is used to fill the axle. Change the oil as follows:

• Drive the vehicle a short distance to warm up the oil.

• Place a suitable container underneath the axle and remove the oil drain plug at the bottom of the axle.

Front Axle and Front Suspension

- The oil level/filler plug can be removed immediately from the axle cover. It will also speed up the draining of the oil.
- Wait until the oil has drained, clean the drain plug and refit the plug to the axle and tighten it.
- Fill the axle housing with the oil and amount given above until the oil level can be seen at the lower edge of the filler hole. Clean the plug, fit it and tighten it.

4.4. Front Axle – Removal and Installation

- Chock the rear wheels and jack up the front end of the vehicle. Place the jack underneath the centre of the front axle.
- Disconnect the propeller shaft flange from the flange on the front axle and tie it with a piece of wire to the chassis frame. Do not allow the shaft to hang down under its own weight.

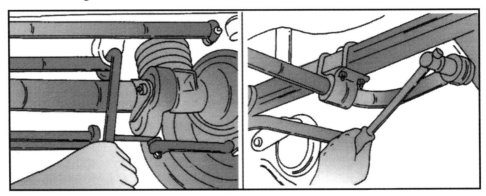

Fig. 4.3 – Removal of the suspension arm from the frame on the L.H. side and removal of the stabiliser bar (anti-roll bar) on the R.H. side.

- Remove both shock absorber mountings at the lower end (Fig. 4.1). The axle must be lifted slightly to compress the dampers.
- Slacken the bolts securing the suspension arms to the frame without removing them fully. Fig. 4.3 shows the operation in the L.H. view. Refer to the R.H. view and detach the stabiliser bar from the chassis frame.

Fig. 4.4 – Use two open-ended spanners to remove the union nuts from the hose-to-pipe connections.

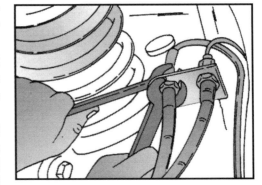

- Remove the split pin out of the castle nut of the steering lever and separate the steering linkage ball joint with a suitable puller.
- Unscrew the brake pipes on the L.H. and R.H. sides. The hexagons of the hoses must be held with an open-ended spanner. The union nuts are slackened with a second spanner. Fig. 4.4 shows the operation. Protect the open pipes against entry of foreign matter.
- On the round object on the axle disconnect the pipe. This is the control unit for the differential lock. Also disconnect the cable for the electrical control indicator.
- Remove both longitudinal members from the frame. Remove the nuts with a socket and take off the washers and rubber bearings.
- Lift the vehicle until the coil springs can be removed, fully unscrew the suspension arm securing bolts until the arms can be freed. Remove the front axle towards the front.

The installation of the front axle is carried out as follows:

- Place the axle onto the jack and lift it up until it is in the approximate fitting position.
- Place the coil springs onto the axle so that the coil ends are contacting the stops on the spring seats.
- Fit the bolt to the suspension arm. The vehicle must now be lowered until the longitudinal suspension arm can be inserted into the frame. Fit the rubber bearings and the washers and fit and tighten the nuts to 20.0 kgm (144 ft.lb.).
- Re-connect the shock absorbers at the bottom. Tighten the mounting to 12.0 kgm (86.5 ft.lb.).
- Refit the stabiliser bar. Tighten the bolts to 20.0 kgm (144 ft.lb.).
- Tighten the bolts securing the wishbone to 20.0 kgm (144 ft.lb.). Fig. 4.3 shows where the attachment takes place.
- Re-connect the steering linkage to the steering lever. Tighten the castle nut to 9.0 – 10.0 kgm (65 – 72 ft.lb.). Fit a new split pin.
- Re-connect the brake pipes to the front axle. After tightening of the union nuts make sure that there is at least a gap of 20 mm between the coil springs and the hoses. Otherwise slacken the union nut(s), twist the hose and re-tighten the union nut(s). Move the wheel towards the left and right to make sure that the brake hoses cannot contact the wheels.
- Re-connect the cable for the control indicator and the pipe to the differential control unit.
- Re-connect the propeller shaft.
- After installation bleed the brake system. Check the oil level in the axle and correct if necessary.

4.5. Longitudinal Suspension Arm – Removal and Installation

The removal of the arm can be carried out when the front of the vehicle is jacked up. Remove the attachment on the axle and on the frame and remove the arm.

A bearing bush is pressed into the arm which can be replaced under a press. During installation make sure that the bush protrudes on both sides by the same amount. We recommend to leave the bush replacement to a workshop.

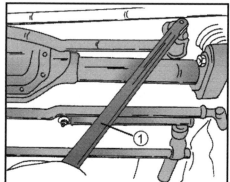

Fig. 4.5 – The suspension arm is attached at the position shown. A socket and extension (1) is required to remove the bolt.

During installation insert the arm into the frame and the axle and fit the bolts. Tighten the frame-side bolts to 12.0 kgm (86.5 ft.lb.) and the control arm-side bolts to 18.0 kgm (130 ft.lb.). Fig. 4.5 shows where the arm is fitted to the frame.

4.6. Front Wheel Hubs and Wheel Bearings

4.6.1. REMOVAL AND INSTALLATION

The wheel hub and wheel bearings can only be removed as a single item and must be replaced as such. Repair kits are available.

- Place the front end of the vehicle on chassis stands and remove the wheel.
- Remove the brake caliper and tie it with a piece of wire to the front suspension.
- Do not allow it to hang down on the brake hose. Remove the brake disc.

Front Axle and Front Suspension

Fig. 4.6 – Removal of the hub grease cap with the special puller.

1   Front wheel hub
2   Special puller
3   Grease cap

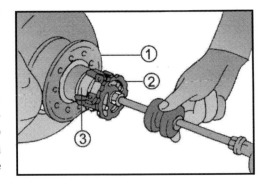

- Remove the hub grease cap. Normally a special extractor with an impact hammer as shown in Fig. 4.6 is used. Otherwise try to knock off the cap by carefully inserting a screwdriver at different points of the circumference.

- Unlock the outer grooved nut and unscrew it with a peg spanner. Normally the special wrench 460 589 00 07 00 is used, but you can try to slacken it by hitting the grooves with a drift and hammer. The nut must then be replaced. Remove the lock plate and unscrew the inner grooved nut in the same manner.

- Remove the front wheel hub. A tight hub can be removed with a puller. The puller is bolted to the wheel hub flange. The outer bearing will come away together with the hub.

- If the inner wheel bearing race has remained on the axle stump you will have to remove it with a suitable puller. Finally remove the oil seal from the axle stump. Thoroughly clean all parts of the wheel hub and the axle stump and check for visible wear.

Refit the wheel hub as follows:

- Push the assembled wheel hub over the stump and drive it in position, using a plastic or rubber mallet. Fit the inner grooved nut. Tighten the nut with the peg spanner to 20.0 kgm (144 ft.lb.), at the same time rotating the hub to settle the bearing. After the torque has been reached, slacken the nut by 1/8 of a turn.

- Fit the lock washer and tighten the outer nut to 20.0 kgm (144 ft.lb.).

Fig. 4.7 – Checking the end float of the wheel bearings. The illustration shows the check with the wheel hub assembled.

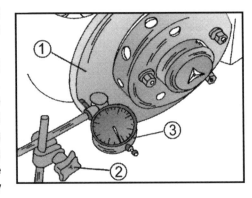

- Attach a dial gauge as shown in Fig. 4.7 and set the dial gauge to a pre-tension of 2 mm. The illustration shows a different hub, but the method is the same. Grip the hub flange and move it in and out at the same time observing the dial gauge reading. The final reading should be between 0.02 and 0.04 mm. The wheel hub must be rotated before any new measurement takes place, but not during the actual measurement.

- After the measurement peen the lock plate into the grooves of the nuts.

- Refit the brake caliper. M14 bolts are tightened to 19 – 20 kgm (137 – 144 ft.lb.), M16 bolts are tightened to 25 – 28 kgm (189 – 202 ft.lb.).

- Fill the grease cap with a little grease and knock it over the wheel hub. Use the grease available from your dealer (available in tubes of 150 grams). Only 15 grams are smeared into the grease cap.

- Refit the front wheel and lower the vehicle to the ground. Tighten the wheel bolts.

4.6.2.   WHEEL HUB - OVERHAUL

- Withdraw the outer bearing race from the hub. A two or three-arm puller is required, with the claws placed under the edge of the bearing race.

- In the inside of the wheel hub you will find an oil seal carrier with an oil seal. Remove the part by levering them out with a screwdriver.
- Thoroughly clean all parts and check for wear.
- Insert a new oil seal into the oil seal carrier. We recommend to take the old parts to your parts supplier to ensure you obtain the correct parts.
- Coat the oil seal carrier face, where it comes into contact with the wheel hub, with sealing compound and drive the carrier over the wheel hub without damaging it. Check with your workshop which type of sealing compound is used.
- Drive the outer wheel bearing with a suitable piece of tube over the wheel hub.
- Fill the wheel hub with the recommended wheel bearing grease (approx. 50 g per wheel hub). Make sure that the grease enters the bearing rollers. Excessive grease must be wiped off.

4.7. Joint Housing and Drive Shaft

4.7.1. REMOVAL AND INSTALLATION

If the joint housing has been completely cleaned it will have to be filled with 800 grams of multi-purpose grease. If the following operations are carried out you will also have to consider that the pre-tension of the steering knuckle mounting must be adjusted. We therefore must recommend that you read the instructions in full. Basically we recommend that the work is entrusted to a Mercedes-Benz dealer. Removal, however, takes place as follows. Fig. 4.8 shows the parts in question. We must point out that the operations are, in our opinion, rather complicated.

Fig. 4.8 – Component parts of the joint housing and drive shaft.
1   Seal retainer
2   King bolt
3   Steering knuckle arm
4   Joint housing with drive shaft
5   Spacer washer
6   Spacer washer
7   Screw plug

Note: If the axle housing, the joint housing or the king bolts must be replaced, do not attempt the work yourself. Also note that the shims mentioned in the description must not be mixed up or lost.

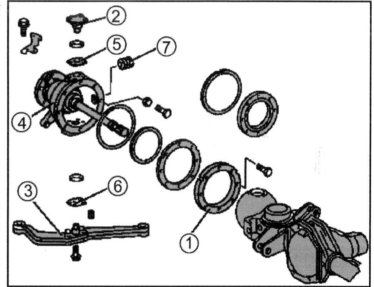

- Remove the fixed caliper and the brake disc.
- Withdraw the split pins from the tie rod ball joint nuts and remove the nuts.
- Remove the steering damper from the front axle.
- Separate the track rod ball joint with a suitable puller from the steering lever.
- Remove the wheel hub as already described.
- On the outside of the axle remove the protective shield from the joint housing.
- On the inside of the joint housing unscrew the bolts securing the oil seal carrier and allow it to hang down.
- Detach the king bolt (2) in Fig. 4.8 at the top and the steering knuckle arm (3) at the bottom and remove them. The shims and the taper roller bearings on the king pin must be marked to be refitted to their original position during installation.

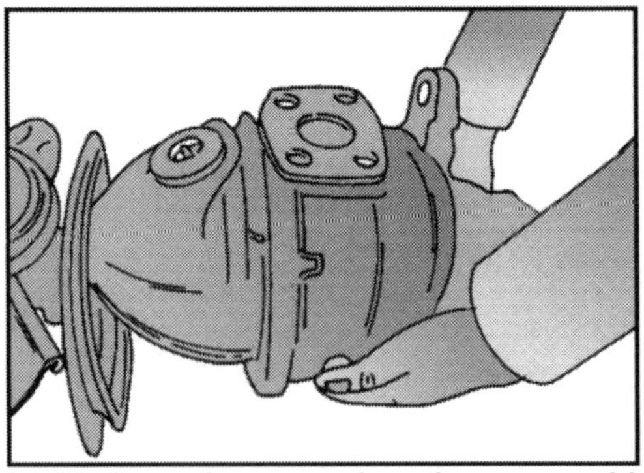

Fig. 4.9 – Removal of the joint housing with the drive shaft.

- Remove the joint housing with the taper roller bearings which now be removed as shown in Fig. 4.9. The oil seal carrier can also be removed. Make a note where the separation of a split gasket is located, as it must be fitted in the same position. Replace the gasket if necessary.
- Remove the taper roller bearing for the steering knuckle king pin towards the top and withdraw the outer bearing race with a suitable puller. In the inside remove the end cover.
- Thoroughly clean all parts and check them for re-use before commencing the installation.
- Insert the end cover into the joint housing.
- Drive the outer race of the taper roller bearing into the axle, using a suitable drift.
- Place the seal carrier with the gasket onto the axle so that the chamfer of the gasket matches the chamfer on the housing. Note that on some models a closed ball gasket is fitted. In this case the chamfer must face towards the ball.
- Install the joint housing with the drive shaft.
- Fit the joint housing with the taper roller bearing at the lower end to the axle and refit the steering knuckle arm (3) in Fig. 4.8. Tighten the bolts to 15 – 17 kgm (108 – 122 ft.lb.). Make absolutely sure to refit the shims and the taper roller bearings into their original positions.
- Fit the king bolt (2) to the top and attach it with the bracket. Tighten the bolts to 11 – 12.5 kgm (79 – 90 ft.lb.).
- Fit the protective shield to the outside of the joint housing (2.0 – 2.5 kgm/14.5 – 18 ft.lb.).
- Fit the seal carrier (1) to the inside of the joint housing (2.0 – 2.5 kgm). If an open gasket is used, arrange the opening at the bottom or at the top, depending on its original position. Later on a closed gasket was used. In this case the paper gasket is fitted between the outer seal carrier and the joint housing.
- Remove the closing plug from the joint housing (not fitted to early models) and fill the housing with the 800 grams of grease mentioned above. Refit the plug.
- Refit the tie rod, tighten the castle nut and tighten it to 9.0 – 10.0 kgm (65 – 72 ft.lb.).
- Refit the steering damper (2.0 – 2.5 kgm/14.5 – 18 ft.lb.).

4.7.2. DRIVE SHAFT – REMOVAL AND INSTALLATION

The drive shaft can be withdrawn after the joint housing has been removed as described above.

In the case of a drive shaft with differential lock an "O" sealing ring is fitted, which must be replaced if damaged. In the case of a shaft without differential lock check the race for signs of wear. A new race must be pressed in position – workshop job.

4.7.3. OIL SEAL ON FRONT AXLE DRIVE

The oil seal can be replaced without removal of the front axle, but the work must be left to a Mercedes-Benz dealer as the drive pinion nut must be removed. It is easily possible that the tightening torque for the nut is exceeded during installation, necessitating the removal of the axle to re-adjust the pinion drive.

4.8. Front Axle – Tightening Torque Values

Front Shock Absorbers:
- To mounting bracket: ....12.0 kgm (86.5 ft.lb.)
- To front axle: ....7.0 kgm (50.5 ft.lb.)
Tie rod to steering lever:..6.5 kgm (47 ft.lb.)
Wheel bolts:...18 kgm (130 ft.lb.)
Tie rod to steering lever:..6.5 kgm (47 ft.lb.)
Longitudinal arm to front axle: ....18.6 kgm (133 ft.lb.)
Longitudinal arm to frame:..12.0 kgm (86.5 ft.lb.)
Grooved nuts to front wheel hub: ....20.0 kgm (144 ft.lb.)
Brake Caliper to Joint Housing:
- M14 thread:... 19.0 – 20.0 kgm (137 - 144 ft.lb.)
- M16 thread: .... 25.0 – 28.0 kgm (180 - 202 ft.lb.)
Joint Housing:
- Seal retainer:...................................... 2.0 – 2.5 kgm (14.5 - 18 ft.lb.)
- Stop bolt (locknut): .... 1.5 – 2.0 kgm (11 - 14.5 ft.lb.)
King pin (top) to joint housing:................ 11.0 – 12.5 kgm (79 - 90 ft.lb.)
Joint housing screw plug: ....10 kgm (72 ft.lb.)
Tie rod to track arm: .... 9.0 – 10.0 kgm (65 - 72 ft.lb.)
Steering knuckle arm to joint housing: .... 15.0 – 17.0 kgm (108 - 122 ft.lb.)
Steering damper to damper bracket:........................ 2.0 – 2.5 kgm (14.5 - 18 ft.lb.)
Protective shield to joint housing:.......................... 2.0 – 2.5 kgm (14.5 - 18 ft.lb.)

5   Propeller Shafts

Fig. 5.1 shows the location of the various propeller shafts. Three shafts are fitted. Shaft (1) is the input shaft for the transfer case, shaft (2) is the front propeller shaft and shaft (3) the rear propeller shaft.

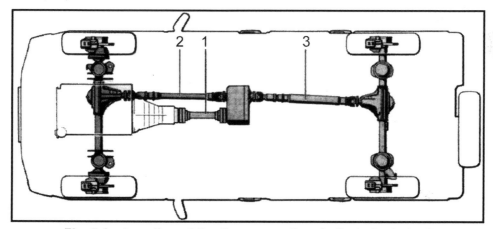

Fig. 5.1 – Location of the three propeller shafts (refer to text).

The shafts can be removed as follows. The description is valid for all shafts, as applicable. Note that self-locking nuts and bolts must be replaced during installation.
- Place chassis stands underneath the vehicle.
- When removing the input shaft to the transfer case (1) check the markings on the shaft at both ends and then remove the shaft from the flange on the transfer case and the shaft flange. Remove the shaft. During installation of the shaft make sure that the markings are in alignment. If a new shaft is required take the old one to your parts supplier as not all shafts are of the same constructions. The shaft is

either designed as a so-called homokinetic propeller shaft or a propeller shaft with universal joint is fitted.

Fig. 5.2 – Removal of the propeller shaft from one of the flanges. A socket and an open-ended spanner are required.

- To remove the front propeller shaft (2) mark the two flanges at both ends and then separate the shaft from the transfer case and the front axle. Fig. 5.2 shows the removal of the bolts and nuts. If the vehicle is moved after removal of the shaft you must secure the bolts in the transfer case flange, as otherwise the bolt heads may be tilted on the transfer case. To do this, fit an M10 nut as a spacer sleeve and then use one of the M8 nuts to tighten the bolt and the M10 nut together.

- To remove the rear propeller shaft (3) mark the two flanges at both ends and then separate the shaft from the transfer case and the front axle. If the vehicle is moved after removal of the shaft you must secure the bolts in the transfer case flange as described above for the front shaft.

The installation is a reversal of the removal procedure. In all cases joint the flanges together with the marks aligned. Tighten the bolts of a homokinetic propeller shaft to the transmission flange to 6.0 kgm (43 ft.lb.) and the bolts of the propeller shaft to the drive flange to 3.5 kgm (25 ft.lb.).

6   Rear Axle and Rear Suspension

The rear suspension is of similar construction as the front suspension, i.e. longitudinal and transverse control (suspension) arms, coil springs and hydraulic telescopic shock absorbers are fitted.

6.1.   Rear Shock Absorbers – Removal and Installation

As there is enough room, a shock absorber can be removed without placing the rear end of the vehicle on chassis stands.

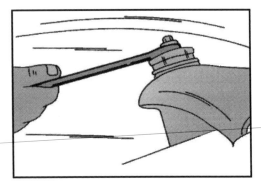

Fig. 6.1 – Removal of the upper shock absorber mounting.

At the lower end of the shock absorber, using an open-ended spanner and a ring spanner, remove the securing bolt and nut. Do not remove the bolt at this stage.

The upper end of the shock absorber is secured by means of a nut to the frame. Rubber mountings and a washer complete the mounting. Undo the nut with a ring spanner or an open-ended spanner as shown in Fig. 6.1.

Drive out the lower bolt and remove the shock absorber.

The installation is a reversal of the removal procedure. Note the different tightening torques. The upper mounting is tightened to 7.0 kgm (50.5 ft.lb.), the lower mounting to 12.0 kgm (86.5 ft.lb.).

If the shock absorber is replaced with the front of the vehicle on chassis stands you will have to place a jack underneath the area of the shock absorber mounting to compress the damper before the mountings are removed.

6.2.   Rear Springs – Removal and Installation

The removal and installation of the rear coil springs are carried out in a similar manner as described for the front springs. Additionally a linkage must be removed. Although there is no need to disconnect the pipes for the differential lock you have to ensure that they cannot be damaged when the axle is lowered.

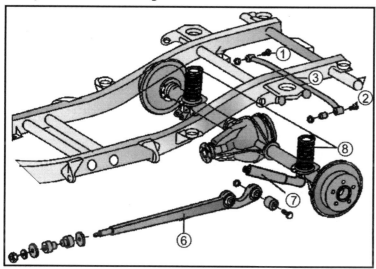

Fig. 6.2 – Details for the removal and installation of the rear axle. Items 4 and 5 are shown in Fig. 6.3.

1	Transverse control arm bolt
2	Transverse control arm bolt
3	Transverse control arm
4	Connector plug (differential lock cylindrical actuator)
5	Pull (if fitted)
6	Trailing arm
7	Shock absorber
8	Coil springs

6.3.   Oil Change in Rear Axle

The front axle has a capacity of 1.6 litres to May 1982 and 1.8 litres after this date. To remove the oil drain plug and the oil level/oil filler plug an Allen key of 14 mm A/F is required. Hypoid oil SAE 90 is used to fill the axle. Change the oil as follows:

•   Drive the vehicle a short distance to warm up the oil.

•   Place a suitable container underneath the axle and remove the oil drain plug at the bottom of the axle. The oil level/filler plug can be removed from the axle cover to speed up the draining of the oil.

•   Wait until the oil has drained, clean the drain plug and refit the plug to the axle and tighten it.

•   Fill the axle housing with the oil and amount given above until the oil level can be seen at the lower edge of the filler hole. Clean the plug, fit it and tighten it.

6.4.   Rear Axle – Removal and Installation

Fig. 6.2 shows details for the removal and installation of the rear axle, with the parts to be removed during the removal of the axle.

•   Chock the front wheels and jack up the rear end of the vehicle. Unscrew the drain plug on the differential housing and drain the oil into a container. Place the jack underneath the centre of the rear axle.

•   Disconnect the propeller shaft flange from the flange on the rear axle and tie it with a piece of wire to the chassis frame. Do not allow the shaft to hang down under its own weight.

•   Remove both shock absorber mountings at the lower end. The axle must be lifted slightly to compress the dampers.

•   Slacken the bolts securing the transverse control arm (3) to the frame. The bolt (1) is only slackened at this stage. In a similar manner treat the bolt (2) when separating the control arm (3) to the axle.

Rear Axle and Rear Suspension

Fig. 6.3 – Location of items (4) and (5), identified in Fig. 6.2.

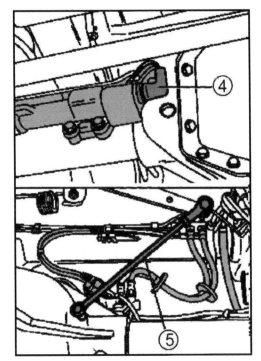

- Unscrew the brake pipes on the L.H. and R.H. sides and the connecting pipes to the differential lock cylindrical actuator. The hexagons of the hoses must be held with an open-ended spanner. The union nuts are slackened with a second spanner. Fig. 4.4 shows the operation, which is similar on the rear brake pipes. Protect the open pipes against entry of foreign matter.
- Disconnect the connector plug (4) for the differential lock cylindrical actuator (Fig. 6.3).
- Unscrew the pressure switch for the differential lock warning light and withdraw it.
- Disconnect both handbrake cables from the handbrake operating levers and withdraw them downwards through the floor panel.
- If fitted unlock and detach the pull rod (5) of the ALB controller (Fig. 6.3).
- Remove the mounting clamps for the handbrake cables from the trailing arm.
- Remove both trailing arms (6) from the frame. Remove the nuts with a socket and take off the washers and rubber bearings.
- Lift the vehicle until the coil springs can be removed, fully unscrew the transverse control arm bolts until the arm can be freed. Remove the rear axle towards the rear from underneath the vehicle. The trailing arms (6) can be removed from the rear axle.

The installation of the rear axle is carried out as follows:

- Place the axle onto the jack and lift it up until it is in the approximate fitting position. If removed, fit the trailing arms to the axle. The arms are tightened to 19 kgm (137 ft.lb.).
- Place the coil springs onto the axle so that the coil ends are contacting the stops on the spring seats.
- Fit the bolt (1) to the transverse control arm (3), but do not tighten the bolt. The vehicle must now be lowered until the trailing arm can be inserted into the frame. Fit the rubber bearings and the washers and fit and tighten the nuts to 20.0 kgm (144 ft.lb.).
- Re-connect the shock absorbers at the bottom. Tighten the mounting to 12.0 kgm (86.5 ft.lb.).
- Tighten the bolts (1) and (2) securing the transverse control arm (3) to 20.0 kgm (144 ft.lb.).
- Re-connect the brake pipes and other disconnected pipes to the rear axle.
- Re-connect the cable for the control actuator (4) indicator and the pipe to the differential control unit.
- Re-connect the pull rod (5) for the ALB controller (if fitted).
- Re-connect the propeller shaft (3.5 kgm/25 ft.lb.).
- After installation bleed the brake system. Check the oil level in the axle and correct if necessary or fill the axle if it has been drained.
- Re-connect the handbrake cables and adjust the handbrake as described in section "Brakes".

6.5. Trailing Arms and Transverse Control Arms

The location of the trailing arm and the transverse control arm can be seen in Fig. 6.2. The removal is straight forward with the rear of the vehicle on chassis stands. Remove the bolts securing the arm to the frame and the rear axle and remove it.

The control arm is fitted with a bearing bush which can be replaced. The new bush is pressed into the arm bores. Both sides of the bush must protrude by the same amount. Consider to have the bush replaced in a workshop.

The installation is a reversal of the removal procedure. Tighten the bolt on the frame side and the axle side to the values given in section 6.8.

6.6. Rear Axle Shafts

6.6.1. REMOVAL AND INSTALLATION

The wheel must be removed, the vehicle must be resting on chassis stands. Proceed as follows:

- Remove the brake drum securing screw and remove the drum.
- Disconnect the return spring for the brake adjuster at the bottom of the brake shoe. A special tool is used in the workshop, i.e. you will have to use a suitable pair of pliers.

Fig. 6.4 – The bolts securing the bearing cover are removed in the manner shown.

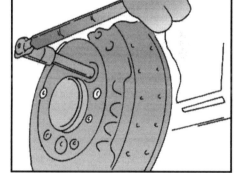

- Unscrew the securing nuts for the bearing cover through the holes in the drive shaft flange, as shown in Fig. 6.4. The shaft must be turned in order to reach all nuts. Make a note of the fitting direction of the nuts, as the new nuts (must always be replaced, see below) must be fitted the same way round. Carefully withdraw the shaft. After removal mark the shaft in accordance with the side of the vehicle, if both shafts are to be removed. A fitted compression ring determines the installation.

- Remove the gasket and the brake back plate. Sometimes the outer race of the taper roller bearing will remain in the axle tube. In this case a suitable puller must be used to remove it.

Fig. 6.5 – Fit the bearing cover gasket to the brake backplate. Ensure that all holes are aligned.

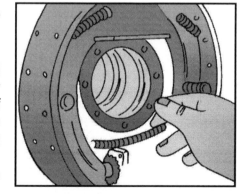

Refit an axle shaft as follows:

- Fit the brake carrier plate to the rear axle and insert the gasket between the bearing cover and the brake back plate, the location of which is shown in Fig. 6.5. Make sure that the "O" sealing ring is fitted to the supporting ring of the rear axle shaft.

- Insert the rear axle shaft in accordance with the marking, but refer to the following note:

Note: Up to a certain chassis number the rear axle shaft bearing is secured with a shrink ring. The shaft has been modified later on and a locking plate and a slotted nut is used. Only fit the later version, if a shaft has been replaced. The new shafts are marked with two arrows in the shaft flange, indicating the direction of rotation – i.e. make sure that the shaft is fitted to the correct side. If wrongly installed, the slotted nut may come loose and major axle damage can take place.

Steering

- Align the holes in the bearing cover with the holes in the brake backplate and the rear axle tube and fit and hand-tighten the bolts. The nuts are self-locking and must always be replaced. Tighten the nuts evenly across, until the bolt heads contact the bearing cover and the cover contacts the brake backplate. From this position tighten each nut by a further ½ of a turn, until the correct tightening torque of 6.3 – 7.5 kgm (45 – 54 ft.lb.) has been obtained. Again the shaft flange must be rotated accordingly to insert a socket with a short extension.
- Engage the return spring with the brake adjuster, refit the brake drum and fit the securing screw. All other operations are carried out in reverse order to the removal procedure.

6.6.2.   AXLE SHAFT REPAIRS (bearing replacement)

If a shrink ring is used to retain the shaft bearing (in most cases), take the shaft to a workshop to have the bearing replaced. You will receive the axle shaft ready for installation as described above.

6.7. Oil Seal on Rear Axle Drive

The oil seal can be replaced without removal of the rear axle, but the work must be left to a Mercedes-Benz dealer as the drive pinion nut must be removed. It is easily possible that the tightening torque for the nut is exceeded during installation, necessitating the removal of the axle to re-adjust the pinion drive.

6.8.   Rear Axle and Suspension – Tightening Torques

Lower shock absorber mounting: .... 12.0 kgm (86.5 ft.lb.)
Upper shock absorber mounting: .... 70.0 kgm (50.5 ft.lb.)
Wheel bolts: .... 18.0 kgm (130 ft.lb.)
Transverse control arm to frame and axle: .... 21.0 kgm (151 ft.lb.)
Trailing arm to frame: .... 12.0 kgm (86.5 ft.lb.)
Trailing arm to axle: .... 21.0 kgm (151 ft.lb.)
Bearing cover of rear axle shafts to axle tube: .... 6.3 – 7.5 kgm (45 – 54 ft.lb.)
Cover to rear axle housing: .... 4.0 – 5.0 kgm (29 – 36 ft.lb.)
Propeller shaft to rear axle flange: .... 3.5 kgm (25 ft.lb.)

7	Steering

7.0   Technical Data

Type	Re-circulating ball steering. With power-assisted steering (optional or standard)
Max. speed of steering pump	7000 rpm
Pump pressure	max. 5 bar
Pressure relief valve opens at	65 bar, plus or minus 5 bar
Oil capacity of mechanical steering	450 cc
Fluid capacity of power-assisted steering	1.6 litre
Type of fluid used	As in automatic transmissions
Fluid used	MB steering fluid

7.1 Mechanical Steering (Type L 1.5 Z)
Power-assisted Steering (Type LS 2B)

7.1.1 REMOVAL AND INSTALLATION

Suitable ball joint pullers to separate the ball joints from the steering linkage and the steering drop arm from the steering shaft must be available to remove the steering. The operations are described for a mechanical and a power-assisted steering:

* Open the bonnet and disconnect the battery.

Fig. 7.1 – The pressure pipe (1) and the return pipe (2) are connected as shown. The plug (3) can be removed to drain the steering.

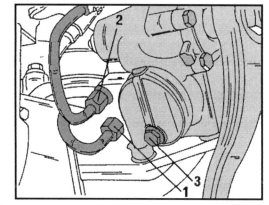

* Jack up the front end of the vehicle. Chassis stands can be placed under the front axle body. The wheels must be allowed to hang down under its own weight.

* Open the fluid reservoir and remove the filter insert. Using a syringe, remove the fluid from the container. The system can also be drained by opening the plug next to the two hydraulic pipes in Fig. 7.1. In this case start the engine and let it run for approx. 10 seconds, until pump and reservoir are drained. Catch as much fluid as possible from the draining point.

* Remove the steering fluid reservoir.

* Refer to Fig. 7.1 and disconnect the high pressure pipe (1) and the return pipe (2). Close the open connections in suitable manner to prevent entry of foreign matter.

* Push the protective gaiter away from the steering shaft connection and remove the universal joint clamp bolt. Push the universal joint with the steering shaft away from the steering worm shaft. Steering shaft and steering worm shaft have marks which must be aligned during assembly.

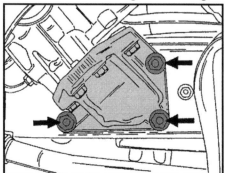

Fig. 7.2 – The arrows point to the securing bolts for the steering.

* Unscrew the drop arm nut. The drop arm is the lever connected to the steering shaft. Use a suitable puller to withdraw the arm. The pressure spindle must press against the steering shaft, the claws of the puller must engage below the arm.

* Remove the three bolts shown in Fig. 7.2 on the chassis sidemember and remove the steering unit together with the mounting bracket. If necessary remove the steering from the bracket, if a new steering is to be fitted (tighten the bolts to 4.0 – 5.0 kgm (29 – 36 ft.lb.) during installation).

The installation of the steering is a reversal of the removal procedure. Note the following points:

* If the steering has been replaced, fit it to the mounting bracket and tighten the bolts to 7.6 – 5.0 kgm (29 – 36 ft.lb.).

* Position the steering with the mounting bracket against the sidemember, at the same time engaging the end of the steering shaft with the universal joint. It is assumed that the front wheels and the steering wheel are still in the straight-

ahead position. Tighten the mounting bracket bolts to 4.0 – 4.5 kgm (29 – 32.5 ft.lb.) and the universal clamp bolt to 2.0 kgm (14.5 ft.lb.). Finally fit the gaiter over the universal joint.

- Push the steering drop arm over the steering shaft. Drop arm and steering shafts are marked. The marks must be opposite each other. Fit the castle nut and tighten to 6.5 kgm (47 ft.lb.).

- Re-connect the high-pressure and the return pipes to the steering (power-assisted steering only).

- Turn the steering wheel from one lock to the other and check that the stop screw on each side contacts the front axle beam. If this is not the case, check the drop arm alignment once more and refit it correctly.

- The steering system must now be bled of air as described in the next section.

- All other operations are carried out in reverse order. After completed installation take the vehicle on the road and check if the steering wheel spokes are correctly aligned. If necessary remove the steering wheel (puller required) and refit it accordingly.

7.1.2. Bleeding the Steering System of Air

The steering system must be bled of air when any of the connections have been opened or air has entered the reservoir due to a low fluid level. The steering system has a capacity of 1.6 litres. Bleed the system as follows, a helper is required:

- Jack up the front end of the vehicle. As a helper must be in the vehicle, place chassis stands in position.

- Remove the reservoir cap and take out the filter insert. Fill the reservoir with steering fluid to the "Max" mark.

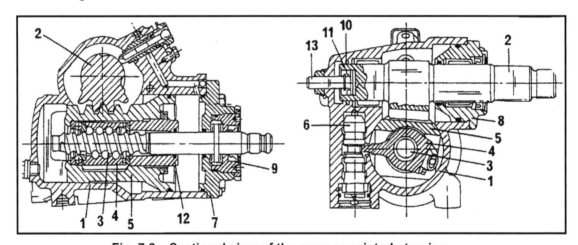

Fig. 7.3 – Sectional view of the power-assisted steering.

1 Steering box housing	6 Regulating valve	11 "O" sealing ring
2 Steering drop arm shaft	7 Bearing cover	12 Screw cover
3 Steering worm	8 Housing cover	13 Adjusting screw
4 Steering nut	9 Bearing insert	
5 Piston	10 Sealing ring	

- Start the engine and turn the steering wheel a few times from one lock to the other. As the fluid level drops, fill more fluid into the reservoir (helper). The system is self-bleeding, i.e. no further operations are required. It is important that the fluid level is always kept above the "Min" mark to prevent fresh air from entering the system. MB recommends Dexron II-D ATF fluid.

- Continue moving the steering wheel until no more air bubbles can be seen in the fluid.
- Fit the filter and the reservoir cap. Unscrew the cap once more and check the fluid level on the dipstick. With the engine running, the fluid level must be seen between the upper and lower mark on the dipstick.

7.2.   Checks on the Steering

Checking the Steering Play

Excessive play in the steering can be adjusted, but this should be left to a Mercedes dealer who has the necessary special tools. The steering can, however, be checked as follows:

- Place the front wheels in the straight-ahead position and reach through the open window and turn the steering wheel slowly to and fro.
- The front wheels must move immediately as soon as you move the steering wheel.
- If there is no play in the straight-ahead position but the steering wheel is more difficult to move as you rotate the steering wheel further you can assume that the steering gear is worn and must be replaced.

Checking the track rod ball joints for excessive play

With the wheel fitted grip the track rod ball joint and move it up and down with a considerable force.

A worn track rod ball joint can be recognised by excessive "up and down" movement. If this exceeds 2 mm, replace the ball joint.

Checking the steering rubber gaiters

Check the rubber gaiter over its entire length and circumference for cuts or similar damage. Also check that the gaiters are securely fastened at both ends. Track rods with worn ball joints or damaged rubber gaiters must be replaced as described earlier on.

Checking the System for Leaks

Sometimes it is possible that fluid is lost for some unknown reason. A quick check may establish where the fluid is lost:

- Ask a helper to turn the steering wheel from one lock to the other, each time holding the wheel in the maximum lock. This will create the max. pressure in the system and any obvious leaks will be shown by fluid dripping on the floor.
- From below the vehicle (on chassis stands) check the area around the steering pinion. Slacken the rubber gaiters on the steering rack and check the ends of the rack. The rack seals could be leaking.
- Check the hose and pipe connections with reference to Fig. 7.1. These must be dry.

7.3.   Tightening Torques – Steering

Steering to frame:... 7.6 kgm (55 ft.lb.)
Track rod ball joint to joint housing: .... 15.0 - 17.0 kgm (108 - 122 ft.lb.)
Steering drag link ball joint nut (drop arm side):
- M14 thread:.. 11.0 kgm (79 ft.lb.)
- M16 thread:.. 12.0 – 15.0 kgm (86.5 - 108 ft.lb.)
- M18 thread:.. 18.5 – 20.5 kgm (133 - 148 ft.lb.)
Union nut for high pressure hose:... 2.5 – 3.0 kgm (18 - 22 ft.lb.)
Return pipe to pump: .... 3.5 – 4.5 kgm (25 - 32.5 ft.lb.)

8   Brake System

8.0.   Technical Data

Type of system	See description below
Effective braking area:	
- Front brakes:	297 sq.cm.
- Rear Brakes:	448 sq.cm.
Total braking area, front and rear:	745 sq.cm.
Caliper piston diameter, front brakes:	44.00 mm
Wheel brake cylinder piston diameter, rear brakes:	17.46 mm

Front Disc Brakes

Thickness of brake pads, incl. back plate:	14.0 mm
Min. thickness of linings:	2.0 mm
Min. thickness including metal plate:	6.0 mm
Brake disc diameter:	303.0 mm
Brake Disc Thickness:	16.0 mm
Min. Thickness of Brake Discs:	13.0 mm
Wear limit of brake discs, per side:	max. 0.05 mm

Rear Drum Brakes

Brake drum diameter:	260.0 mm
Max. permissible drum diameter:	261.0 mm
Max. run-out of drum face:	0.05 mm
Width of Brake Shoes:	55.0 mm
Thickness of new Brake Linings:	7.8 mm
- Repair stage I:	8.3 mm
- Repair stage II:	8.8 mm
Min. thickness of brake linings:	3.5 mm
Wheel bearing clearance:	0.02 – 0.04 mm
Basic adjustment of automatic mechanism:	See main text

Brake Master Cylinder

Cylinder diameter:	23.81 mm

Brake Servo Unit

Diameter:	8 inches

Handbrake

Brakes must apply	When handbrake lever is pulled 5 notches

8.1   Short Description

All models covered in this manual are fitted with a hydraulic dual-circuit brake with vacuum-operated brake servo unit. Fixed brake calipers with 4 pistons are used for the front wheels, with drum brakes at the rear wheels with automatic take-up mechanism. Drum brakes with automatic adjustment have a plug at the inside of the brake back plate, marked "Automatik". The brake system is laid-out as shown in Fig. 8.1.
- In the circuit arrangement shown in Fig. 8.1, the intermediate piston circuit acts on the front wheels, the push rod circuit on the rear wheels. The four cylinders of each front caliper are interconnected. If the front brakes fail, the rear brakes will

operate as normal, but more brake force will be required. The same applies when the rear brakes fail, i.e. the front wheels will work in the normal manner.

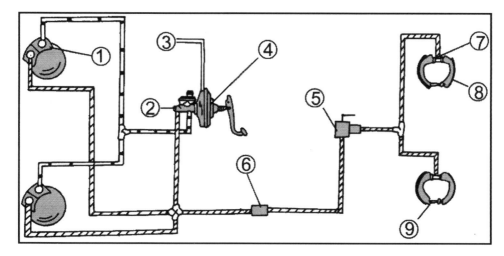

Fig. 8.1 – Layout of the brake circuit.

1 Fixed caliper
2 Tandem brake cylinder
3 To vacuum pump
4 Brake servo unit
5 Brake pressure regulator

6 Pre-pressure valve
7 Wheel brake cylinder
8 Brake shoes
9 Brake adjuster

All vehicles are fitted with a load-depending brake pressure regulator which is connected by means of a linkage to the rear axle. A pre-pressure valve (item "6" in the illustrations) retains a fluid pressure of between 0.5 – 1.2 bar after the brakes have been released.

The handbrake acts onto the rear brakes via a system of cables.

8.2   Adjusting the Brakes

A regular adjustment of the front disc brakes and the rear drum brakes is not necessary, as an automatic adjustment mechanism will adjust the brakes when necessary.

Note: Brake shoes with automatic take-up device must be adjusted if the brake shoes have been replaced. The operation is described in conjunction with the replacement of the brake shoes.

8.3   Front Disc Brakes

As already mentioned, fixed brake calipers with four pistons are fitted to the front wheels. The assemblies consist of a caliper cylinder bolted rigidly to the front axle.

8.3.0.   Brake Pad Replacement

If the remaining brake pad material thickness is less then 2 mm (0.08 in), a warning light will light up in the dashboard, indicating that the brake pads must be replaced. Very early vehicles are built without the warning light. The thickness of the brake pad linings can also be checked through the openings in the brake caliper after the wheels have been removed. Proceed as follows:

* Place the front end of the vehicle on chassis stands (underneath the front axle beam).
* Using a suitable drift, drive out the two retaining pins as shown in Fig. 8.2 from the outside towards the inside. Remove the spring plate.

Brake System

Fig. 8.2 – Removal of the brake pad retaining pins.

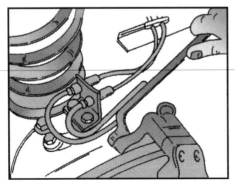

- Remove the brake pads. Sticking pads can be removed by feeding a wire loop through the holes of the pads and pulling them out with a short pull – *do not cut yourself on the wire!*
- Carefully push the pistons into their bores, using a piece of hardwood. The fluid reservoir could overflow. If necessary remove some brake fluid.
- Check the thickness of the brake pad linings. If it has reached the thickness of approx. 2 match-sticks, replace the pads as a set. Never replace a single pad, even if the remaining three appear to be in good condition.

If brake pads have worn more than expected, there is a possibility that the pistons have seized inside the bores. In this case it may be necessary to overhaul the brake calipers or have them overhauled. The same applies if the rubber dust boots on the cylinder housing are damaged.

Check the brake disc faces and clean them thoroughly before new pads are fitted. If possible measure the brake disc thickness and compare the result with the dimensions given in Section 8.0. If the minimum thickness has been reached, replace the disc(s).

Refit the brake pads as follows:

- Clean the contact areas for the brake pads inside the caliper housing and insert both pads into the caliper.
- Place the spring plate over the brake pads and drive in the retaining pins from the inside towards the outside. The ends of the retaining pins have a clamping sleeve, which must hold the pin securely after installation.
- Check the fluid level in the reservoir and top-up if necessary. Then operate the brake pedal a few times to set the brake pads against the brake disc faces. Re-check and if necessary correct the fluid level once more.
- Treat the new brake pads with care during the first 100 miles or so, remember that the new material must "bed in" before they reach their full performance. To speed up the process, brake the vehicle several times from a speed of approx. 50 mph to 25 mph. Allow the brakes to cool between each braking operation.

8.3.1 Brake Caliper – Removal and Installation

- Push a bleeder hose over one of the bleed screws in the brake calipers and insert the other end of the hose into a jar. Open the bleed screw and operate the brake pedal until the brake fluid has been drained.

Fig. 8.3 – The two bolts secure the caliper to the front axle.

- Remove the brake pads as described in the last section.
- Unscrew the union nut from the brake pipe connection on the caliper. Close the open connections in suitable manner to prevent entry of foreign matter.
- Unscrew the fitting bolt and the locking bolt, shown in Fig. 8.3 and lift off the caliper. The bolts cannot be interchanged, as they have a different diameter.

The installation is carried out in reverse order. The fitting bolt must be tightened to 25 – 280 kgm (180 – 201 ft.lb.), the locking bolt to 19 – 22 kgm (137 – 158 ft.lb.). The brake system must be bled of air after installation.

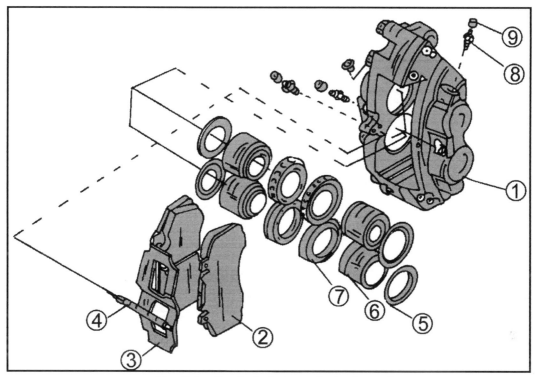

Fig. 8.4 – Exploded view of a brake caliper.

1 Brake caliper cylinder
2 Brake pads
3 Spring plate
4 Retaining pin
5 Cylinder seal

6 Piston
7 Dust sealing ring
8 Bleed screw
9 Rubber dust cap

8.3.2   Brake Calipers - Overhaul

Before a brake caliper is dismantled note the following points:
*   The two halves of the caliper must not be separated.
*   Always replace the cylinder sealing rings after a caliper has been dismantled. These are contained in repair kits.
*   Never refit pistons or the caliper if the surfaces show signs of wear, pitting or other damages. In this case fit a new caliper.
*   Only use the recommended brake fluid. Never use brake fluid which has been stored for long periods.
*   Pistons and sealing rings must be coated with clean brake fluid or brake paste before installation.

Fig. 8.4 shows an exploded view of a brake caliper. Dismantle a caliper as follows, but first enquire if a repair kit can be obtained:
*   Clamp the caliper into a vice and remove the dust seal from cylinder and piston (Fig. 8.5).
*   Remove the pistons from the caliper cylinder bores. MB workshops use a special tool for this operation. We recommend to clamp three of the pistons in position and blow out the remaining one with compressed air (applied to the brake hose connection). A piece of wood must be placed into the caliper bore to prevent the

piston from hitting the metal. Fingers must be kept away from this area. This method, however, means that each piston must be treated separately.

Fig. 8.5 – Remove the rubber dust seals in the manner shown from the end faces of the pistons.

- Remove the sealing ring out of the cylinder bores as shown in Fig. 8.6, using a blunt instrument.
- Thoroughly clean all parts if the cylinder appears to be in good condition. All parts contained in the repair set must be used.

Fig. 8.6 – Cylinder sealing rings are lifted out with a small blunt instrument.

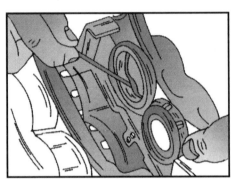

- Coat a new sealing ring with brake fluid or brake paste and insert into the groove in the inside of the caliper.
- Fill the inside of the dust seal with brake paste and attach the seal to the piston.
- Fit the piston with rotating movements into the caliper bore.

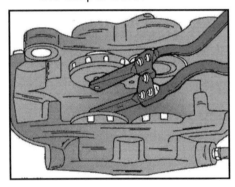

Fig. 8.7 – The rubber dust seals must be pressed in position with a pair of pliers, operating on the principle shown.

- Fit the rubber dust seal over the piston, but note that two pistons must be fitted. To spread the pressure evenly, a pair of pliers, as shown in Fig. 8.7 is most suitable for this operation.
- Thoroughly clean the brake caliper. The caliper and the brake pads can now be refitted. Refer to the instructions in the sections earlier on in this section.

8.4. Rear Brakes

The brake drums are secured with a cross-headed screw and can be removed after unscrewing the screw. If a drum is difficult to remove, release the brake shoes in the manner described for the adjustment of the rear brakes through the holes on the inside of the brake back plates.

Refer to Section 8.2 for further details. Remove the brake shows as follows after the drums have been removed. Fig. 8.8 shows a view of the fitted brake shoes on one side and should be referred to.

- Refer to the illustration and remove the two springs (7) and (8) with a pair of pliers or a screwdriver. Take care when removing the springs.
- Remove the brake shoe hold-down pins from both brake shoes. To do this, compress the spring, turn the spring seat by 90°, until the slot in the seat is   in line with the head of the pin and release the spring. The pin head will slide through the spring seat and the parts can be removed.
- Pull the two brake shoes apart at the upper end (Fig. 8.9) and disengage them carefully from the slots in the wheel cylinder pistons. Take care not to damage the

rubber boots. The push rod (10) will be released and can be removed. Lift the brake shoes out of the adjuster cylinder and unhook the return spring (9).

Fig. 8.8 – View of a rear brake assembly, shown with an MB adjuster.

1 Brake back plate
2 Brake shoe adjuster
3 Wheel brake cylinder
4 Trailing brake shoe
5 Leading brake shoe
6 Support bridge
7 Return spring
8 Return spring
9 Return spring, lower
10 Push rod
11 Spring
12 Spring seat
13 Spring seat
14 Shoe hold-down spring

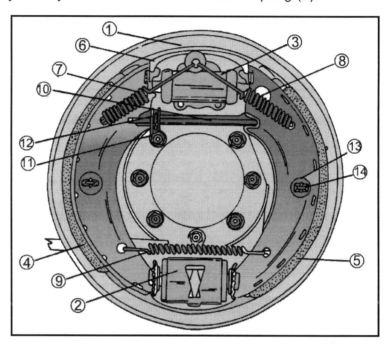

• Disconnect the lever on one of the brake shoes from the handbrake cable.

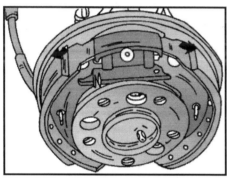

Fig. 8.9 – Push the upper ends of the brake shoes apart until the push rod in the centre can be removed.

• Note the engagement of the springs which will be found during removal. A compression spring with spring seat is fitted to the push rod, as it is shown in Fig. 8.10.

• Remove bolt adjuster bolts out of the adjuster housings and clean them thoroughly. Coat the threads with a good long-lasting grease and screw them back into the adjusters. Check that they can be screwed in and out without heavy spots.

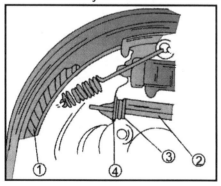

Fig. 8.10 – Arrangement of the springs on the push rod.

1   Front brake shoe
2   Push rod
3   Spring
4   Spring seat

Refit the brake shoes as follows and compare the assembled brake with Fig. 8.8, to make sure that all items have been fitted correctly.

• Engage the lever on the brake shoe with the end of the handbrake cable and loosely place the brake shoe in position.

• Fit the rear shoe with the hold-down pin, the spring and the spring seat to the brake back plate. The spring seat is again turned by 90° until the head of the hold-down spring can be guided through the slot in the spring seat. Then turn the spring seat by a quarter of a turn.

• Engage the upper return spring to the rear brake shoe. Use a hook, as shown in Fig. 8.11 and stretch the spring until it can be engaged.

• Fit the push rod between the brake shoes in the manner shown in Fig. 8.12. Fit the spring and the spring seat: Fig. 810 shows the attachment of the spring.

Brake System

Fig. 8.11 – Return springs can be fitted with a wire hook.

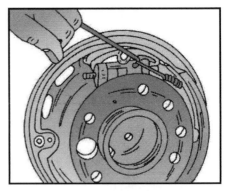

- Fit the second brake shoe, engage the lower return springs and set the brake shoes in the correct position. Fit the return spring in the manner shown in Fig. 8.11.
- Fit the brake shoe hold-down spring as described for the other brake shoe.

The following operations must now be carried out to set the shoes in the basic position:

Fig. 8.12 – Fitting the push rod between the two brake shoes. Make sure the correct side is facing towards the outside.

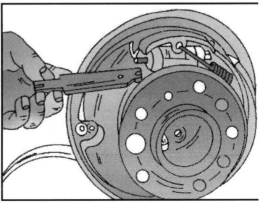

If the brake shoes or the brake adjuster have been replaced, it will be necessary to carry out certain adjustments on the shoe adjuster, before the brake drum can be refitted. First screw the two adjuster bolts towards the inside or unscrew it, until dimension "a" in Fig. 8.13 is 70.0 mm. Additionally dimension "b" must be set to 0.5 – 0.6 mm, between the adjuster wheel and the edge of the adjuster housing.

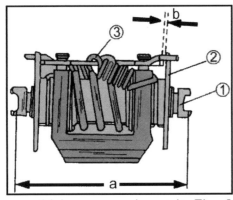

Fig. 8.13 – View of the automatic adjuster. Dimensions "a" and "b" must be set to the values given when brake shoes are adjusted.
1   Adjusting screw
2   Adjusting wheel
3   Tensioning spring

- Fit the brake drums and tighten them with the screw.
- To set the adjuster in the centre position, to check the gap "b" on each brake shoe. Insert a feeler gauge of 0.5 – 0.6 mm thickness as shown in Fig. 8.14 into the inspection hole. If the gap is not the same on both sides, you must adjust the adjuster in its elongated hole.

Fig. 8.14 – Check the gap "b" in Fig. 8.13 with a feeler gauge, inserted as shown. The check must be carried out on both brake shoes.

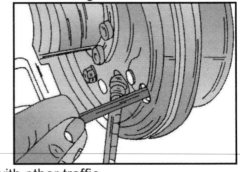

- Tighten the adjuster bolt to 4.0 kgm.
- Lower the vehicle to the ground and tighten the wheel nuts. The handbrake must be adjusted as described later on.
- After completing all the operations, road test the vehicle and operate the brakes in the following manner, taking care not to interfere with other traffic.
- All brake system types are automatically adjusted when the vehicle is driven in the normal direction. In order to adjust the front disc brakes, apply the brakes five times when driving forward and five times when driving backwards.
- If Mercedes adjusters are fitted, the adjusting screw for the leading brake shoe is adjusted when driving forward, the adjusting screw for the trailing brake shoe is adjusted when driving backwards. Brake the vehicle accordingly.

8.4.1 Wheel Brake Cylinders

Wheel brake cylinders can be removed after removal of the brake shoes. Remove the brake pipe at the inside of the brake back plate and unscrew the cylinder from the plate.

Wheel brake cylinders can be overhauled in normal manner, but we suggest to first find out, if a repair kit is available for your type of cylinder.

The cylinder is refitted in reverse order. The bolts are tightened to 1.0 kgm (7.2 ft.lb.). The brakes must be bled of air after installation.

8.4.2 Brake Drums

Brake drums can be re-ground twice, before they must be replaced. The larger diameter of the re-ground drums is compensated by fitting brake shoes with oversize brake shoe linings, which have a normal thickness of 7.8 mm. Linings with a thickness of 8.3 mm (first repair stage) and 8.8 mm (second repair stage) are available. Brake drums must be re-ground in a workshop, as special mandrels are required to clamp the drums into a lathe.

8.5. Master Brake Cylinder

All models are fitted with a tandem master cylinder with a double reservoir, supplying both circuits of the dual circuit with brake fluid. The brake lines are split as shown in Fig. 8.1.

The brake fluid level is indicated by means of a warning light in the dashboard, when it is below the "Min" mark.

8.5.0. Removal and Installation

The master cylinder is fitted to the front face of the brake servo unit and is removed from the engine compartment.

- Push a bleeder hose over one of the bleed screws in a front brake caliper (remove the rubber dust cap first), suspend the other end of the hose into a container, open the screw and pump the brake pedal until the system has been drained.

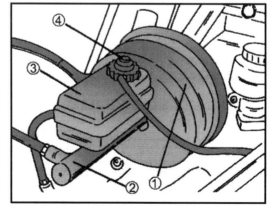

Fig. 8.15 – The fitted brake master cylinder.
1　Brake servo unit
2　Master brake cylinder
3　Reservoir
4　Reservoir cap

- Withdraw the cable plug from the brake fluid level contact switch on the side of the reservoir cap.
- Grip the reservoir with both hands and move it to and fro, at the same time pulling it out of the rubber grommets in the cylinder.
- Disconnect the brake pipes from the cylinder and push them carefully to one side. Close the pipe ends in a suitable manner to prevent entry of foreign matter.
- Unscrew the cylinder. A rubber sealing ring is inserted between cylinder and brake servo unit. Take care to collect it. Fig. 8.15 shows the cylinder as it is fitted to the brake servo unit.

Brake System

The installation is a reversal of the removal procedure. Always replace the sealing ring. Tighten the cylinder to 2.0 – 3.0 kgm (14.5 – 29 ft.lb.). There is no need to adjust the brake servo push rod.
Finally fill the reservoir and bleed the brake system as described later on.

8.5.1. Master Cylinder - Overhaul

Master brake cylinders are no longer overhauled. A new cylinder must be fitted if the old one fails. Always quote the model and the chassis number when ordering a new cylinder, as cylinders are sometimes changed and a different cylinder may have been allocated to your particular vehicle.

8.6. Handbrake

8.6.0. Handbrake Adjustment

Before the handbrake is adjusted make sure that the brake shoe linings have not been worn to the limits. If this is the case replace the brake shoes. The adjustment is carried out at the underside of the handbrake lever, inside of the underside of the vehicle. Both cables are individually secured. Adjustment is carried out as follows:

- Place the rear end of the vehicle on chassis stands (underneath the axle tubes). The wheels must be "in the air".
- Slacken the locknuts of both handbrake cables at the bottom of the handbrake lever (do not remove them).
- Apply the handbrake lever to the first "click" and adjust the adjusting nuts until both wheels are difficult to rotate **in the direction of drive.**
- Without disturbing the adjusting nuts tighten the locknuts against the adjusting nuts.
- Release the handbrake lever and check that both wheels can be rotated freely. Then pull the lever to the 5th notch and check that both wheels are fully locked, when rotated with a fair pressure.
- Lower the vehicle to the ground.

8.7. Brake Servo Unit

Brake servo units should not be dismantled, as special tools are required to dismantle, assemble and test the unit. Different servo units are fitted to the range covered in this manual. Always make sure to fit the correct unit of the part is replaced. Remember that a failure of the servo unit to act will not affect the efficiency of the brake system but, of course, additional effort will be required for the same braking distance to be maintained.

Note: If you coast downhill without the engine running, for what ever reason, remember that the vacuum in the unit will be used up after a few applications of the brake pedal and the brake system will from then onwards operate without the power-assistance. Be prepared for his.
Fig. 8.16 shows the arrangement of the brake servo unit. Remove the unit by referring to this illustration.

- Remove the master cylinder as already described.
- Disconnect the vacuum hose from the brake servo unit.
- Disconnect the brake servo push rod from the brake pedal. To do this, remove the lock and pull out the pin.

- Remove the brake servo securing nuts from the inside and lift it out from the engine compartment side.

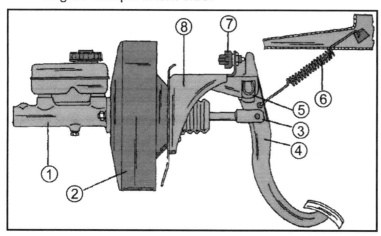

Fig. 8.16 – Brake servo unit and master brake cylinder.

1   Brake master cylinder
2   Brake servo unit
3   Push rod
4   Brake pedal
5   Pedal pin clip
6   Return spring
7   Stop light switch
8   Mounting bracket

The installation is a reversal of the removal procedure. Tighten the securing nuts to 2.0 – 3.0 kgm.

8.8.   Bleeding of the Brake System

Bleeding of the brake system should be carried out at any time that any part of the system has been disconnected, for whatever reason. If only one of the brake circuits (caliper or wheel brake cylinder) has been opened, either bleed the front or the rear circuit. If both circuits have been opened, first bleed the primary circuit and then the secondary circuit. Fig. 8.1 can be used to follow the circuits. Note that the front calipers have three bleed screws. The upper screw must be bled first. Fig. 8.17 shows the location of the three bleed screws of a front caliper. The procedure given below should be followed and it should be noted that an assistant will be required, unless a so-called "one-man" bleeding kit is available.

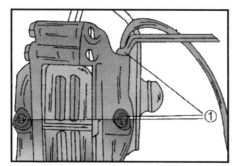

Fig. 8.17 – The location of the three bleeding screws of a front brake caliper.

Always use clean fresh brake fluid of the recommended specification and never re-use fluid bled from the system. Be ready to top up the reservoir with fluid (a brake bleeding kit will do this automatically) as the operations proceed. If the level is allowed to fall below the minimum the operations will have to be re-started.

- Obtain a length of plastic tube, preferably clear, and a clean container. Put in an inch or two of brake fluid into the container and then go to the first bleed point. This is the upper bleeder screw in Fig. 8.17. Take off the dust cap and attach the tube to the screw, immersing the other end of the tube into the fluid in the container.

- Open the bleed screw about three quarters of a turn and have your assistant depress the brake pedal firmly to its full extent while you keep the end of the tube well below the fluid level in the container. Watch the bubbles emerging from the tube and repeat the operation until no more are seen. Depress the brake pedal once more, hold it down and tighten the bleed screw firmly.

- Check the fluid level, go to the next point and repeat the operations in the same way. Install all dust caps, depress the brake pedal several times and finally top up the reservoirs.

8.9   Changing the Brake Fluid

The brake fluid should be changed every two years. In general this is normally not carried out, but we highly recommend it if heavy loads or passengers are carried.

Empty the brake system by opening all bleeding screws and pumping the pedal. Old fluid should be collected in a jar as described above.

After filling the fluid reservoir, bleed the system in the manner described above. In this case it is more important to observe the fluid level in the reservoir, as it will sink rapidly. It is of advantage to have an additional helper, one to operate the brake pedal and another one to top-up the reservoir.

Make sure to fit the rubber dust caps over the bleeder screws after the system has been bled. Operate the brake pedal a few times to check the pedal pressure. If the pedal "lifts" during the pumping operation, re-bleed the system.

8.10   Brake Pressure Regulator

The brake pressure regulator can be adjusted. The job, however, must be carried out in a workshop, as pressure gauges are necessary to check and/or adjust the pressure settings.

8.11.   Checking the Brake Pad and Brake Shoe Lining Thickness

The remaining thickness of the brake pad and the brake shoe linings can be measured with the brake calipers and brake drums fitted. In the case of the front disc brakes, remove both wheels and check the pad thickness through the "window" in the caliper, as shown in Fig. 8.18.

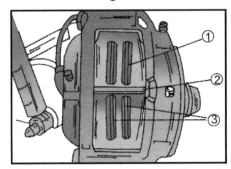

Fig. 8.18 – After removal of the front wheel you will be able to check the lining thickness.
1   Metal cover
2   Retaining pin
3   Brake pads

The linings must have a minimum thickness of 2 mm. In the case of the rear brakes, remove the plugs at the inside of the brake back plate (approx. In the centre on the L.H. and R.H. side) and shine a torch into the openings. The edges of the brake shoes can be seen. If the thickness of the lining has approached the thickness of the brake shoe, replace the brake shoes as a set.

9   602 and 603 DIESEL ENGINES

9.0.   General Technical Data

Fitted Engines:
- 250 GD: OM602
- 300 GD: OM603

Number of Cylinders:
- 602 engine: Five
- 603 engine: Six

Injection Order:
- Five cylinder: 1 – 2 – 4 – 5 – 3
- Six cylinder: 1 – 5 – 3 – 6 – 2 - 4

Arrangement of cylinders: In-line

Camshaft: Overhead camshaft, No. marked in end face
Arrangement of valves: Overhead
Cylinder bore, all engines: 87.00 mm
Piston stroke, all engines: 84.00 mm

Capacity:
- 602 engine: 2497 cc
- 603 engine: 2996 cc

Compression Ratio, all engines: 22 : 1

Max. B.H.P. (DIN):
- 602 engine to end of 1990:   63 kW (84 BHP) at 4600 rpm
- 602 engine from 1991:   69 kW (94 BHP) at 4600 rpm
- 603 engine: 80 kW (109 BHP) at 4600 rpm

Max. Torque:
- 602 engine to end of 1990:   15.4 kgm at 2800 rpm
- 602 engine from 1991:   15.8 kgm at 2500 – 3100 rpm
- 603 engine: 18.5 kgm at 2800 rpm

Crankshaft bearings: 6 (602). 7 (603) friction bearings
Cooling system: Thermo system with water pump, thermostat, cooling fan with fluid clutch, tube-type radiator

Lubrication: Pressure-feed lubrication with gear-type oil pump, driven with chain from crankshaft. With full-flow oil filter
Air cleaner: Dry paper element air cleaner

Valve Timing – New Timing Chain – Both engines:
- Inlet valve opens: 11° A.T.D.C
- Inlet valve closes: 17° A.B.D.C.
- Exhaust valve opens: 28° B.B.D.C.
- Exhaust valve closes: 15° B.T.D.C

Valve Timing – Used Timing Chain (after 12 000 miles) – Both engines:
- Inlet valve opens: 12° A.T.D.C
- Inlet valve closes: 18° A.B.D.C.
- Exhaust valve opens: 27° B.B.D.C.
- Exhaust valve closes: 14° B.T.D.C

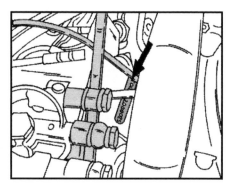

Fig. 9.1 – The location of the engine number (both engines).

The engines covered in this section were introduced during 1988. A five-cylinder engine (OM602) or a six-cylinder engine (OM603) can be fitted to the models given above. The six-cylinder engine was fitted the first time during 1990. The five-cylinder engine has a performance of 94 BHP since model year 1991. Earlier models have a power of 84 BHP.

602 and 603 Diesel Engines

The engine number of these engines can be found at the position shown in Fig. 9.1, i.e. on the side of the starter motor in the cylinder block.

The following sections describe operations which are different. When compared to the previously described 616 and 617 engines.

9.1. Engine – Removal and Installation

The removal and installation is in general carried out in the same manner as described for the 616 and 617 engines in Section 1.1. Although some of the connections and parts are different, you should have no problems following the described operations.

9.2. Engine – Dismantling and Assembly

As a complete strip-down of the engine is in most cases not necessary, and many of the operations can be carried out with the engine fitted, you will find in the following text a description of individual operations which can be carried out with the engine fitted and removed. Combining these, will give you the complete dismantling of the engine.

9.3. Engine - Overhaul

9.3.0. Cylinder Head and Valves – Technical Data

Cylinder Head:

Cylinder head height:	142.9 - 144.0 mm
Max. Distortion of Cylinder Head Faces:	
- Longitudinal direction:	0.08 mm
- Across the face:	0.00 mm
Max. deviation of faces between upper and lower sealing faces (parallel to each other):	0.10 mm

Depth of valve head faces and cylinder head sealing face:

- Inlet valves:	+0.17 to 0.23 mm
- Exhaust valves:	+0.12 to 0.28 mm
- With re-cut valve seats:	1.0 mm – all valves

Valves

Valve Head Diameter ("D" in Fig. 9.10):

- Inlet valves:	37.90 – 38.10 mm
- Exhaust valves:	34.90 – 35.10 mm
Valve seat angle:	45° + 15'

Valve Stem Diameter ("D1" in Fig. 9.10):

- Inlet valves:	7.970 – 7.955 mm
- Exhaust valves:	8.960 – 8.945 mm

Valve Length ("L" in Fig. 9.10):

- Inlet valves:	106.50 – 106.30 mm
- Exhaust valves:	106.50 – 106.30 mm
Valve Seat Width:	
- Inlet valves:	2.5 mm
- Exhaust valves:	3.5 mm

Valve Identification:

- Inlet valves:	E 601 02
- Exhaust valves:	A 601 02

Valve Seats
Valve seat width:
- Inlet valves: 2.5 mm
- Exhaust valves: 3.5 mm

Valve seat angles: 45° - 15'
Upper correction angle: 15°
Lower correction angle: 60°

Valve Seat Inserts (D in Fig. 9.8)
Insert outer diameter:
- Inlet valves – Std.:   40.100 – 40.084 mm
- Exhaust valves – Std.:   37.100 – 37.084 mm
Insert inner diameter ("D1" in Fig. 9.8):
- Inlet valves – Std.:   33.400 – 33.600 mm
- Exhaust valves – Std.:   30.500 – 30.600 mm

Basic bore in cylinder head ("D2" in Fig. 9.8):
- Inlet valves – Std.:   40.000 – 40.016 mm
- Exhaust valves – Std.:   37.000 – 37.016 mm
Valve seat height, all valves: 6.97 – 7.00 mm
Upper edge of valve seat rings to cylinder head face:
- Inlet valves: 2.37 – 2.25 mm
- Exhaust valves: 2.44 – 2.25 mm

Valve Springs
Colour code: yellow-green or purple-green
Outer diameter: 33.20 mm
Wire diameter: 4.25 mm
Free length: 50.80 mm
Length under load of 72 to 77 kg: 27.00 mm
- Wear limit: 27.00 mm at 65 kg

Valve Guides
Inlet valve Guides:
- Outer diameter – Std.:   14.044 – 14.051 mm
- Outer diameter – Repair size: 14.214 – 14.222 mm
- Inner diameter: 8.000 – 8.015 mm
Basic bore in cylinder head:
- Std.:   14.030 – 14.035 mm
- Repair size: 14.198 – 14.203 mm

Exhaust Valve Guides:
- Outer diameter – Std.:   14.044 – 14.051 mm
- Outer diameter – Repair size: 14.214 – 14.222 mm
- Inner diameter: 9.000 – 9.015 mm

Basic bore in cylinder head:
- Std.:   14.030 – 14.035 mm
- Repair size: 14.198 – 14.203 mm

Interference fit of valve guides – All guides:
- Std.:   0.009 – 0.021 mm
- Repair size: 0.011 – 0.024 mm

Camshaft
Camshaft Bearings:
- 5 cyl. engine: 6
- 6 cyl. engine   7
Journal diameter: 30.944 – 30.950 mm
Camshaft Bearing Clearance:
- New condition: 0.050 – 0.091 mm
- Wear limit: 0.11 mm
Camshaft End Float:
- New condition: 0.07 – 0.15 mm
- Wear limit: 0.18 mm

9.3.0.1.   Cylinder Head – Removal and Installation

The following information should be noted when work is carried out on a cylinder head:
- The cylinder head is made of light-alloy. Engine coolant, engine oil, the air required to ignite the fuel and the exhaust gases are directed through the cylinder head. Glow plugs, injectors, pre-combustion chambers and valve tappets are fitted to the cylinder head. Also in the cylinder heads you will find the camshaft.
- The exhaust manifold and the inlet manifold are bolted to the outside of the head. The fuel enters the head on one side and exits on the other side, i.e. the head is of the well-known "crossflow" type.
- The cylinder head is fitted with various sender units, sensors and switching valves, responsible for certain functions of the temperature control.
- As the cylinder head is made of light alloy, it is prone to distortion if, for example, the order of slackening or tightening of the cylinder head bolts is not observed. For the same reason never remove the cylinder head from a hot engine.
- A cylinder head cannot be checked in fitted position. Sometimes the cylinder head gasket will "blow", allowing air into the cooling system. A quick check is possible after opening the coolant reservoir cap (engine fairly cold). Allow the engine to warm-up and observe the coolant. Visible air bubbles point in most cases to a "blown" gasket. Further evidence is white exhaust smoke, oil in the coolant or coolant in the engine oil. The latter can be checked at the oil dipstick. A white, grey emulsion on the dipstick is more or less a confirmation of a damaged cylinder gasket.
- If you are convinced that water has entered the engine and you want to get home or to the nearest garage, unscrew the injectors and crank the engine with the starter motor for a while to eject the water. Refit the injectors, start the engine and drive to your destination without switching off the engine. This is the only method to avoid serious engine damage (bent connecting rods for example).

The cylinder head must only be removed when the engine is cold. The head is removed together with the exhaust manifold, but the inlet manifold must be separated from the cylinder head before the head can be lifted off. New cylinder head gaskets are wrapped in plastic and must only be unwrapped just before the gasket is fitted. The cylinder head can be removed with the engine fitted and these operations are described below, but note that operations may vary, depending on the equipment fitted:
- Place the engine bonnet in vertical position. Disconnect the battery earth cable.

- Drain the cooling system (Section 1.8.1.) and remove the radiator.
- Remove the air cleaner.
- Cut the cable binder securing the engine cable harness.
- Remove the single poly V-belt from the front of the engine ad described earlier on in the manual in the section dealing with the cooling system.
- Remove the bolt securing the guide tube for the oil dipstick.
- Disconnect all coolant, fuel and vacuum hoses and the electrical cables connected to the cylinder head or any other unit on the cylinder head which cannot be removed together with the cylinder head (also see below).
- Separate the throttle control linkage at the ball joint connection.
- Disconnect the vacuum pipes from the exhauster (vacuum) pump. One hose and one union nut must be removed.
- Use suitable clamps and clamp-off the fuel hoses and disconnect the fuel hoses at the fuel filter or remove the fuel filter bracket and tie it up with a piece of wire.
- In the case of an engine with EGR system disconnect the pipe between the EGR valve and the exhaust manifold.
- Disconnect the exhaust pipe flange from the exhaust manifold and unscrew the exhaust pipe support bracket from the transmission.
- If an automatic transmission is fitted remove the bolt securing the dipstick for the transmission fluid.
- Disconnect the injection pipes. Protect the open ends to prevent entry of foreign matter.

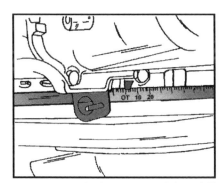

- Remove the inlet (intake) manifold.

Fig. 9.2 – Dead centre position of the engine.

- Disconnect the electrical leads from the glow plugs.
- Remove the cylinder head cover. Six screws must be removed. Two are located on each long side of the cover and two on the timing side of the engine. If an automatic transmission is fitted, there is a regulating rod fitted across the cylinder head cover, which must be separated on one side at the ball joint. A sticking cylinder head cover must not be freed by tapping it with a hammer. If difficult to remove, try to unstick it by pushing it by hand to one side. Use a plastic mallet, if necessary.

Fig. 9.3 – Mark the chain and sprocket with a spot of paint before removal of the sprocket.

- Remove the securing clip for the heater assembly feed pipe with a wire hook.
- Rotate the engine until the piston of No. 1 cylinder is at top dead centre in the firing position., i.e. the "0" mark must be opposite the adjusting pin, as shown in Fig. 9.2. A 27 mm socket can be applied to the crankshaft pulley to rotate the crankshaft. Never attempt to rotate the

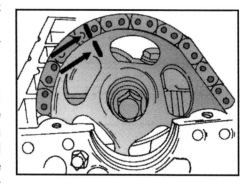

crankshaft by applying a socket to the camshaft timing wheel bolt. The crankshaft must be rotated in the direction of rotation.
- Remove the chain tensioner as described later on. The chain tensioner plug must be unscrewed by applying a spanner to the hexagon. The plug is located above the water pump and the thermostat cover, next to the large tube.

- Mark the camshaft sprocket and the timing chain at opposite points, as shown in Fig. 9.3, using a spot of paint.
- Unscrew the camshaft sprocket bolt. To counterhold the camshaft against rotation, insert a strong screwdriver blade or steel bolt into one of the holes of the camshaft sprocket.
- Remove the camshaft sprocket from the shaft without disengaging the timing chain from the crankshaft sprocket. Pull the chain tight and use a piece of wire to tie chain and sprocket together.
- Remove the camshaft as described under the relevant heading.
- Remove the slide rail from the cylinder head as described later on.
- In the inside of the chain case remove two 8 mm socket head bolts with an Allen key. An extension and a socket is required to reach the bolts.

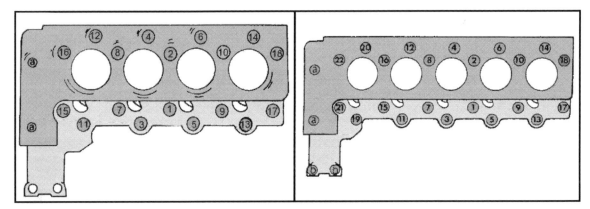

Fig. 9.4 – Tightening sequence for the cylinder head bolts for the 602 engine (2.5 litres) in the L.H. view and the 603 (3.0 litres) in the R.H. view. The bolts "a" on the L.H. side are the smaller bolts mentioned in the text. Slacken the bolts in reverse order.

- Unscrew the cylinder head bolts in reverse order to the one shown in Fig. 9.4 for the engine in question. A multi-spline bit must be used to slacken the bolts (MB Part No. 601 589 00 10 00). A normal Allen key is not suitable as it will damage the bolt heads. Immediately after removal of the bolts measure their length. If the dimension from the end of the bolt to the underside of the bolt head is more than 83.6, 105.6 or 118.5 mm, depending where the bolts are located, replace the bolts. New bolts have a length of 80 mm, 102.0 mm or 115.0 mm. i.e. bolts which nearly approach the max. length should also be replaced.

Note: Certain bolts are fitted through the camshaft bearings. As the cylinder head bolts are of different length, mark them before removal to assure refitting in the original positions.

- Lift off the cylinder head. If a hoist or other lifting equipment is available, hook a rope to the two lifting eyes and lift off the head. Remove the cylinder head gasket.
- Immediately after removal, clean the cylinder head and block surfaces of old gasket material.
- If necessary, overhaul the cylinder head as described in Section 1.9.0.2. after dismantling.

Install the cylinder head in the following manner:
- Place a new cylinder head gasket in position.
- Place the cylinder head carefully in position, taking care to engage the dowel sleeves. Use a soft-faced mallet to tap the head in position.
- Coat the threads of the cylinder head bolts and the underside of the bolt heads with oil. It is assumed that original bolts have been measured for their re-use.

- Insert the cylinder head bolts as originally fitted (and hopefully marked) and tighten them in the sequence shown in Fig. 9.4 in several stages. The tightening is carried out in stages as follows:
- Tighten all bolts in the correct order to 2.5 kgm (18 ft.lb.).
- Tighten all bolts in the correct order to 4.0 kgm (29 ft.lb.).
- Wait 10 minutes.
- Angle-tighten all bolts in their correct tightening order. To do this, insert the multi-spline bit with the socket into each bolt and fit the tommy bar so that it is in line with the longitudinal axis of the engine. Tighten the bolt until the tommy bar is at right angle to the engine, i.e. the bolt has been tightening by 90° (1/4 of a turn). Do not use the torque wrench for this operation.
- Re-tighten each bolt in the order given by a further 90° in the manner described above.
- Fit the two socket head screws to the inside of the timing chain chamber and tighten them to 2.5 kgm (18 ft.lb.).

Note: *Multi-spline head socket bolts require no re-tightening after they have been fitted as described above.*

Cylinder heads are sometimes modified (for example after Oct. 1984). When for example fitting a second head cylinder head at some stage, make sure it is the correct one.

- Refit the slide rail to the head as described later on (Section 1.3.5.3.).
- Fit the camshaft sprocket together with the timing chain to the end of the camshaft, making sure that the paint marks made during removal are in line. The sprocket must engage with its bore over the dowel pin in the camshaft.
- Fit the camshaft sprocket bolt and tighten the bolt to 6.5 kgm (47 ft.lb.). Counterhold the camshaft by inserting a strong screwdriver blade or steel bolts through one of the openings in the sprocket.
- Refit the timing chain tensioner and tighten the plug to 8.0 kgm (58.5 ft.lb.).
- Check the marking for top dead centre for the No. 1 cylinder in the camshaft (see Fig. 9.5). A notch is machined into the camshaft which should be in line with a mark machined into the cylinder head. The alignment can be seen by looking from above and comparing it with Fig. 9.5.

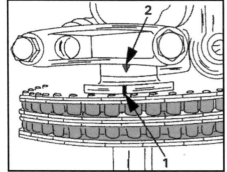

Fig. 9.5 – Alignment of the notch in the camshaft flange (1) and the lug on the No. 1 camshaft bearing cap (2) assures the T.D.C. position of the engine.

- Re-connect the glow plug cables.
- Refit the inlet manifold and the injectors and re-connect the injection pipes.
- Fit the tube elbow with a new "O" sealing ring.
- Fit the exhaust pipe to the exhaust manifold.
- The remaining operations are carried out in reverse order to the removal procedure. Check and, if necessary adjust, the throttle cable operation.

9.3.0.2. Cylinder Head - Dismantling

The following description assumes that the cylinder head is to be replaced. If only a top overhaul is asked for, ignore the additional instructions. The cylinder head must be removed.

602 and 603 Diesel Engines

The valve stem oil seals can be replaced with the cylinder head fitted. Signs of worn oil seals are blue exhaust smoke when the vehicle is coasting (gear engaged), when the engine is accelerated after idling for a while or blue smoke when starting the cold engine. If the oil consumption has reached 1 litre per 600 miles, replace the valve stem oil seals as described under a separate heading.

Proceed as follows during dismantling:
- Remove all auxiliary parts from the cylinder head, including the exhaust manifold.
- Remove the camshaft. All camshaft bearing brackets must be removed and the camshaft lifted out. Each bearing bracket is marked with a number. A corresponding number is marked into the cylinder head, i.e. there is no need to mark the bearing brackets.
- A valve spring compressor is required to remove the valves. Valves are held in position by means of valve cotter halves. Compress the springs and remove the valve cotter halves with a pair of pointed pliers or a small magnet.

If a valve spring compressor is not available, it is possible to use a short piece of tube to remove the valve cotter halves. To do this, place the tube over the upper valve spring collar and hit the tube with a blow of a hammer. The valve cotter halves will collect in the inside of the tube and the components can be removed. The valve head must be supported from the other side of the cylinder head. Keep the hammer in close contact with the tube to prevent the cotter halves from flying out.

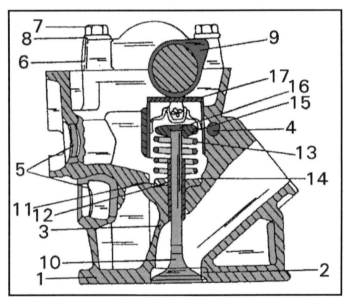

Fig. 9.6 – Sectional view of the cylinder head and an inlet valve.
1. Cylinder head
2. Inlet valve seat ring
3. Inlet valve guide
4. Oil passage
5. Welsh plug
6. Bearing cap
7. Bolt, M8 x 45
8. Washer
9. Camshaft
10. Inlet valve
11. Thrust ring
12. Lock ring
13. Valve spring
14. Valve stem oil seal
15. Valve spring retainer
16. Valve cotter halves
17. Valve clearance element

- Remove the valve spring collar and the valve spring. The valve springs (one spring per valve) are identified with a paint spot and only a spring with a paint spot of the same colour must be fitted. A thrust ring is fitted underneath each valve spring and can be removed. Figs. 9.6 and 9.7 show sectional views of the two valve assemblies.
- Remove valve stem oil seals carefully with a screwdriver or a pair of pliers.
- Remove the valves one after the other out of the valve guides and pierce them in their fitted order through a piece of cardboard. Write the cylinder number against each valve if they are to be re-used.

A few words should be said about the camshaft. The camshaft of a five-cylinder engine has six bearings, the shaft of a six-cylinder engine has seven bearings. All bearings have the same diameter of 31.0 mm. The lower part of the bearing location is machined directly into the cylinder head. The camshaft is located in axial direction by means of a retaining ring, which is secured to the cylinder head and engages into a groove at the front end of the cylinder head.

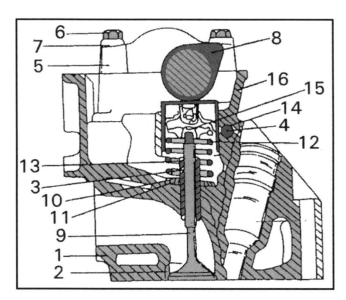

Fig. 9.7 – Sectional view of the cylinder head and an exhaust valve.
1. Cylinder head
2. Exhaust valve seat ring
3. Exhaust valve guide
4. Oil passage
5. Bearing cap
6. Bolt, M8 x 45
7. Washer
8. Camshaft
9. Exhaust valve
10. Thrust ring
11. Lock ring
12. Valve spring
13. Valve stem oil seal
14. Valve spring retainer
15. Valve cotter halves
16. Hydraulic valve tappet

The camshaft flange is marked with a line. Next to the line is an identification number. If a shaft is replaced, only fit a shaft with the same number. The parts lists will have the correct camshaft for the engine in question.

9.3.0.3.   Cylinder Head - Overhaul

The cylinder head must be thoroughly cleaned and remains of old gasket material removed. The checks and inspections are to be carried out as required.

Valve Springs: Valve springs are checked in the manner described for the 616/617 engines.

Valve Guides: Valve guides for inlet and exhaust valves are made of cast iron and have different diameters, Guides for exhaust valves are shorter and have a larger inner diameter.

Clean the inside of the guides by pulling a petrol-soaked cloth through the guides. Valve stems can be cleaned best by means of a rotating wire brush. Measure the inside diameter of the guides. As an inside micrometer is necessary for this operation, which is not always available, you can insert the valve into its guide and withdraw it until the valve head is approx. level with the cylinder head face. Rock the valve to and fro and check for play. Although no exact values are available, it can be assumed that the play should not exceed 1.0 - 1.2 mm (0.04 -0.047 in.). Mercedes workshops use gauges to check the guides for wear.

Guides are removed with a shouldered mandrel from the combustion chamber side of the cylinder head. If guides with nominal dimensions can be used, drive them in position, until the retaining ring is resting against the cylinder head. If repair guides are fitted, the locating bores in the cylinder head must be reamed out to take the new guides. As dry ice is required to fit the new valve guides, we recommend to have the work carried out in a workshop.

Before a valve guide is replaced, check the general condition of the cylinder head. The guides must be reamed after installation, and after the cylinder head has cooled down, if applicable, to their correct internal diameter, given in Section 9.3.0, noting the different diameters for inlet and exhaust valves.

Valves must always be replaced if new valve guides are fitted. The valve seats must be re-cut when a guide has been replaced. If it is obvious that seats cannot be re-ground in the present condition, new valve seat inserts must be fitted.

602 and 603 Diesel Engines

Again this is an operation for a specialist and the work should be carried out in a workshop.

Valve Seats: If the camshaft bearings are excessively worn, fit a new or exchange cylinder head. In this case there is no need to renovate the valve seats.

Check all valve seats for signs of pitting or wear. Slight indentations can be removed with a 45° cutter. If this operation is carried out properly, there should be no need to grind-in the valves. Use correction cutters to bring the valve seating area into the centre of the valve seat. Make sure that the valve seat width, given in Section 9.3.0. is obtained. This again is achieved by using cutters of different angles (for example 15° and 60°). Valve seat inserts can be fitted to the cylinder head. Replacement of valve seat inserts will require that the old seat insert is removed by machining. The machining must not damage the bottom face of the head recess.

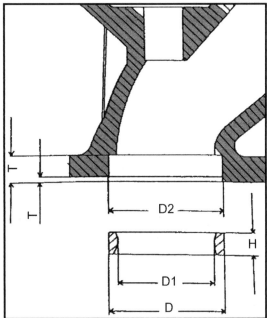

Fig. 9.8 – Principal dimensions of a valve seat.

Description
D   Outer diameter of seat ring
D1 Inner diameter of seat ring
D2 Locating bore in cylinder head
H   Height of valve seat ring
T   Dimension between head face and
    upper face of valve seat ring

Dimensions
D   40.100 - 40.084 mm, inlet valve
D1 33.400 - 33.600 mm, exhaust valves
D2 40.000 - 40.016 mm, inlet valves
H   6.97 - 7.0 mm
T   2.37 - 2.25 mm, inlet valves
    2.44 - 2.25 mm, exhaust valves

As this is a critical operation, we advise you to bring the cylinder head to your Mercedes Dealer who has the necessary equipment and experience to do the job. Fig. 9.8 shows a valve seat. It may be possible to obtain a reconditioned cylinder head in exchange for the old one to avoid time delay. In this case remove all ancillary parts from the old head and refit them to the new head.

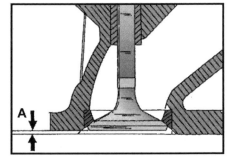

Fig. 9.9 – The maximum dimension "A" between the valve face and cylinder head face is shown on the L.H. side.

If the valve seats have been re-cut, use the valve and measure the dimension "A" in Fig. 9.9. To do this, insert the valve into the respective bore and, using a depth gauge, measure the gap between the cylinder head face and the valve face. The dimension must be between 0.1 and 0.5 mm in the case of new valves. The wear limit is 1.0 mm.

Valves can be ground into their seats in the conventional manner.

Valves: The stems of inlet valves and exhaust valves have been specially treated, i.e. the ends of the valve stems must not be ground off.

Valves can be cleaned best with a rotating wire brush. Check the valve faces for wear or grooving. If the wear is only slight, valves can be re-ground to their original angle in a valve grinding machine, but make sure that there is enough material left to have an edge on the valve head. The valve head thickness must be 0.5 - 0.7 mm in the case of the inlet valves and 0.5 - 0.6 mm in the case of the exhaust valves.

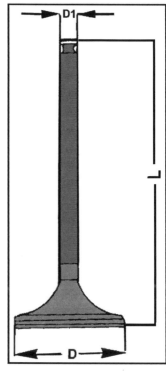

Fig. 9.10 – Principal valve dimensions.
D = Valve head diameter
D1 = Stem diameter
L = Length

Measure the valves in accordance with the values given in Section 9.3.0 and Fig. 9.10 and replace any valve which is outside the limits given. Note that the valves are not filled with sodium, as is the case with other Mercedes engines.

Check the valve stem diameters and in this connection the inside diameters of the valve guides. If there is a deviation from the nominal values, it may be necessary to replace the valve guides (see above). Also check the end of the valve stems. There should be no visible wear in this area.

Always quote the model year and the engine number when ordering new valves, as different valves are used. These are marked by means of a number in the end of the valve stem. The numbers can be found in Section 9.3.0.

Sometimes it is only required to replace the exhaust valves, if these for example are burnt out at their valve head edges.

Cylinder Head: Thoroughly clean the cylinder head and cylinder block surfaces of old gasket material and check the faces for distortion. To do this, place a steel ruler with a sharp edge over the cylinder head face and measure the gap between ruler and face with feeler gauges. Checks must be carried out in longitudinal and diagonal direction and across the face. If a feeler gauge of more than 0.10 mm (0.004 in.) can be inserted, when the ruler is placed along or across the cylinder head, have the cylinder head face re-ground. The dimension between the face of the valve heads and the cylinder head face ("A" in Fig. 9.9) will change after regrinding, but the workshop will correct it accordingly.

A further check must be carried out on the pre-combustion chambers for the fuel injection. These must protrude by 7.6 - 8.1 mm. Mercedes workshops correct this dimension by fitting sealing washers of different thicknesses, to correct the protrusion.

Camshaft: Place the camshaft with both end journals into "V" blocks or clamp the shaft between the centres of a lathe and apply a dial gauge to the centre journal, as shown in the section dealing with the 616/617 engines. Slowly rotate the shaft to check for wear. If it exceeds 0.01 mm, fit a new shaft. Make sure to fit the correct shaft if the shaft is to be replaced. Check the identification number when ordering a new shaft.

Replacing Valve Stem Oil Seals (Cylinder Head fitted): Valve stem oil seals are available in repair kits. Included in the repair kits are protective sleeves which must be pushed over the valves during installation of the seals. Valve stem seals are different in diameter and can also be identified by their shape (Fig. 9.11).

Normally a special tool is used to fit the seals, but a well fitting piece of tube of suitable diameter can be used. Take care not to damage the sealing lip and the spring.

The valve cotter halves and the valve springs must be removed to replace the seals. To prevent the valves from dropping into the combustion chambers, the pistons must be at the top dead centre position.

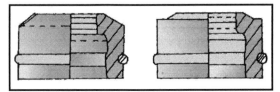

Fig. 9.11 – Sectional view of the valve stem oil seals. On the left for the exhaust valves; on the right for the inlet valves.

- Remove the camshaft (see description later on).

- Remove the valve cotter halves of the first cylinder as described in Section 9.3.0.2.

- Use a pair of pliers or a screwdriver to remove the valve stem seals, without damaging the valve stems.

- Coat the new seals with engine oil and carefully push them over the valve stems. The protective sleeve must be used for the inlet valves. Push the seals over the valve guides until properly in position.

- Fit the valve springs with the paint spot towards the bottom, fit the upper spring cup and compress the springs until the valve cotter halves can be inserted. Make absolutely sure that the cotter halves have properly engaged before the crankshaft is rotated.

- Lift the camshaft sprocket slightly to prevent disengagement of the timing chain and rotate the crankshaft until the valves of the next cylinder are closed. This will take place in the firing order of the engine (see Section 9.0). As already mentioned, take care when rotating the crankshaft. Both valves of a cylinder must be at the same height, before the valve cotter halves are removed.

- Refit the camshaft and associated parts.

Note: Operate the valve spring compressor very slowly, as valve cotter halves sometimes stick to the valve stems. Observe the valve spring during compression. Only the spring should move, not the valve. Prevent the valve from pressing against the piston.

9.3.0.4. Cylinder Head - Assembly

The assembly of the cylinder head is a reversal of the dismantling procedure. Note the following points:

- Lubricate the valve stems with engine oil and insert the valves into the correct valve guides.

- Valve stem seals are different for inlet and exhaust valves. Make sure to order the correct seals. The repair kit contains fitting sleeves and these must be used to fit the seals (see last Section).

- The sleeves are fitted over the valve stem before the seal is pushed in position.

- Fit the valve spring and valve spring collar over the valve and use the valve lifter to compress the spring. Insert the valve cotter halves and release the valve spring lifter. Make sure that the cotter halves are in position by tapping the end of the valve stem with a plastic mallet. Place a rag over the valve end - just in case.

- Fit the camshaft as described later on and carry out all other operations in reverse order to the dismantling procedure.

9.4. Timing Cover – Removal and Installation

The timing cover closes the crankcase at the front. It is located by two dowels and secured by two bolts on the cylinder head, at the bottom by five bolts to the oil sump and 14 bolts to the cylinder block. The sealing between timing cover and engine is ensured by using sealing compound. The following parts are fitted to the timing cover (see Fig. 9.12):

Fig. 9.12 – The timing cover and attached parts.
1. Bearing pin for drive belt tensioner
2. Crankshaft oil seal
3. TDC timing pointer
4. Oil dipstick guide tube
5. Flange face for exhauster pump

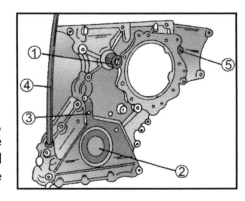

Water pump, fuel filter, the power steering pump, the bearing pin for the tensioning device of the drive belt for alternator, etc., the front crankshaft oil seal, the TDC indication pointer and the guide tube for the oil dipstick.

The timing cover can be removed with the engine fitted.

- Open the bonnet, and drain the engine oil and the cooling system. Remove large air intake hose.
- Remove the large nut in the centre of the cooling fan and remove the fan.
- Disconnect the battery earth cable.
- Remove the four Allen head bolts in the inside of the water pump pulley.
- Withdraw the cable plug from the connector on the magnetic body for the fan clutch, remove the bolts and withdraw the clutch from the magnetic body.
- Completely remove the tensioning device for the single drive belt. First remove the bolt at the upper end of the shock absorber. Remove the cover from the tensioning lever, unscrew the bolt and remove the washer. Remove the tensioning lever together with the shock absorber and the tensioning spring from the bearing pin in the timing cover, shown in Fig. 9.12 with (1).
- If a power-assisted steering is fitted, remove the steering pump pulley.
- Remove the two bolts securing the steering pump, lift off the pump without disconnecting the hoses. Place the pump to one side where it is out of the way.
- Remove the front bolt of the two fuel filter securing bolts.
- Remove the crankshaft pulley and the crankshaft pulley hub. A gear may be engaged to prevent the crankshaft from rotating. A puller may be necessary. Otherwise try two tyre levers.
- Remove the T.D.C. transmitter (indicates electrically when the piston of No. 1 cylinder is at T.D.C. firing point). The T.D.C. transmitter is located on the R.H. side of the timing cover, as can be seen in Fig. 9.13.

Fig. 9.13 – The TDC transmitter (arrow) is fitted to the timing cover.

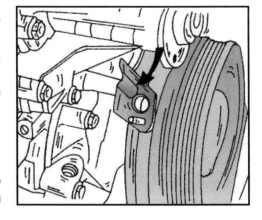

- Unscrew the exhauster pump (vacuum pump) from the timing cover.
- Remove the alternator together with the mounting bracket.
- If an automatic transmission is fitted, disconnect the oil pipes from the oil cooler. Plug the open ends in suitable manner.
- Remove the oil sump securing bolts in the area of the timing cover and then slacken the remaining oil sump bolts.
- Remove the cylinder head cover. Two screws are fitted on each side of the cover, two further screws are inserted into the small side on the timing gear end. A breather hose must be disconnected at the centre of the cover. If an automatic transmission is fitted you will have a throttle operating linkage across the cylinder head cover. Disconnect it on one side from the ball joint connection.

- Using a 6 mm Allen key and an extension of at least 440 mm in length, unscrew the two 8 mm cylinder head bolts from the inside of the timing chain chamber. These are the bolts shown with "a" in Fig. 9.4.
- Unscrew the oil dipstick guide tube from the timing cover.
- Unscrew the oil filler elbow and remove it.
- Remove the injection pump securing bolts and the nuts at the pump mounting flange.
- Remove the remaining timing cover bolts and take off the cover. Mark the position of the bolts in a suitable manner, as bolts of different lengths are used. Take care not to damage the cylinder head gasket during the cover removal, as this would mean a replacement is needed.

Refit the timing cover as follows:
- Carefully clean the sealing faces of the timing cover and the cylinder block from old sealing compound. Also check the sealing face of the cover for damage to prevent oil leaks later on.
- Coat the sealing face of the cover with sealing compound. Mercedes workshops use "Curil T" for this purpose, available under Part No. 001 989 47 20. Carefully fit the timing cover, without damaging the cylinder head gasket.
- Fit the screws into the timing cover, noting their different lengths.
- If the crankshaft oil seal has been replaced, fit it into the timing cover and over the crankshaft end.
- The remaining operations are carried out in reverse order to the removal procedure. Tension the single belt as described earlier on. Start the engine and check for oil leaks.

Modifications to Timing Cover and Cylinder Head

The following, important modifications were carried out over the years on cylinder heads and other associated parts, but it should be noted that not all engines are affected:

Model Year 1989: The combustion chamber in the cylinder head has been enlarged on all engines. Cylinder heads of earlier engines cannot be fitted to cylinder blocks of engines manufactured from model year 1989. The pre-combustion chambers have been adapted to the new cylinder head.

Engines with EGR system have a pressure valve in the cylinder head cover, which prevents the build-up of excessive vacuum (depression) in the engine. A breather hole is drilled into one side of the cylinder head cover (on the R.H. side of the oil filler neck). This hole must not be blocked by oil or other foreign matter. Always check the hole if the cylinder head cover has been removed.

9.5.   Pistons and Connecting Rods

9.5.0.   Technical Data

All dimensions are given in metric units.

Pistons

Class A: . . . . 86.970 - 86.976 mm
Class X: . . . . More than 86.975 - 86.983 mm
Class B: . . . . More than 86.982 - 86.988 mm

Piston Running Clearance:
- New: . . . . 0.017 – 0.043 mm

- Wear limit: ....0.12 mm

Max. weight difference within engine:
- New ....4 grams
- Wear limit ....10 grams

Piston Pins:
Pin diameter:..26.995 – 27.000 mm
Piston pin running clearance:
- In small end bush :...0.018 – 0.029 mm
- In piston:...0.004 – 0.015 mm

Piston Rings:
Piston Ring Gaps:
- Upper rings:....................................0.20 – 0.40 mm (wear limit 1.5 mm)
- Centre rings:....................................0.30 – 0.40 mm (wear limit 1.0 mm)
- Lower rings:.....................................0.20 – 0.40 mm (wear limit 1.0 mm)

Side Clearance in Grooves:
- Upper rings:...............................0.090 – 0.120 mm (wear limit 0.20 mm)
- Centre rings:...............................0.050 - 0.080 mm (wear limit 0.15 mm)
- Lower rings:................................0.030 - 0.065 mm (wear limit 0.10 mm)
Connecting Rods
Distance from centre small end bore to
        centre big end bore: ....145.0 mm
Width of con rod at big end bore: ....24.000 mm
Basic bore diameter of big end bore: ....47.95 mm
Basic bore diameter of small end bore: ....29.500 mm

Small End Bush:
- Outer diameter: ....29.50 mm
- Inner diameter: ....27.000 mm
Max. twist of connecting rods: ....0.10 mm per 100 mm
Max. bend of connecting rods: ....0.045 mm per 100 mm
Max. weight difference in same engine: ....5 gram (per set)
Connecting Rod Bolts:
- Thread:.. M9 x 1
- Diameter of stretch neck :.. 7.4 mm
- Min. diameter of stretch neck: .... 7.1 mm
Connecting rod bearing details:.............................See under "Crankshaft"

9.5.1.   Piston and Connecting Rods – Removal

The pistons are made of light-alloy. Each piston has a star-shaped cavity, a pre-combustion chamber and two round recesses for the valve heads. The exit of the pre-combustion chamber is connected with the combustion cavity. Fig. 9.14 shows a view of the piston.

Three piston rings are fitted to each piston. The two upper rings are the compression rings, i.e. they prevent the pressure above the piston crown to return to the crankcase. The lower ring is the oil scraper ring. Its function is to remove excessive oil from the cylinder bore, thereby preventing the entry of oil into the combustion chamber. The three rings are not the same in shape. The upper ring has a rectangular section, the centre ring has a chamfer on the inside and the lower ring is chrome-plated on its outside. Only the correct fitting of the piston rings will assure the proper operation of the piston sealing.

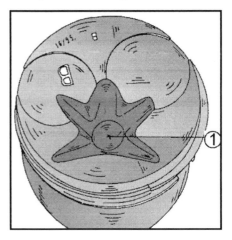

Fig. 9.14 – View of the piston, showing the combustion chamber with (1). The two recesses for the valves prevent contact between the valve heads and the piston crown.

Pistons and connecting rods are pushed out towards the top of the cylinder bores, using a hammer handle after connecting rod bearing caps and shells have been removed. Before removal of the assemblies note the following points:

- Pistons and cylinder bores are graded in three diameter classes within specified tolerance groups and marked with the letters A, X and B. The class number is stamped into the upper face of the cylinder block, next to the particular cylinder bore, as shown in Fig. 9.15.

Fig. 9.15 – Identification (marking) of piston crown and cylinder block face with the group code letters.

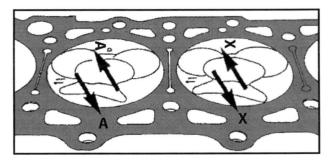

- The class number of the piston must always be identical with the letter stamped next to the cylinder bore. Piston diameter, the class number and the two last numbers of the piston spare part number are stamped into the piston crown. An arrow with the inscription "Vorn" (front), indicating the fitting direction is also stamped into the piston crown.

Fig. 9.16 – The connecting rods are marked at the position shown to indicate the bearing shell diameter.

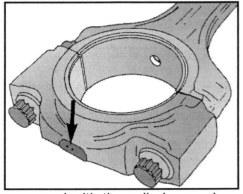

- For repairs, only pistons with group code letter "X" are available. These pistons can also be used if the code letters "A" or "B" are stamped into the cylinder block. If the cylinder bores are re-bored, their size will be increased to take the group "X" pistons, plus the allowance for the piston running clearance.

- Mark each piston and the connecting rod before removal with the cylinder number. This can be carried out by writing the cylinder number with paint onto the piston crown. Also mark an arrow, facing towards the front of the engine (the arrow in the piston crown will be covered by the carbon deposits). When removing the connecting rod, note the correct installation of the big end bearing cap. Immediately after removal mark the connecting rod and the big end bearing cap on the same side. This is best done with a centre punch (cylinder No. 1 one punch mark, etc.).

- Mark the big end bearing shells with the cylinder number. The upper shells have an oil drilling (to lubricate the piston pin).

- The big end bearing shells can be of two different diameters. At the lower end of the connecting rod bearing cap, at the position shown in Fig. 9.16, you will see one or two punch marks. If one punch mark is present, bearing caps with a blue paint mark (on the edge of the bearing shells) are fitted. If two punch marks are visible, as shown in the illustration, bearing shells without colour code are used.

- Big end bearing journals can be re-ground to four undersizes (in steps of 0.25 mm between sizes). Corresponding bearing shells are available.
- Remove the bearing caps and the shells and push the assemblies out of the cylinder bore. Any carbon deposits on the upper edge of the bores can be carefully removed with a scraper.
- Remove the piston pin snap rings. A notch in the piston pin bore enables a pointed drift to be inserted, as shown for the 616/617 engines in Fig. 1.27, to remove the rings. Press the piston pins out of the pistons. If necessary heat the piston in boiling water.
- Remove the piston rings one after the other from the pistons, using a piston ring pliers if possible (Fig. 9.17). If the rings are to be re-used, mark them in accordance with their pistons and position.

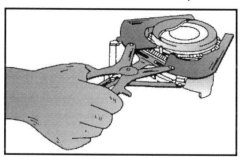

Fig. 9.17 – Removal or installation of piston rings with a pair of piston ring pliers. Never expand rings more than necessary to prevent breakage.

9.5.2.   Measuring the Cylinder Bores

The operations are carried out as described for the 616/617 engines.

9.5.3.   Checking Pistons and Connecting Rods

The operations are carried out as described for the 616/617 engines, but note the following:

- Piston pins and small end bushes must be checked for wear or seizure. One individual connecting rod can be replaced, provided that a rod of the same weight group is fitted. Connecting rods are marked with either one or two punch marks (arrow, Fig. 9.16) and only a rod with the same mark must be fitted.
- Before re-using the connecting rod bolts check their diameter at the position shown in Fig. 9.18. If this is smaller than 7.1 mm, replace the bolt. A second check is carried out by placing the connecting rod bearing on one of the connecting rod bolts. If the bearing cap is moving under its own weight, renew bolt. The check is shown in Fig. 1.29.

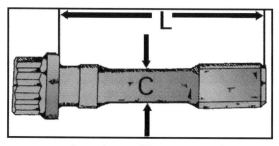

Fig. 9.18 – Connecting rod bolts can stretch in their length "L". By measuring the stretch neck "c", you will know if the bolts can be re-used.

- Connecting rods should be checked for bend or twist, particularly when the engine has covered a high mileage. A special jig is necessary for this operation and the job should be carried out by an engine shop. The max. values are given in Section 9.5.0.

The following information concern the connecting rods:
- Connecting rods which were over-heated due to bearing failure (blue-ish colour) must not be refitted.
- Connecting and bearing caps are matched to each other and must be fitted accordingly.

- New connecting rods are supplied together with the small end bearing bush and can be fitted as supplied.

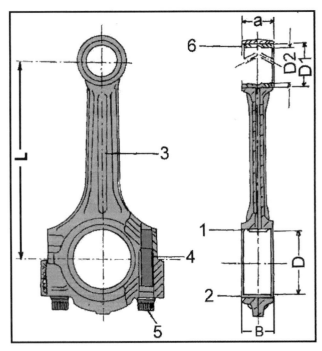

Fig. 9.19 – Sectional view of a connecting rod.
1   Upper bearing shell
2   Lower bearing shell
3   Connecting rod
4   Spring pins (roll pins)
5   Connecting rod bolt
6   Small end bush
L   145.0 mm
B   24.00 mm
D   47.95 mm
D1   29.50 mm
D2   27.00 mm

Fit the bearing cap with the inserted bearing shells and clamp the connecting rod into a vice. Tighten the bolts to the specified torque, using an internal micrometer, measure the big end bore diameter at various points. If the value of 51.119 mm is exceeded, or the bore is out of round, replace the complete connecting rod.

- If the piston pin has excessive clearance in the small end bush, fit a new bush. When pressing in the new bush, align the oil bore in the bush with the oil bore in the connecting rod. The small end bush must be reamed to the diameter "D2" in Fig. 9.19 to obtain the correct piston pin running clearance and again we recommend to have the job carried out by an engine shop.

9.5.4.   Checking the Big End Bearing Clearance

These operations are described in connection with the crankshaft.

9.5.5.   Piston and Connecting Rods - Assembly

If new pistons are fitted, check the piston crown markings to ensure the correct pistons are fitted. If the original pistons are fitted, arrange them in accordance with the cylinder number markings.

Fig. 9.20 – The arrow in the piston crown (1) must face the front end of the engine when the locating lugs for the bearing shells (2) are on the L.H. side of the cylinder block.

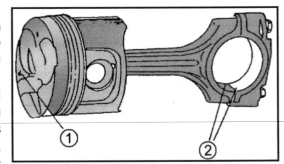

- If connecting rods have been replaced check the bottom of the big end bearing caps. Either one or two punch marks are stamped into the centre of the cap, as shown in Fig. 9.16. These numbers refer to the bearing shells to be fitted. Shells with blue colour code (marked at the side of the shells) must be fitted If one punch mark is stamped into the cap.

- Insert the connecting rod into the piston and align the two bores. Make sure that the arrow in the piston crown and locating lugs for the bearing shell location are facing the L.H. side of the engine, as shown in Fig. 9.20.

- Generously lubricate the piston pin with engine oil and insert it into the piston and connecting rod, using thumb pressure only. Never heat the piston to fit the piston pin. Fit the circlips to both sides of the piston, making sure of their engagement around the groove. Move the piston up and down to check for free movement.

- Using a pair of piston ring pliers, fit the piston rings from the top of the piston, starting with the bottom ring. The two compression rings could be mixed up and Fig. 9.21 should be referred to avoid mistakes. Under no circumstances mix-up the upper and lower compression rings.

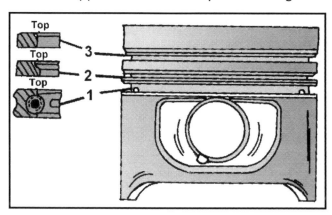

Fig. 9.21 - Sectional view of a piston, concentrating on the piston rings.
1 Slotted control ring with expander ring, chrome plated
2 Chamfered compression ring
3 Square compression ring, contact case asymmetrically ground and chrome plated

Note: If the engine operates with an EGR system, the pistons are cooled by oil splash jets, if applicable, introduced for model year 1991.

9.5.6. Pistons and Connecting Rods - Installation

- Generously lubricate the cylinder bores with oil. Markings on connecting rods and bearing caps must be opposite each other. The arrows in the piston crowns must face towards the front of the engine.

- Arrange the piston rings at equal spacings of 120° around the circumference of the piston skirt and use a piston ring compressor to push the rings into their grooves. Check that all rings are fully pushed in.

- Insert the second bearing shell into the connecting rod bearing cap, with the locating tab on the L.H. side and fit the assembly over the connecting rod. Check that connecting rod/cap marks are facing each other.

- Coat the contact areas for the cap bolts with engine oil and fit and tighten the bolts to 3.0 kgm (22 ft.lb.) in several stages. From this position tighten each bolt by a further 90° – 100° (approx. 1/4 of a turn) without using the torque wrench. It is assumed that the stretch bolts have been measured as previously described.

- Rotate the crankshaft until the two remaining crankpins are at bottom dead centre and fit the two other piston/connecting rod assemblies in the same manner.

- Check the pistons and connecting rods once more for correct installation and that each piston is fitted to its original bore, if the same parts are refitted.

- With a feeler gauge measure the side clearance of each big end bearing cap on the crankpin. The wear limit is 0.50 mm (standard 0.11 – 023 mm).

9.6. Cylinder Block

9.6.0. Technical Data

Cylinder Bore Diameter:
- Nominal diameter   - Group A: .... 87.000 - 87.006 mm
                                - Group X: .... More than 87.006 - 87.012 mm
                                - Group B: .... more than 87.012 - 87.018 mm
- Max. wear, longitudinal and across: .... 0.10 mm (0.004 in.)
Max. out-of-round or taper of bores:
- New condition: .... 0.014 mm

602 and 603 Diesel Engines

- Wear limit: ....0.05 mm
Measuring point for bores: ....Upper edge, centre and lower edge, in longitudinal and transverse direction

Measuring point for bores: ....As for other engines

Crankcase
Permissible unevenness of:
- Upper crankcase face: ....0.10 mm
- Lower crankcase face: ....0.05 mm
Difference between upper and lower sealing face: .... 0.10 mm (0.004 in.)

9.6.1. Servicing

Special attention should be given to the cylinder block each time the crankshaft has been removed, irrespective whether the bores are to be re-machined or not.

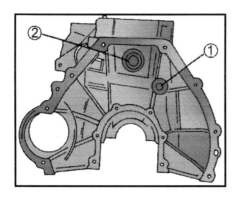

Fig. 9.22 – View of the rear end of the cylinder block, showing the steel ball (1) for the main oil gallery and the welsh plug (2).

Thoroughly clean all cavities and passages and remove all traces of foreign matter from the joint faces. If any machining or honing of the bores takes place, it is essential that all swarf is removed before assembly of the engine takes place. The main oil gallery is closed off by steel balls of 17 mm diameter at the front and 15 mm diameter at the rear. The steel balls must be removed in order to clean the main oil gallery. The steel balls can be refitted unless they show deep grooves. Figs. 9.22 and 9.23 show where these steel balls are located. Fig. 9.23 also shows other parts of the cylinder block, which should also be checked for wear, but note that not all parts are fitted to these engines. We must point out that the special drift 601 589 06 15 00 is used to drive the steel balls in position to ensure their correct seating. If possible always clean oil galleries with compressed air.

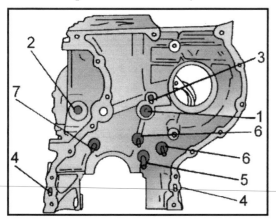

Fig. 9.23 – View of the front end of the cylinder block, showing the location of the various parts.
1 Welsh plug
2 Steel ball, 17 mm dia.
3 Oil splash jet
4 Roll pin
5 Bearing pin, oil pump chain tensioner
6 Bearing pin, tensioning rail
7 Bearing pin, slide rail

The following instructions apply to the advanced engineer:
If oil leaks can be detected at the front or rear of the cylinder block and the mentioned special drift cannot be obtained, it will be possible to close off the bores with threaded plugs. The operations are carried out in a similar manner as described for the 616/617 engines.

Replacing the Welsh Plugs: Refer to the description in the section covering the 616/617 engines.

Cylinder Block (crankcase) Modifications

The crankshaft bearing bores of engines were reduced by 2 mm with the introduction of model year 1985. The main bearing cap bolts were reduced from M12 to M11 at the same time. The bolts are stretch bolts and must be less than 63.8 mm in length if they are to be re-used. The upper surface of the cylinder block has also been modified and must only be used together with the modified cylinder head. The coolant drain plug in the cylinder block has an M18 thread (earlier blocks with M14 thread).

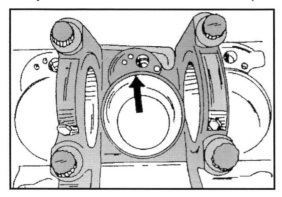

Fig. 9.24 – The arrow shows the oil splash jet (engine with EGR system).

If an EGR system is fitted, you will find oil feed bores and oil cooling jets for the pistons. The jets are fitted at the position shown in Fig. 9.24. These cylinder blocks cannot be fitted to other models. Always seek advise from your Mercedes Dealer, if you are intending to fit a replacement cylinder block.

9.7.   Crankshaft and Bearings

9.7.0.   Technical Data

All dimensions in metric units.
Machining tolerances:

Max. out-of-round of journals:	0.005 mm
Max. taper of main journals:	0.010 mm
Max. taper of crankpins:	0.015 mm
Max. run-out of main journals*:	
Journals Nos. II and IV:	0.07 mm
Journal No. III:	0.10 mm

> *   Crankshaft placed with Nos. I and IV journals (602) or I and VII journals (603) in "V" blocks.

Main Bearing Journal Diameter:

Nominal:	57.950 - 57.965 mm
1st repair size:	57.700 - 57.715 mm
2nd repair size:	57.450 - 57.465 mm
3rd repair size:	57.200 - 57.215 mm
4th repair size:	56.950 - 56.965 mm

Basic Bearing Bores:

For main bearings:	62.500 - 62.519 mm
For big end bearings:	51.600 - 51.619 mm

Crankpin Diameter:

Nominal dimension:	47.950 - 47.965 mm
1st repair size:	47.000 - 47.715 mm
2nd repair size:	47.450 - 47.560 mm
3rd repair size:	47.200 - 47.215 mm
4th repair size:	46.950 - 46.965 mm

Width of Crankpins:

Nominal Dimension :	27.960 - 28.044 mm

Repair sizes: ....Up to 28.30 mm

Bearing Running Clearances:
Main bearings:.. 0.03 - 0.07 mm (best 0.055 mm)
Big end bearings: .... 0.03 - 0.07 mm (best 0.50 mm)
Wear limit: .... 0.080 mm
Bearing End Float:
Main bearings:.. 0.10 - 0.25 mm
Big end bearings: .... 0.12 - 0.26 mm
Wear limit - Main bearings: .... 0.30 mm
Wear limit - Big end bearings: .... 0.50 mm

Bearing Shells (all engines):

	Main Bearings	*Big End Bearings*
Nominal Dimension:	2.25 mm	1.80 mm
1st repair size:	2.37 mm	1.92 mm
2nd repair size:	2.50 mm	2.05 mm
3rd repair size:	2.62 mm	2.17 mm
4th repair size:	2.75 mm	2.30 mm

Connecting Rod Bolts:
Thread: ....M9 x 1
Diameter of stretch neck: ....7.4 mm
Min. diameter of stretch neck: ....7.1 mm
Tightening torque: ....3.0 ± 0.5 kgm (22 ± 0.3 ft.lb.) + 90° − 100°

9.7.1. Crankshaft - Removal and Installation

The engine must be removed to take out the crankshaft. The operations are similar on all engines.

- Remove the transmission from the engine. Take care not to distort the clutch shaft.
- Counterhold the flywheel in a suitable manner and evenly slacken the clutch securing bolts. Use a centre punch and mark the clutch and flywheel at opposite points. Lift off the clutch plate and the driven plate. Immediately clean the inside of the flywheel and unscrew the flywheel.
- Remove the drive plate for a torque converter of an automatic transmission in the same manner.
- With the flywheel still locked, remove the crankshaft pulley bolt and remove the crankshaft pulley/damper as described later on.

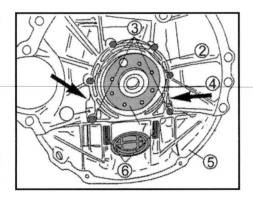

Fig. 9.25 – View of the cylinder block rear end, showing the attachment of the seal flange.
1   Roll pin
2   Oil seal flange
3   Screw, M6 x 22 mm
4   Crankshaft oil seal
5   Oil sump
6   Bolt, M6 x 85 mm
7   Crankshaft

- Remove the cylinder head as described and the timing cover as described earlier on. Remove the oil sump and oil pump.
- Remove the pistons and connecting rods as described.

- The crankshaft end float should be checked before the crankshaft is removed. To do this, place a dial gauge with a suitable holder in front of the cylinder block and place the gauge stylus against the end flange of the crankshaft, as shown in Fig. 9.26. Use a screwdriver to push the crankshaft all the way to one end and set the gauge to "0". Push the shaft to the other side and note the dial gauge reading. The resulting value is the end float. If it exceeds 0.30 mm (0.012 in.) replace the thrust washers during assembly, but make sure to fit washers of the correct width. These are located left and right at the centre bearing. Note that only two washers of the same thickness must be fitted.

- Unscrew the oil seal flange from the rear of the cylinder block. Fig. 9.25 shows a view of the fitted oil seal flange.

Fig. 9.26 – Checking the crankshaft end float.

- Unscrew the main bearing bolts evenly across. The bearings caps are marked with the numbers 1 to 6 or 1 to 7, depending on the engine. The numbers are stamped into the centre of the caps, as shown in 1.38. No. 1 cap is located at the crankshaft pulley side.

- Remove the bearing shells from the bearing journals (they could also stick to the caps) and immediately mark them on their back faces with the bearing number.

- Lift the crankshaft out of the cylinder block and remove the remaining thrust washers from the centre bearing location and the remaining bearings shells.

- Keep the shells together with the lower shells and the bearing caps. These shells have an oil bore and a groove and must always be fitted into the crankcase when the crankshaft is installed.

9.7.2.   Inspection of Crankshaft and Bearings

Main and crankpin journals must be measured with precision instruments to find their diameters. All journals can be re-ground four times and the necessary bearing shells are available, i.e. undersize shells can be fitted.

Place the crankshaft with the two end journals into "V" blocks and apply a dial gauge to the centre main journal. Rotate the crankshaft by one turn and read off the dial gauge. If the reading exceeds 0.06 mm, replace the crankshaft.

Check the main bearing and big end bearing running clearance as follows:

- Bolt the main bearing caps without shells to the crankcase, oil the bolt threads and fit each cap. Tighten the bolts to 9.0 kgm (65 ft.lb.) if the engine has been manufactured before October 1984. From 1985, when bearing cap bolts with double hexagon and shoulder are used, tighten the bolts to 5.5 kgm (39.6 ft.lb.) and then angle-tighten them a further 90° - 100°. Bearing caps are offset and can only be fitted in one position.

- Referring to Fig. 1.39 measure the bearing bores in directions A, B and C and write down the results. If the basic diameter is exceeded (see Section 9.3.0.), the bearing cap and/or the cylinder block must be replaced.

- Remove the bearing caps and refit them, this time with the well cleaned bearing shells. Re-tighten the bolts as specified.

- Measure the diameter of each bearing in accordance as shown in Fig. 1.39 on the R.H. side and write down the results. Deduct the journal diameter from the bearing diameter. The resulting difference is the bearing running clearance, which should be between 0.031 - 0.073 mm, with a wear limit of 0.080 mm.

- Check the big end bearing clearances in a similar manner, but bolt the bearing caps to the connecting rods. Tighten the nuts to the value given in the technical data and angle-tighten as above. The bearing clearance should be between 0.031 - 0.073 mm, with the same wear limit.

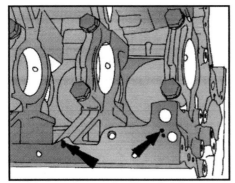

Fig. 9.27 – The arrows show where the identification of the main bearing bore tolerances are marked in the crankcase.

Selection of bearing shells is rather complicated, and we advise you to take the cylinder block to an engine shop, if the above measurements have revealed that new bearing shells are necessary. Fig. 9.27 shows where the cylinder block is marked to identify the main bearing shells. The crankshaft is marked with colour spots at the positions shown in Fig. 9.28.

Fig. 9.28 – The arrows point to the colour spots on the crankshaft webs which indicate the side of the bearing shells in the bearing caps.

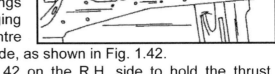

9.7.3.   Crankshaft - Installation

Thoroughly clean the bearing bores in the crankcase and insert the shells with the drillings into the bearing bores, with the tabs engaging the notches. Fit the thrust washers to the centre bearing, with the oil grooves towards the outside, as shown in Fig. 1.42.

Use the two forefingers as shown in Fig. 1.42 on the R.H. side to hold the thrust washers against the bearing cap and fit the cap in position.

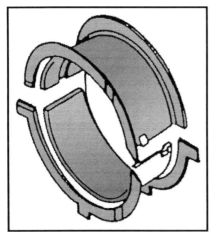

Fig. 9.29 – Correct installation of the bearing shells and thrust washers.

Lift the crankshaft in position and fit the bearing caps with the inserted shells (again shells well oiled and locating tabs in notches). Fit the two thrust washers to the centre bearing cap, again with the oil groove towards the outside. Fig. 9.29 shows the correct installation of the bearing shells. Place this cap in position, guiding the two thrust washers in order not to dislodge them. Use the forefingers to hold the washers as shown in Fig. 1.42. Note that the thrust washers have been changed. Quote the engine number when new washers are ordered.

Check the numbering of the bearing caps and fit the well oiled bolts. Tighten the bolts from the centre towards the outside in several steps to a torque reading of 9.0 kgm (65 ft.lb.) if bolts with hexagonal heads are used. If the bolts have a double-hexagonal head and a shoulder, tighten them to 5.5 kgm (39.5 ft.lb.) and from this position a further 90° – 100°.

Rotate the crankshaft a few times to check for binding (hard spots).
Re-check the crankshaft end float as described during removal. Attach the dial gauge to the crankcase as shown in Fig. 9.26. The remaining operations are carried out in reverse order to the removal procedure. The various sections give detailed description

of the relevant operations, i.e. piston and connecting rods, rear oil seal flange, timing mechanism, flywheel and clutch or drive plate, oil pump, oil sump and cylinder head.

9.7.4. Flywheel or Drive Plate (Automatic)

Figs. 9.30 and 9.31 show the end of the crankshaft together with the flywheel and the driven plate respectively. Always check the height of the old flywheel before fitting a new one.

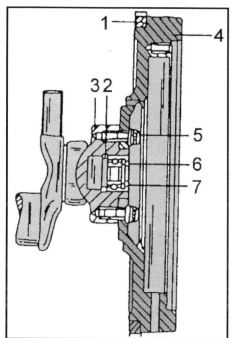

Fig. 9.30 – Arrangement of the flywheel with manual transmission.

1 Starter ring gear
2 Spacer washer
3 Crankshaft
4 Flywheel
5 Stretch bolts, M10
6 Ball bearing
7 Retaining ring

Both flywheel and drive plate can be replaced with the engine fitted without re-balancing of the crankshaft. Proceed as described:

- Remove the transmission (Section 3.1.).
- Counterhold the flywheel in suitable manner and remove the clutch after having marked its relationship to the flywheel. Remove the drive plate in a similar manner. 8 bolts are used to secure the flywheel. A hole has been drilled between two of the bores and a similar hole is drilled into the crankshaft. These two bolts must be aligned when the flywheel or the drive plate is fitted. Fig. 9.32 shows the alignment bore in the case of the flywheel. The drive plate has a similar hole.

Fig. 9.31 – Arrangement of the flywheel with automatic transmission.
1 Starter ring gear
2 Flywheel
3 Drive plate
4 Spacer washer
5 Stretch bolts
6 Crankshaft

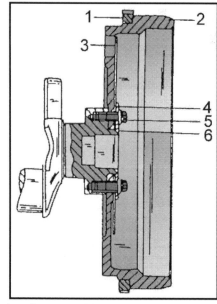

- Remove the flywheel or the drive plate. Distance washers are used in the case of the drive plate, which can also be removed. Measure the diameter of the mounting bolts at their smallest section (stretch neck). If less than 8.1 mm, replace the bolts. The measurement is carried out as shown earlier on for the connecting rod bolts (also see Fig. 9.18).
- If the flywheel or the starter ring looks worn, take the wheel to your dealer to have the flywheel re-machined and/or the ring gear replaced.

To replace the ring gear of a drive plate, unscrew the ring gear with the steel ring from the drive plate. When refitting the new ring gear, align the bores for the ring gear mounting and the converter and on the drive plate.

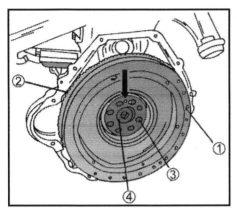

Fig. 9.32 – The arrow points to the alignment bore in flywheel and crankshaft flange. Drive plates are drilled in the same manner.

1   Flywheel
2   Starter ring gear
3   Stretch bolt, M10 x 22
4   Ball bearing

Fit the flywheel or the drive plate with the alignment bores in line. Fit a distance washer underneath and on top of the drive plate. Tighten the bolts evenly across to 3.0 - 4.0 kgm (22 - 29 ft.lb.) and from this position a further 90° - 100°.

The angle is important to give the stretch bolts their correct tension.

Engines for manual transmissions are fitted with a ball bearing in the end of the crankshaft. The removal and installation of the bearing follows the description for the 616/617 engines.

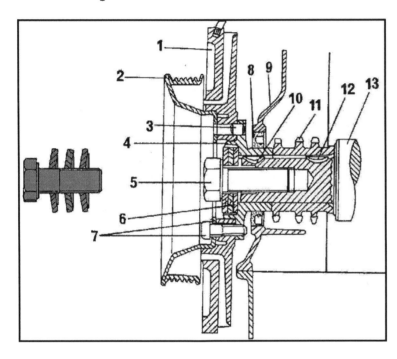

Fig. 9.33 – Sectional view of the crankshaft front end.

1   Vibration damper
2   Crankshaft pulley
3   Dowel pin, 8 x 8
4   Pulley hub
5   Bolt, M18 x 1.5
6   Spring discs
7   Bolts, M8 x 25
8   Oil seal
9   Timing cover
10 Woodruff key
11 Timing gear
12 Woodruff key
13 Crankshaft

9.7.5.   Crankshaft Pulley and Vibration Damper

The engine is fitted with a crankshaft pulley and a vibration damper. The mounting bolts for the crankshaft pulley are automatically aligned if a dowel pin in inserted into the corresponding bore. Fig. 9.33 shows a sectional view of the front end of this engine.

Remove the parts as follows, noting that a puller may be necessary to withdraw the hub:

*   Remove the radiator.
*   Release the tension of the drive belt, as described during earlier on under the heading in question.
*   Engage a gear and apply the handbrake to lock the engine against rotation. In the case of a vehicle with automatic transmission remove the starter motor and lock the starter motor ring gear in a suitable manner.
*   Unscrew the crankshaft pulley with the vibration damper.

- Remove the centre bolt from the crankshaft pulley hub and withdraw the hub with a suitable puller. Make a note of the fitting position of the three spring discs, as they must face the same way during installation.

The crankshaft pulley has a certain diameter. If replaced, quote the engine type and number.

The installation of the crankshaft pulley and the hub or the vibration damper proceed as follows:

- Rotate the crankshaft until the Woodruff key is visible and slide the hub with the key way over the key and the shaft end. Place the three spring discs correctly over the centre bolt, as shown in Fig. 9.33, coat the bolt threads with engine oil and fit the bolt. Tighten the bolt to 32.0 kgm. The crankshaft must still be locked against rotation.
- Fit the vibration damper and the crankshaft pulley.
- The remaining operations are carried out in reverse order.

9.7.6.   Rear Crankshaft Oil Seal and Oil Seal Carrier

The rear crankshaft oil seal is located inside a flange which is bolted to the rear of the crankcase. Two dowels locate the flange correctly in relation to the crankshaft centre. The flange is fitted with sealing compound ("Loctite").

Transmission and flywheel and/or drive plate must be removed to replace the oil seal. If only the oil seal needs replacement, lever it out carefully with a screwdriver without damaging the flange. If the oil seal carrier is to be removed, remove the bolts around the outside edge and two bolts from below. Apply two screwdrivers to the points shown by the arrows in Fig. 9.25 and carefully lever the carrier off the crankcase. The oil seal can now be removed from the inside.

Clean the carrier and crankcase faces and fit a new oil seal to the carrier (removed or still fitted). The sealing lip of the new oil seal is offset to prevent it from running on the same crankshaft area. Fill the space between the sealing lip and the dust protection lip with grease.

Coat the carrier face with sealing compound and fit it to the block, with the dowel pins engaged. Slightly tap the carrier in position. Great care must be taken during installation in order not to damage the oil seal.

Fit the bolts. First tighten the two lower bolts and then the other bolts. The torque is 1.0 kgm (7.2 ft.lb.).

Carry out all other operations in reverse order.

9.7.7.   Front Crankshaft Oil Seal

The front crankshaft oil seal is located in the timing cover. Oil leaks at this position can also be caused by a leaking timing cover gasket. Check before replacing the oil seal.

The hub or the vibration damper and the crankshaft pulley must be removed as already described before the oil seal can be replaced. The seal can be carefully removed with a screwdriver. Screw a self-tapping screw into the outside of the seal and apply the screwdriver plate under the screw head. If the spacer ring on the crankshaft shows signs of wear, remove it with a suitable puller.

Thoroughly clean the surrounding parts. Burrs on the timing cover bore can be removed with a scraper. Fill the space between sealing lip and dust protection lip with grease and carefully drive a new oil seal into the timing cover and over the crankshaft until the ring outer face is flush. Refit the vibration damper or hub as described in Section 9.7.5.

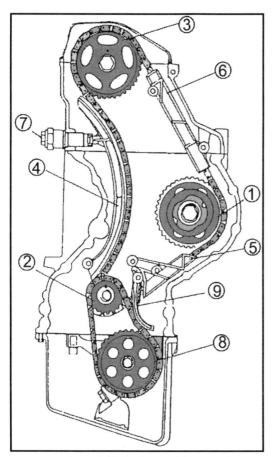

Fig. 9.34 – Timing chain and chain drive in fitted position.

1. Injection pump drive gear
2. Crankshaft sprocket
3. Camshaft sprocket
4. Tensioning rail
5. Slide rail
6. Slide rail
7. Chain tensioner
8. Oil pump drive sprocket
9. Tensioning lever for oil pump drive chain

9.8.   Timing Mechanism

The component parts covered in this section can be removed with the engines fitted. The arrangement of the timing chain and the other timing gear components are shown in Fig. 9.34.

The endless timing chain is engaged with the camshaft sprockets, the injection pump sprocket and the crankshaft sprocket. The chain is guided by two slide rails. The tension of the chain is ensured by means of a hydraulic chain tensioner, which is located in the crankcase and pushes onto a tensioning rail. The camshaft sprocket is fitted by means of an M8 bolt and located by a Woodruff key. Technical data concerning the camshaft are given in Section 9.3.0.

A second, smaller chain is used to drive the oil pump. The chain is fitted around a second sprocket on the crankshaft and around the pump drive sprocket and has its own chain tensioner.

9.8.0.   Chain Tensioner – Removal and Installation

The chain tensioner is fitted into the R.H. side of the cylinder head. The tensioning force of the chain tensioner is a combination of the fitted compression spring and the pressure of the engine oil. The oil contained inside the tensioner also absorbs shock loads from the timing chain. A chain tensioner cannot be repaired, i.e. must be replaced if suspect.

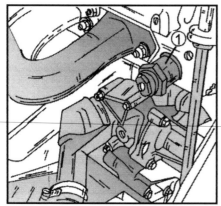

Fig. 9.35 – The chain tensioner (1) is located at the side of the engine.

The chain tensioner can simply be unscrewed from the side of the engine, but a hand press is required to refit it properly. A bench-mounted electric drill is, however, sufficient to pre-load the tensioner. Looking at the chain tensioner you will see a large and a small hexagon. Only apply a socket to the large hexagon. Unscrewing the tensioner by applying the socket to the smaller hexagon will result in the tensioner falling internally apart. Fig. 9.35 shows where the chain tensioner is located.

The chain tensioner must be filled with oil before installation. This requires the use of a hand press (or the drill mentioned above) and a glass jar, filled with SAE 10 engine oil.

Hold the tensioner with the thrust bolt facing downwards into the oil. The oil must be above the flange of the hexagon. Using the hand press, push the thrust bolt about 7 to 10 times into the tensioner. As the tensioner is filled with oil, the pressure required to compress the tensioner will increase. After filling the tensioner with oil, check that some force is required to compress it by hand.

Fit a new gasket seal and screw the chain tensioner in position. Tighten the tensioner to 8.0 kgm (58 ft.lb.). The thrust bolt of the tensioner must engage with the tensioning rail as can be seen in Fig. 9.34.

9.8.1.   Removal and Installation of Timing Chain

Fig. 9.34 shows the arrangement of the timing chain. The replacement of the timing chain is a complicated operation. The description for the removal and installation, is however, given for the 616/617 engines and can be carried out in a similar manner on these engines.

Two slide rails guide the chain on one side, a long tensioning rail, operating in conjunction with the hydraulic chain tensioner, is fitted to the other side.

9.8.2.   Tensioning Rail - Replacement

The location of the tensioning rail can be taken from Fig. 9.34. The cylinder head and the timing cover must be removed to replace the tensioning rail. The complete tensioning rail must be replaced, as the plastic coating cannot be replaced separately. Remove the rail as follows:
*   Remove the cylinder head as already described.
*   Remove the timing cover and the chain tensioner.
*   Using paint, mark the relationship between the timing chain and the crankshaft sprocket, similar, as shown in Fig. 1.12 for the camshaft sprocket and mark the camshaft sprocket and chain as shown in this illustration.
*   Counterhold the camshaft and remove the camshaft sprocket bolt. Remove the sprocket. Note that the drive sleeve is held to the sprocket with a socket head bolt inside the sleeve.
*   Swivel the tensioning rail towards the inside and withdraw from the pivot pin.

Check the plastic coating for wear or damage and replace the rail if necessary. The installation of the tensioning rail is a reversal of the removal procedure. Tighten the camshaft sprocket bolt to 6.5 kgm (47 ft.lb.). The camshaft must be held against rotation at the other end. When fitting the timing chain to the camshaft sprocket make sure that the paint marks are in line.

9.8.3.   Slide Rails - Removal and Installation

The position of the slide rails is shown in Fig. 9.34. An impact hammer, together with a M6 threaded bolt of 100 mm in length is required to remove the slide rail bearing bolts. The 6 mm bolt is screwed into the end of the bearing bolt and the impact hammer (slide hammer) attached to the end of the bolt. Provided that these tools can be obtained, the rail can be removed as described below. Proceed as follows to replace the slide rail on the, cylinder head (6 in Fig. 9.34):
*   Disconnect the battery, the air suction hose and the radiator.
*   Remove the tensioning device for the single drive belt. The bearing pin for the tensioning lever of the tensioning device is at the same time the bearing pin for this slide rail.
*   Remove the cylinder head cover.

- Remove the camshaft sprocket as already described.
- Withdraw the two bearing pins with the impact hammer and a threaded insert, as shown in Fig. 1.55 and lift out the slide rail. If no slide hammer is available, try the following: Slide a piece of tube over the bearing pin and place a washer over the tube. Screw in a 6 mm bolt and tighten it. With the washer pressing against the tube, the bearing pin will be dislodged as soon as the tube is under tension.

Refit the slide rail as follows:

- Coat the two bearing bolts on the flange with sealing compound.
- Fit the slide rail in position and insert the bearing bolts. Fit the 6 mm bolt and the slide hammer to the end of the bearing bolt and knock the bolt in position, this time hitting the weight of the slide hammer towards the front. Fit the second bearing bolt in the same manner. Counterhold the slide rail during the bearing bolt installation with a screwdriver to prevent distortion. A locating nose in the bearing bolt bore of the slide rail will engage in the locating groove of the upper bearing bolt when the bolt is in position.
- The remaining operations are carried out in reverse order to the removal procedure. Pay attention to the paint marks on timing chain and camshaft sprocket when the parts are refitted.

Replace the lower slide rail (5, Fig. 9.34) as follows:

- Remove the parts as given above to gain access to the timing cover. Then remove the timing cover as described and remove the slide rail from the two bearing bores. Fit the new slide rail in position and refit the timing cover.

9.8.4. Crankshaft Sprocket - Removal and Installation

- Remove the timing cover and turn the engine until the piston of No. 1 cylinder is at top dead centre in the firing stroke. Check on the camshaft position as the crankshaft pulley is removed (timing marks cannot be checked).
- Remove the tensioner lever for the oil pump chain ("9", Fig. 9.34).
- Remove the oil pump chain sprocket and withdraw the sprocket, at the same time disengaging the chain from the crankshaft sprocket.
- Mark the crankshaft sprocket and the oil pump drive sprocket to ensure installation in the correct position to each other.
- Mark the timing chain and the camshaft sprocket as shown in Fig. 1.12.
- Remove the camshaft sprocket. The chain can remain in engagement with the sprocket teeth.
- Use a suitable puller and extract the crankshaft sprocket from the end of the crankshaft. Immediately check the condition of the Woodruff key in the crankshaft. A damaged key can be removed with a side cutter. The Woodruff key for the crankshaft pulley hub can be dealt with in the same manner.

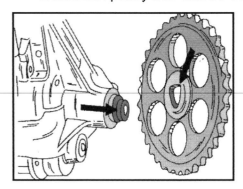

Fig. 9.36 – Fitting the oil pump drive sprocket. The flats shown by the arrows must be engaged.

Take the new crankshaft sprocket and align the paint mark of the old sprocket with the same tooth of the new sprocket, i.e. the same tooth must be marked in relation to the key groove.

- If removed, insert the two Woodruff keys. Their flat faces must lie parallel.
- Insert the sprocket into the timing chain (in accordance with the markings) and drive the sprocket over the crankshaft end, using a suitable piece of tube. Make sure that the key is not dislodged.

- Refit the camshaft sprocket and the timing chain. Rotate the engine several turns and check that the timing marks at the top of the camshaft are aligned as shown in Fig. 1.54, with the No. 1 piston at top dead centre.
- Fit the oil pump drive sprocket together with the small chain. The inside of the pump sprocket has a locating flat, shown by the arrow in Fig. 9.36, which must be engaged with a corresponding flat on the oil pump shaft.
- Refit the chain tensioner lever and the timing cover. All other operations are carried out in reverse to the removal procedure.

9.8.5. Camshaft - Removal and Installation

Except for the number of bearing journals and cams, a similar camshaft is fitted to all 602/603 engines. The shaft of the five-cylinder engine has six bearing locations, the shaft of the six-cylinder has seven. To identify the camshaft a number is stamped into the rear face.

The camshaft is located in the cylinder head. The lower part of the bearings are machined directly into the cylinder head. Removable bearing caps are used to hold the shaft in position. The camshaft is located in axial direction by a crescent-shaped collar. A camshaft is removed after removal of the bearing caps and camshaft sprocket.

- Disconnect the battery earth cable and set the engine bonnet into vertical position. Also remove the air intake hose.
- Remove the cylinder head cover. 6 screws must be removed. Disconnect the throttle linkage at the ball joint connection if an automatic transmission is fitted.
- Rotate the engine (in direction of rotation) until the piston of No. 1 cylinder is at T.D.C. compression stroke, i.e. the "0" mark in Fig. 9.2 must be opposite the timing pointer. The crankshaft can be turned by using a 27 mm socket, applied to the crankshaft pulley bolt. Never rotate the crankshaft by applying a socket or spanner to the camshaft sprocket bolt, even if it looks an easy method.
- Remove the chain tensioner as already described.
- Mark the camshaft sprocket and the timing chain with a spot of paint (see Fig. 9.3).

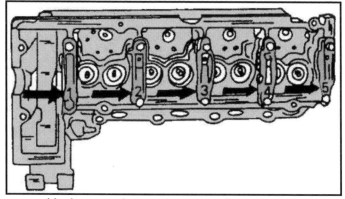

Fig. 9.37 – Camshaft bearing caps are marked as shown.

- Remove the camshaft sprocket bolt. Insert a metal rod or strong screwdriver into one of the holes to prevent the sprocket from rotating.
- Remove the sprocket from the end of the camshaft. Hold the timing chain tight and tie it suitably together.

Under no circumstances allow the chain to disengage itself from the crankshaft sprocket.

- Slacken the camshaft bearing cap bolts in several stages and alternatively until the tension has been released and can be removed. Lay the caps out in their order of removal. The caps are marked, as shown in Fig. 9.37, with their number and are to be treated accordingly.
- Lift the camshaft out of the cylinder head.
- Remove the locating collar from the cylinder head. Fig. 9.38 shows a sectional view of the cylinder head at the camshaft end with the location of the collar. The collar serves to locate the camshaft in axial direction.

- The valve tappets can be removed with a suction tool, but make sure they are inserted into their original bores.
- If a new camshaft is fitted, refer to the identification numbers (shown in Fig. 9.37) or consult your dealer. A new shaft should be inserted into the bearing bores (well oiled) to carry out the following checks:
- Insert the locking collar into the cylinder head. The collar must have sharp edges, otherwise replace it.

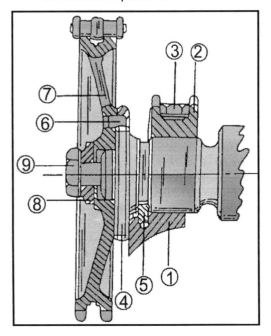

Fig. 9.38 – Sectional view of the camshaft end of the cylinder head.

1   Cylinder head
2   Bearing cap
3   Bolt, M8 x 45
4   Camshaft
5   Locking collar
6   Dowel pin
7   Camshaft sprocket
8   Washer
9   Bolt, M10 x 50

- Coat the camshaft journals and place the shaft into the bearing bores. The tappets should not be fitted.
- Fit the camshaft bearing caps in accordance with their numbers and tighten the bolts from the centre towards the outside with 2.5 kgm (18 ft.lb.).
- Screw a bolt, M10 x 30, into the end of the camshaft and tighten it until the shaft begins to turn. Rotate the shaft to notice any "bearing crush". If you feel that the camshaft shows "hard spots", slacken the bearing caps one at a time. When the troublesome bearing cap has been reached, check the bearing clearance with "Plastigage" as described for the crankshaft. The clearance must be between 0.050 and 0.081 mm.
- Remove the camshaft.
- Lubricate the tappets with engine oil and insert them into their original bores.
- Insert the camshaft into the bearing bores, with the groove entering the locking collar.
- Fit the bearing caps and tighten them from the centre towards the outside. The tightening must be carried out carefully to prevent distortion of the shaft through the pressure of the tappets.
- Fit the camshaft sprocket together with the timing chain over the camshaft (hold the chain tight during installation). The dowel pin in the shaft must engage with the hole in the sprocket. Fit the bolt and tighten it to 6.5 kgm (47 ft.lb.). The camshaft must be prevented from rotating. Refit the chain tensioner as described.
- Check the timing marks on the camshaft in accordance with Fig. 9.5. The marks must align when the piston of No. 1 cylinder is at top dead centre.
- Refit the cylinder head cover.
- All other operations are carried out in reverse order to the removal procedure. After the engine has been assembled start it up and check the areas which were separated for oil leaks.

9.8.6   Valve Timing

As the valve timing cannot be adjusted, it is sufficient to obtain the timing mark alinment in Fig. 9.5 to ensure that valves, cams, etc. are in the correct position. Only re-start the engine after you have carried out the check.

9.9. Hydraulic Valve Clearance Compensation

The function of the hydraulic valve clearance compensating elements is to eliminate valve clearance, i.e. the dimensional changes in the valve train (valve lash) due to heat expansion and wear are compensated by the elements. The rocker arm is in constant contact with the cam. The compensating elements cannot be repaired, but can be checked for correct functioning as described below. Figs. 9.39 and 9.40 show sectional views of a valve with clearance compensation. We will give a short description of the operation. All references refer to Fig. 9.39.

The hydraulic valve compensating elements are fitted into the rocker levers and operate the valves directly via a ball socket (11). Each element consists of the following components:

- The thrust pin (5) with oil supply chamber and the return bores and the ball valve (check valve), i.e. items (9), (7) and (10). The ball valve separates the supply chamber from the work chamber.

- The guide sleeve (6) with the work chamber (b), the thrust spring (8) and the closing cap (4).

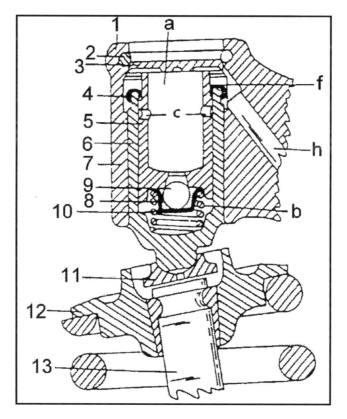

Fig. 9.39 - Sectional view of a valve clearance compensating element.

1	Rocker lever	7	Ball guide	13	Valve
2	Lock ring	8	Thrust spring	a	Oil chamber
3	Washer	9	Ball, 4 mm	b	Work chamber
4	Closing cap	10	Thrust spring	c	Return bores
5	Thrust pin	11	Ball socket	f	Ring groove
6	Guide sleeve	12	Valve spring retainer	h	Oil bores

When the engine is stopped and the tappet is held under load from the cam, the element can completely retract. The oil displaced from the work chamber (b) flows through an annular gap, i.e. the clearance between the guide sleeve and the thrust pin to the oil supply chamber (a).

When the cam lobe has moved past the valve tappet, the thrust pin (5) will be without load.

The thrust spring (8) forces the thrust pin upwards until the valve tappet rests against the cam.

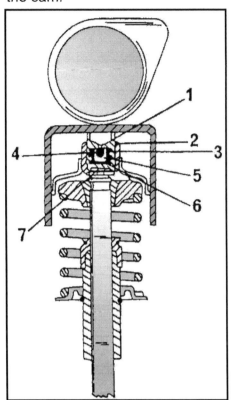

Fig. 9.40 – Sectional view of a valve and a compensating element.
1 Thrust pin
2 Lock ring
3 Thrust spring
4 Ball guide
5 Ball
6 Thrust spring

The vacuum resulting from the upward movement of the thrust pin in the work chamber (b) opens the ball valve and the oil can flow from the supply chamber (h) into the work chamber (b). The ball valve closes when the valve tappet presses against the cam and puts the thrust pin under load. The oil in the work chamber acts as a "hydraulic rigid connection" and opens the valve in question.

When the engine is running and depending on the engine speed and the cam position, the thrust pin is only pushed down slightly.

The oil contained in the oil supply chamber (a) is sufficient to fill the work chamber (b) under all operating conditions of the engine. Oil or leak oil which is not required, as well as air are able to escape via the annular gap between the washer (3) and the rocker lever. The oil ejected from the work chamber flows via the annular gap between the guide sleeve and the thrust pin and the two return bores (c) into the oil supply chamber.

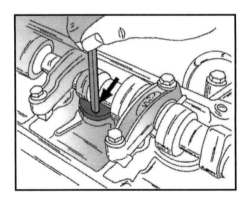

Fig. 9.40 – Checking of a hydraulic compensating element.

If the tappets are removed, note the following points:

• Always keep the tappets in an upright position, i.e. the open side towards the top.

• After removal of a tappet (see below), mark the cylinder number and the compensating element in suitable manner. Always fit original parts in their same locations.

Checking a hydraulic compensating element: As the elements are in continuous contact with the camshaft, you will rarely hear noises from the area of the hydraulic elements. If noises can be heard, check the elements as follows:

• Start the engine and run it approx. 5 minutes at 3000 rpm.

• Remove the cylinder head cover.

• Rotate the crankshaft until the cam for the tappet to be checked is pointing vertically towards the top.

• Use a drift, as shown in Fig. 9.41 and push the tappet towards the inside, or try to move the tappet with the fingers.

• If the tappet cannot be depressed or excessive clearance can be felt between the tappet and the back of the cam, replace the tappet. The tappet is supplied together with the hydraulic compensating element. Mercedes workshops can reset the tappet to its original position, but this operation is beyond the scope of the home mechanic.

Tappet Removal and Installation:

*   Remove the camshaft as described later on.
*   Use a suction tool to remove the tappets. Mark them, if they are to be refitted.
*   Fit the tappets into their original bores, if re-used. Refit the camshaft as described and carry out all other operations in reverse order to the removal procedure.

9.10.   Tightening Torque Values

Cylinder Head Bolts:
- 1st stage:..1.5 kgm (11 ft.lb.)
- 2nd stage: ....3.5 kgm (25.0 ft.lb.)
- 3rd stage: ....90° angle-tightening
- 4th stage: ....Wait 10 minutes
Cylinder head bolts (in timing case): .... 2.5 kgm (18 ft.lb.)
Connecting Rod Bearing Caps:
- 1st stage:..3.0 kgm (22 ft.lb.)
- 2nd stage: ....Angle-tighten 90° – 100°
Main Bearing Cap Bolts:
- Without stretch bolts:..9.0 kgm (65 ft.lb.)
- With stretch bolts – 1st stage: ....5.5 kgm (40 ft.lb.)
                            – 2nd stage: ....Angle-tighten 90° – 100°
Camshaft sprocket bolt:..6.5 kgm (47 ft.lb.)
Chain tensioner: ....8.0 kgm (58 ft.lb.)
Cylinder head cover bolts:...1.0 kgm (7.2 ft.lb.)
Camshaft bearing caps: ....2.5 kgm (18 ft.lb.)
Injectors into combustion chambers:...........................7.0 kgm (60.5 ft.lb.) + 1.0 kgm
Threaded ring for combustion chamber in head:..........................7.0 kgm (50.5 ft.lb.)
Vacuum pump to head: ....1.0 kgm (7.2 ft.lb.)
Vacuum pump housing:..1.0 kgm (7.2 ft.lb.)
Crankshaft pulley hub to crankshaft:.......................................32.0 kgm (230.5 ft.lb.)
Crankshaft pulley to hub:..2.5 kgm (18 ft.lb.)
Flywheel or driven plate:
- 1st stage:..3.0 – 4.0 kgm (22 – 30 ft.lb.)
- 2nd stage: .... Angle-tighten by 90° – 100°
Inlet manifold to cylinder head:..1.0 kgm (7.2 ft.lb.)
Alternator to mounting bracket:
- Bolts fitted from the front: ....2.5 kgm (18 ft.lb.)
- Bolts fitted from the side:..4.5 kgm (32.5 ft.lb.)
Bolt for T.D.C. transmitter (sensor): ....1.0 kgm (7.2 ft.lb.)
Bolt for belt tensioner: ....2.5 kgm (18 ft.lb.)
Fuel filter bolts: ....2.5 kgm (18 ft.lb.)
Plug in injection pump: ....3.0 – 3.5 kgm (22 – 25 ft.lb.)
Injection pump flange: ....2.0 – 2.5 kgm (14.5 – 18 ft.lb.)
Bolt for rear support bracket:......................................2.0 – 2.5 kgm (14.5 – 18 ft.lb.)
Banjo bolts for fuel pipes: ....2.5 kgm (18 ft.lb.)
Oil drain plug in sump:..2.5 kgm (18 ft.lb.)
Oil sump to cylinder block:
- M6 bolts:..1.0 kgm (7.2 ft.lb.)
- M8 bolts:..2.5 kgm (18 ft.lb.)
Exhaust manifold to cylinder head: ....2.5 kgm (18 ft.lb.)

M115 and M102 Petrol Engines

Centre bolt, fan to water pump: ....2.5 kgm (18 ft.lb.)
Timing Cover
- M6 bolts: ....1.0 kgm (7.2 ft.lb.)
- M8 bolts: ....2.5 kgm (18 ft.lb.)
Engine mounting bracket, sides: ....4.5 kgm (32 ft.lb.)
Engine mounting, nut from below: ....4.5 kgm (32 ft.lb.)
Exhaust manifold to exhaust pipe flange: ....3.0 kgm (22 ft.lb.)
Exhaust pipe to transmission bracket: ....2.0 kgm (14.5 ft.lb.)
Oil pipes to automatic transmission: ....2.5 kgm (18 ft.lb.)
Earth strap to chassis: ....2.3 kgm (17.0 ft.lb.)
Coolant drain plug (block): ....2.8 kgm (20 ft.lb.)
Bolt for injection timing advancer: ....4.0 kgm (30 ft.lb.)
Nut for injection timing advancer: ....7.0 kgm (50.5 ft.lb.)
Oil filter to crankcase: ....3.0 kgm (22 ft.lb.)

10   M115 and M102 PETROL ENGINES

Although not identical, both engine types are described in this section. Important differences are given whenever necessary.

10.0.   General Technical Data

Fitted Engines:
- 230 G: M115, 90 or 102 BHP, carburettor
- 230 GE to end of 1984:   M115 E23, fuel injection
- 230 GE, from 1985:   M102, fuel injection, without and with cat.

Type of fuel system:
- M115 to 1981:   With Stromberg carburettor
- M115 from 1982:   With mechanically controlled fuel injection
                                      system (KA)
- M102 from 1985:   With mechanically/electronically controlled fuel
                                      injection system (KE)

Number of Cylinders: Four
Arrangement of cylinders: In-line
Arrangement of valves: Overhead
Valve Clearances
 M115 engines, cold – Inlet valves   0.10 mm
 M115 engines, cold – Exhaust valves   0.20 mm
 M115 engines, warm – Inlet valves   0.15 mm
 M115 engines, warm – Exhaust valves 0.25 mm
 M102 engine: Hydraulic compensating elements

Cylinder bore:
- M115 engines: 93.75 mm
- M102 engine: 95.60 mm

Piston stroke:
- M115 engines: 83.60 mm
- M102 engine: 80.25 mm

Capacity:
- M115 engines: 2307 cc
- M102 engine: 2299 cc

Compression Ratio:
- M115 engine, carburettor: 8.0 : 1 or 9.0 : 1
- M115 engine, injection, M102:   9.0 : 1

Max. B.H.P. (DIN):
- M115 engine, carburettor: 66 kW (90 BHP) at 5000 rpm (comp. 8 : 1)
- M115 engine, carburettor: 75 kW (102 BHP) at 5250 rpm (comp. 9 : 1)
- M115 engine, injection: 92 kW (125 BHP) at 5000 rpm
- M102 engine, from 1986:   92 kW (125 BHP) at 5000 rpm
- M102 engine, with converter: 90 kW (122 BHP) at 5100 rpm

Max. Torque:
- M115 engine, 90 BHP: 16.7 kgm at 2500 rpm
- M115 engine, 102 BHP: 17.2 kgm at 3000 rpm
- M115 engine, 125 BHP: 19.2 kgm at 4000 rpm
- M102 engine, 125 BHP: 19.2 kgm at 4000 rpm

Note: The above performance values are given as available, as the M115 engines since introduction and during the transition to the M102 engines different values may be applicable, depending on the country of sale and registration.

Crankshaft bearings	5:
Cooling system	Thermo system with water pump, thermostat, cooling fan with or without electro-magnetic clutch, tube-type radiator
Lubrication	Pressure-feed lubrication with gear-type oil pump, driven with chain from crankshaft. With full-flow oil filter
Air cleaner	Dry paper element air cleaner

10.1.   Engine – Removal and Installation

It is recommended to remove the engine without the transmission. The following instructions are based on the M115 engines. Any differences applicable to the M102 engine are mentioned when necessary. Remember that the engine is a heavy unit and a suitable hoist or hand crane is required to lift the engine out of the engine compartment.

- Place suitable covers over both wings to prevent damage to the paint work. Bring the engine bonnet into vertical position.
- Disconnect the positive battery lead from the battery,
- Remove the radiator grille.
- Remove the crossmember together with the bonnet lock and remove the protective panel in front of the radiator. Also disconnect the cable leading to the signal horn.
- Open the radiator filler cap and drain the cooling system. The engine must be cold.
- Disconnect the upper and lower radiator hoses from the radiator connections, disconnect the two heater hoses and remove the radiator.
- Remove the cap from the ignition coil and withdraw the centre lead out of the coil. Also disconnect the lead from the terminal "1" of the ignition coil.

M115 and M102 Petrol Engines

- Disconnect the earth cable from the engine.
- Remove the impulse sender for the diagnostic socket from the bracket.
- Locate and withdraw the cable plug from the connections of the oil pressure switch and the coolant temperature sender.
- Disconnect the breather hose from the cylinder head cover.
- Disconnect a vacuum hose from the intake air temperature regulator and in the case of a fitted carburettor a vacuum hose from the carburettor.
- In the case of an M102 engine also disconnect the cable from the idle air distributor.
- In the case of a carburettor disconnect the following cable connectors: From the thermo time switch and the shut-off valve. Also disconnect a suction hose from the carburettor and the warm air suction hose from the exhaust manifold.
- Unscrew the vacuum pipe leading to the brake servo unit from the inlet manifold.

Depending on the installation carry out the following operations:

- Remove the accelerator regulating shaft. To do this, remove a clip from the bracket, separate the regulating linkage and pull the linkage towards the rear.
- Disconnect the throttle operating cable. To do this, remove the plastic guide out of the slotted lever and remove the cable from the lever. At the end of the cable compress a plastic clip and guide the cable through the bracket towards the rear.
- Disconnect all coolant pipes and coolant hoses, vacuum hoses, oil and fuel lines and electrical leads from the engine. Mark any connections if not sure where they were connected. These include the cables connected to the alternator and the starter motor.
- Remove the lower bolt securing the starter motor.
- Separate the exhaust pipe from the exhaust manifold. Two bolts must be removed from the clamp bracket and two nuts from the clamp bracket at the end of the support bracket. Swing the bracket downwards.
- Attach suitable ropes or chains to the engine lifting eyes and attach the other ends to a hoist or hand crane. Operate the lifting equipment until the rope/chains are just tight.
- Remove the bolts connecting the engine to the transmission (from above and below). Place a mobile jack underneath the transmission to bring the transmission in the best position to lift out the engine.
- Unscrew both bolts for the front engine mountings from below.
- Carefully lift the engine, push it away from the transmission and lift it out towards the front of the engine compartment. Continuously check that none of the cables, leads, etc, can get caught in the engine. Stop the lifting operation immediately as soon as problems can be seen. Under no circumstances force the assembly out of the engine compartment.

The installation is a reversal of the removal procedure. The following points should be noted in particular:

- Do not refit any parts to the engine until the engine mountings and engine mounting brackets have been connected and the engine is resting in its mountings without the lifting equipment. Make sure that the engine mountings are in good condition.
- The ignition timing and the idle speed must be checked after installation.
- Tighten the bolts and nuts to the following tightening torques:

Engine mountings:	3.5 – 4.0 kgm
Engine to transmission:	5.5 kgm
Radiator drain plug:	0.6 – 1.0 kgm
Exhaust pipe flange to exhaust manifold:	2.0 kgm

- Check the engine coolant if the old coolant is re-used.
- Replace the air cleaner element if it has been in use for a long time.

10.2. Engine – Dismantling and Assembling

General instructions to be observed during the dismantling of the 616/617 engines. Refer to section 1.1.

10.3.   Engine - Overhaul

10.3.0.   Cylinder Head and Valves – Technical Data

Cylinder Head:	M115 Engines	M102 Engine
Cylinder head height:	84.4 – 85.0 mm	98.5 mm
Min. height after machining:	83.8 mm	97.8 mm
Max. Distortion of Cylinder Head Faces:		
- Longitudinal direction:	0.15 mm	0.15 mm
- Across the face:	0.05 mm	0.05 mm
Max. deviation of faces between upper and lower sealing faces (parallel to each other):	0.10 mm	0.10 mm
Depth of valve head faces and cylinder head sealing face:		
- New inlet valves:	+0.10 mm	1.7 mm
- New exhaust valves:	-0.16 mm	0.5 mm
- With re-cut valve seats:		
- Inlet valves:	-0.9 mm	2.6 mm
- Exhaust valves:	-17 mm	1.4 mm

Valves		
Valve Head Diameter:		
- Inlet valves:	47.10 – 46.90 mm	43.00 mm
- Exhaust valves:	37.20 – 37.00 mm	39.00 mm
Valve seat angle:	45° + 15'	45° + 15'
Valve Stem Diameter:		
- Inlet valves:	8.970 – 8.950 mm	7.97–7.955 mm
- Exhaust valves:	10.96 – 10.94 mm	8.96–8.938 mm
Valve Length:		
- Inlet valves:	128.80 – 128.40 mm	114.90 mm
- Exhaust valves:	113.40 – 113.30 mm	115.80 mm
Valve Seat Width:		
- Inlet valves:	1.8 – 3.0 mm	1.8 – 2.5 mm
- Exhaust valves:	1.5 – 2.5 mm	1.5 – 2.5 mm

Valve Seats		
Valve seat width:		
- Inlet valves:	1.8 – 2.5 mm	1.8 – 2.5 mm
- Exhaust valves:	1.5 – 2.5 mm	1.5 – 2.5 mm
Valve seat angles:	45° - 15'	45° - 15'
Upper correction angle:	70°	15°
Lower correction angle:	70°	60°

M115 and M102 Petrol Engines

Valve Seat Inserts
Insert outer diameter:
- Inlet valves – Std.:   48.600 – 48.590 mm   46.09 - 46.1 mm
- Inlet valves – Repair size: 49.300 mm   46.30 mm
- Exhaust valves – Std.:   42.100 – 42.590 mm   42.09 - 42.1 mm
- Exhaust valves – Repair size: 43.300 mm   43.00 mm

Insert inner diameter:
- Inlet valves – Std.:   48.500 – 48.516 mm   38.00 mm
- Exhaust valves – Std.:   42.500 – 42.016 mm   36.00mm

Valve Springs
Colour code:
- M115 engines, inner springs: white
- M115 engines, outer springs: red, yellow/red or purple/red
- M102 engine: yellow/red or purple/white,
                                yellow/brown or purple/brown

Outer diameter:
- M115 engines, inner springs: 22.20 mm
- M115 engines, outer springs: between 33.2 and 34.2 mm
- M102 engine: 33.9 or 34.2 or 34.7 mm

Wire diameter: Depending on colour code and engine

Free length:
- M115 engines, inner springs: 45.00 mm
- M115 engines, outer springs: 50.0 or 49.0 mm, depending on colour
- M102 engine: 48.50 mm

Valve Guides	M115 Engines	M102 Engine
Inlet valve Guides:		
- Outer diameter – Std.:	14.05 – 14.03 mm	14.044-14.051 mm
- Outer diameter – Repair size I (red):	14.23 – 14.21 mm	-----------
- Outer diameter – Repair size II (white):	14.43 – 14.41 mm	-----------
- Inner diameter:	9.000 – 9.015 mm	8.00-8.015 mm
Valve guide length:	55 mm	46 mm
Basic bore in cylinder head:		
- Std.:	14.02 – 14.04 mm	14.03-14.035 mm
- Repair size I (red):	14.20 – 14.22 mm	------------
- Repair size II (white):	14.40 – 14.32 mm	-----------
Exhaust Valve Guides:		
- Outer diameter – Std.:	15.05 – 15.03 mm	14.044-14.051 mm
- Outer diameter – Repair size I (red):	15.23 – 15.21 mm	------------
- Outer diameter – Repair size II (white):	15.43 – 15.41 mm	------------
- Inner diameter:	11.000 – 11.008mm	9.999-9.015 mm
Basic bore in cylinder head:		
- Std.:	15.00 – 15.02 mm	14.03-14.035 mm
- Repair size I (red):	15.20 – 15.22 mm	-------------
- Repair size II (white):	15.40 – 15.42 mm	-------------
- Repair size:	---------------	14.198-14.203 mm

Interference fit of valve guides – All guides:
- Std.:   0.01 – 0.03 mm   0.009-0.021

Camshaft	M115 Engines	M102 Engine
Bearing bore diameter:		
- Standard:	35.00 – 35.02 mm	32.00-32.05 mm
or:	49.00 – 49.02 mm	
Bearing journal diameter:		
- Standard:	34.95 – 34.92 mm	31.933-31.95 mm
or:	48.90 – 48.92 mm	
Camshaft Bearing Clearance:		
- New condition:	0.05 – 0.084 mm	0.05 – 0.91 mm
- Wear limit:	0.09 mm	0.11 mm
Camshaft End Float:		
- New condition:	0.07 – 0.15 mm	0.07 – 0.15 mm
- Wear limit:	0.15 mm	0.18 mm

10.3.1.   CYLINDER HEAD – REMOVAL AND INSTALLATION

Note the following points before any work is carried out on the cylinder head:

- The M102 engine is fitted with hydraulic valve clearance compensating elements, i.e. there is no need to adjust the valve clearance.
- The cylinder head must only be removed when the engine is cold. The removal takes place together with the inlet manifold and the exhaust manifold. New cylinder head gaskets are wrapped in plastic and must only be unwrapped just before the gasket is fitted. The cylinder head can be removed with the engine fitted and these operations are described below:

Remove as follows:

- Place the engine bonnet into vertical position and drain the cooling system.
- Remove the air cleaner.
- Disconnect the coolant hose from the coolant distributor and between the thermostat housing and the water pump.
- Disconnect all coolant, fuel and vacuum hoses and the electrical cables to the cylinder head or any other unit on the head which cannot be removed together with the head.

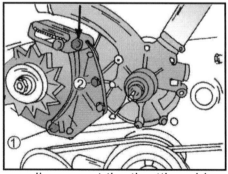

Fig. 10.1 – Alternator mounting (M115 engine). Bolts are identified by the arrow and the numbers. Slacken the alternator of an M102 engine to remove the drive belt. The belt of an M115 engine can remain on the pulley.

- In the case of a carburettor engine (M115) remove the return spring from the throttle operating lever, in the case of an injection engine disconnect the throttle valve return spring from the throttle valve housing and disconnect the throttle cable.
- Remove the inlet manifold support at the top (if fitted). In the case of a carburettor engine a nut is used, in the case of an injection engine two bolts are used, one on each side of the fuel distributor.
- Loosen the oil dipstick tube on the exhaust manifold, slacken the pipe clamp and pull out the oil dipstick. Close the end of the guide tube in suitable manner (for example with tape).
- Remove the upper hose clamp of the by-pass hose and remove the vent hose between water pump housing and thermostat housing cover.

M115 and M102 Petrol Engines

- In the case of an engine without single belt drive refer to Fig. 10.1 and slacken the bolt (1) and swing the alternator together with the mounting bracket towards the outside. A tight alternator bracket can be freed by slackening the bolt (2) as well. If a single belt drive is fitted remove it as described in section "Cooling System" for this engine.
- Disconnect the exhaust pipe from the exhaust manifold. Push the pipe away from the manifold.
- Remove the cylinder head cover. To do this, remove the five dome nuts (M102) or the Allen head bolts (M115). In the case of an M102 engine remove the cover with the parts attached shown in Fig. 10.2. A sticking cylinder head cover must not be freed by tapping it with a hammer. If difficult to remove, try to unstick it by pushing it by hand to one side. Use a plastic or rubber mallet if necessary.

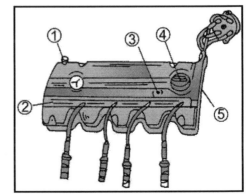

Fig. 10.2 – The cylinder head cover is removed together with the items shown.
1   Rubber buffer
2   Plug cable guide tube
3   Plastic plug
4   Oil filler cap
5   Plug cable guide tube

- Rotate the engine until the piston of No. 1 cylinder is at top dead centre in the firing position. A 27 mm socket can be applied to the crankshaft pulley bolt to rotate the crankshaft. Never attempt to rotate the crankshaft by applying a socket to the camshaft timing wheel bolt. Fig. 10.3 shows how the "0" mark on the timing scale is in line with the pointer in the timing cover when the correct engine position is obtained.

Fig. 10.3 – The engine is set to the T.D.C. firing point.

- In the case of an M102 engine remove the plug (1) in Fig. 10.4 (the chain tensioner is underneath) and withdraw the spring (2). Remove the sealing washer (3).
- In the case of an M115 engine, the pressure plunger of the chain tensioner must be pushed back.

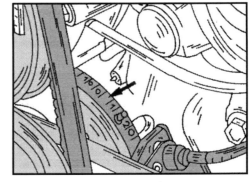

Fig. 10.4 – Removal of the plug for the chain tensioner. The numbers are referred to in the text.

- Mark the camshaft sprocket and the timing chain on opposite points, as shown already in Fig. 1.12, using a spot of paint.
- Remove the ignition distributor (if fitted).
- Remove the inner glide rail from the cylinder head.
- Unscrew the camshaft sprocket bolt. To counterhold the camshaft against rotation, use a 24 mm open-ended spanner, applied to the opposite end of the camshaft as shown in Fig. 10.5, if the head of an M102 engine is removed. This is not possible on the M115 engine. In this case insert a drift or similar in the manner shown in Fig. 10.5 on the R.H. side to lock the camshaft.

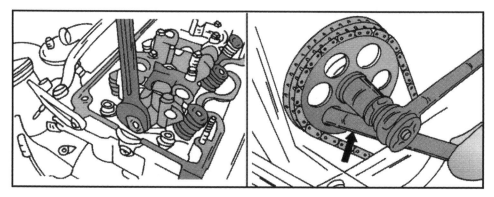

Fig. 10.5 – Prevent the camshaft from rotation. In the L.H. view for the M102 engine, in the R.H. view for the M115 engine.

- Withdraw the camshaft sprocket after the bolt has been removed.
- On certain models with EGR remove the EGR valve out of the inlet manifold. Also on these vehicles remove a nut in the vicinity of the valve (on one side of the engine).
- Unscrew the cylinder head bolts in reverse order to the one shown in Fig. 10.6. Special wrenches are required to slacken the bolts (8 and 10 mm in the case of an M115 engine, a multi-spline bit in the case of an M102 engine). A normal Allen key is not suitable, as it will damage the bolt heads. Immediately after removal of the bolts measure the length if an M102 engine is dealt with. *If the dimension between the end of the bolt to the underside of the bolt head is more than 122.0 mm, replace the bolts.* New bolts have a length of 119.0 mm.

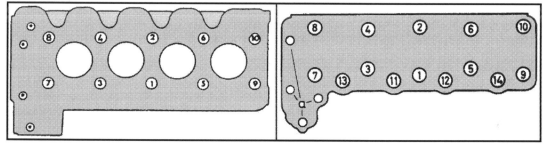

Fig. 10.6 – Tightening sequence for the cylinder head bolts. Bolts are slackened in reverse order. On the left for the M102 engine, on the right for the M115 engine.

- Remove the bolts in the timing chain case (4 in total) by means of a 6 mm Allen key. A suitable extension is required to reach the bolts.
- Lift off the cylinder head. If a hoist or lifting equipment is available hook a rope to the two lifting eyes and lift off the head. In the case of the M115 engine push the tensioning rail towards the centre before the head is removed.
- Immediately after removal clean the cylinder head and block surfaces of old gasket material.
- If necessary overhaul the cylinder head as described in section 10.3.3 after dismantling it.

Note that the cylinder head is positioned by means of two dowel pins. A cylinder head with hydraulic valve clearance compensating elements must not be fitted to an earlier engine.

Install the cylinder head as follows:
- Place a new cylinder head gasket in position. The gasket is different for the two engines. Make sure to obtain the correct one (quote engine type).
- Coat the threads of the cylinder head bolts with oil. It is assumed that the original bolts have been measured for the re-use (M102 engine).

M115 and M102 Petrol Engines

- Insert the cylinder head bolts and tighten them with the correct bolt wrench as follows, using the diagram in Fig. 10.6 as applicable:

M102 Engine
- Tighten the bolts in several stages to 4.0 kgm (30 ft.lb.), using the correct multi-spline bit.
- Re-tighten the cylinder head bolts in the same order, but this time to 7.0 kgm (50.5 ft.lb.). Allow the engine to stand for at least 10 minutes.
- Fit the three socket head bolts to the inside of the timing chain chamber and tighten them to 2.5 kgm (18 ft.lb.).
- In the order shown tighten each cylinder head bolt by 90° and from this position once more by 90°. To obtain the correct angle, place the tommy bar in parallel with the cylinder head and tighten each bolt until it is at right angle to the head. The torque wrench must not be used.

M115 Engine
- Tighten the M10 bolts in the order shown in Fig. 10.6 on the right to a torque of 3.0 kgm (22 ft.lb.) and the M12 bolts to 7.0 kgm (50.5 ft.lb.).
- Tighten the bolts again in the order shown, but this time the M10 bolts to 5.5 kgm (40 ft.lb.) and the M12 bolts to 10.0 kgm (72 ft.lb.).
- Fit the M8 bolts inside the timing chain chamber and tighten them to 2.5 kgm (18 ft.lb.).

Proceed as follows:
- Refit the slide rail to the cylinder head as described later on.
- Fit the camshaft sprocket together with the timing chain to the end of the camshaft, making sure that the paint marks made during removal are in line (see Fig. 1.12). The sprocket must face with the wider flange towards the camshaft.
- Fit the camshaft sprocket bolt and tighten the bolt to 8.0 kgm (58 ft.lb.). Counterhold the camshaft as shown in Fig. 10.5.

Fig. 10.7 – Alignment of the notch in the camshaft and the flat on the cylinder head (M102 engine).

- In the case of an M102 engine refer to Fig. 10.4 and fit the sealing ring (3), the compression spring (2) and the plug (1). Tighten the plug to 7.0 kgm (50.5 ft.lb.).
- Check the marking for top dead centre for the No. 1 cylinder/piston in the camshaft. A notch is machined into the camshaft which should be in line with the flat on the cylinder head as shown in Fig. 10.7 for an M102 engine. The M115 engine looks similar.
- Adjust the valve clearances on engines without compensating elements. See separate heading.
- The remaining operations are carried out in reverse order to the removal procedure. Finally adjust the drive belt tension.

Notes after Installation:
M115 engines: A re-adjustment of the valve clearances is not necessary. The cylinder head bolts must be re-tightened when the engine is warm (80° C). Slacken each cylinder head bolt in the order shown in Fig. 10.5 by a quarter of a turn and re-tighten it to 10.0 kgm or 5.5 kgm, depending of the thread size. Each bolt must be treated individually. Also re-tighten the bolts inside the timing chain chamber (2.5 kgm).

M102 Engine: A re-tightening of the cylinder head bolts is not necessary.

10.3.2.   CYLINDER HEAD – DISMANTLING

Various points must be noted when the cylinder head is dismantled:
*   If the camshaft of an M102 engine must be replaced you will have to replace the rocker levers and the rocker shaft. If the camshaft bearings show signs of excessive wear, camshaft and cylinder head must be replaced together.
*   Camshaft journals of a camshaft for an M115 engine can be re-ground. An engine shop dealing with these engines should advise you.

Proceed as follows during dismantling:
*   Remove all temperature switches and sensors from the cylinder head and unscrew the inlet and exhaust manifolds.
*   **M102 engine**: Unscrew the four bolts securing the camshaft bearing brackets and remove the oil pipe from the top of the cylinder head.
*   **M115 engines:** The removal of the camshaft is described later on.
*   Unscrew the spark plugs and detach all other parts from the head.
*   A valve lifter is required to remove the valves. Refer to the description on Page 106 for one of the diesel engines.
*   Remove the valve stem oil seals with a screwdriver or a pair of pliers.
*   Remove the valves one after the other out of the valve guides and pierce them in their fitted order through a piece of cardboard. Write the cylinder number against each valve if they are to be re-used.
*   Completely remove the camshaft bearing brackets and lift out the camshaft (M102 engine). The bearing brackets are marked with a number which is identical to the number marked in the cylinder head. Remove the Woodruff key out of the camshaft, using a side cutter.

Note that the camshaft of a particular engine type is marked with a code number in the rear face of the shaft. If a repair size camshaft is used you will find different numbers stamped into the camshaft. The bearing journals of these shafts are 0.6 mm larger in diameter.

10.3.3.   CYLINDER HEAD – OVERHAUL

The instructions given for the engines covered earlier on also apply to these engines, using any necessary data as given in Section 10.3.0.

10.3.4.   CYLINDER HEAD – ASSEMBLY

The assembly of the cylinder is a reversal of the dismantling procedure. Fit the valves as explained for the engines covered earlier on. The camshaft and the rocker shaft installation is covered under its own heading.

10.4.   Timing Cover (M102)

The timing cover closes the crankcase at the front. It is located by two dowels and is secured by 15 bolts. Water pump ignition distributor, oil pump, oil pressure relief valve, front crankshaft oil seal, ignition timing pointer and TDC transmitter are fitted to the cover. The timing cover can be removed with the engine fitted. A new cover will come with the oil pump, but without the crankshaft oil seal.
*   Open the bonnet and drain the engine oil and the cooling system.
*   Disconnect the battery. Remove the air cleaner. The ventilation pipe must be disconnected from the cylinder head cover. Also disconnect the hose from the connection on the idle air distributor.

- Slacken the single belt drive and remove as already described in section "Cooling System".
- Remove the cylinder head cover together with the spark plug cables and the distributor cap. Do not use a hammer to free a sticking cylinder head cover, but try to move the cover sideways until free.

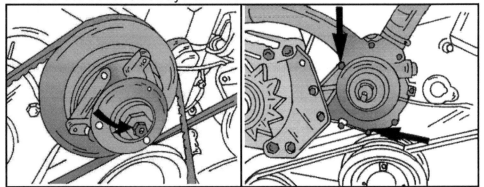

Fig. 10.8 – Details for the removal of the timing cover.

- Remove the cooling fan and remove the nut securing the fan coupling. The washer (arrow in Fig. 10.8) must be held with a 24 mm open-ended spanner to prevent the parts from rotating. Then remove the water pump pulley and the mounting flange by hand.
- Unscrew the magnetic body of the fan coupling. To do this, remove the three bolts shown in the R.H. view of Fig. 10.8, and place the magnetic body to one side.
- Rotate the engine until the piston of No. 1 cylinder is at top dead centre in the firing point (see Fig. 10.3) and then remove the crankshaft pulley and the vibration damper, as described later on. Engage a gear to lock the crankshaft against rotation.

Fig. 10.9 – Location of the TDC transmitter.

- Unscrew and withdraw the TDC transmitter (Fig. 10.9) and the ignition distributor.
- Disconnect the throttle cable and the earth strap.
- Unscrew the support bracket for the front exhaust pipe and push the bracket towards the bottom. Unscrew the exhaust pipe from the exhaust from the exhaust manifold.
- Remove the oil sump and withdraw it towards the front of the engine.
- From underneath the vehicle remove the two engine mounting bolts. Make sure the vehicle is resting on chassis stands before you "crawl" underneath the vehicle.

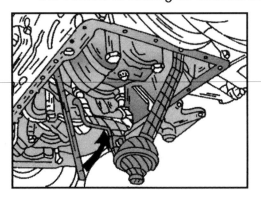

Fig. 10.10 – Attachment of the oil suction strainer.

- Attach a rope or chains to the lifting eyes of the engine and lift the engine with the hoist until the engine mountings are free.
- Unscrew the oil suction strainer from the rear main bearing cap (Fig. 10.10).
- Engage a gear to prevent the crankshaft from rotating.
- Remove the 6 mm Allen head bolts inside the timing chain chamber. An extension is required to reach the bolts.

- Use a cylindrical drift and knock the two dowel pins in the timing cover towards the rear until free of the cover. Unscrew the timing cover bolts. One dowel pin is situated at the L.H. bottom, the other one R.H. top.
- Remove the timing cover together with the spacer ring in a forward direction. Push the cover slightly downwards in order not to damage the cylinder head gasket. The spacer ring on the crankshaft will come away with the timing cover, but note:

If the timing cover cannot be removed because the spacer ring is stuck to the crankshaft, use a puller to withdraw the ring. This requires the removal of the timing cover oil seal to apply the puller. Use a screwdriver carefully to lever out the oil seal. A thick rag should be inserted between crankshaft and oil seal when levering.

Clean the cover and crankcase sealing faces of old sealing compound. The cover and the water pump can be fitted with a gasket. Otherwise a good sealing compound is used.

Turn the cover to the other side and replace the "O" sealing ring in the upper end. The timing cover is fitted as follows:

- Use a new gasket (102 015 00 80) and smear sealing compound at different points to the gasket. Place the gasket against the cylinder block. With a sharp knife cut the protruding ends level with the cylinder block. If no gasket is used coat the cylinder block sealing face with sealing compound.
- Place the timing cover in position at the same time rotating the inner oil pump gearwheel so that the two pilot faces are in alignment with the pump drive sleeve.
- Drive the two dowel pins through the cover and fit the securing screws. Tighten the screws evenly to 2.3 kgm (17 ft.lb.). Note that the bolts are of different length.
- Fit the spacer ring. A new ring must be fitted if the old one shows grooves. Fit a new oil seal into the timing cover as described later on in connection with the crankshaft.
- The remaining operations are carried out in reverse order to the removal procedure. Use a new gasket for the oil sump and the water pump (the latter can also be fitted with sealing compound), tension the drive belt and fill the engine with oil and coolant. If necessary adjust the ignition timing and idle speed or have it adjusted. Start the engine and check for oil leaks around the timing cover.

10.5.   PISTON AND CONNECTING RODS

10.5.0. Technical Data

All dimensions are given in metric units.

Pistons	**M115 Engine**	**M102 Engine**
Piston Diameter - Standard:		
- Group 0:	93.73 mm	95.468 – 94.482 mm
- Group 1:	93.74 mm	95.478 – 95.493 mm
- Group 2:	93.75 mm	95.488 – 95.502 mm
Oversizes:	0.4 and 0.8 mm	0.5 and 1.0 mm
Piston Running Clearance:		
- New:	0.025 – 0.035 mm	0.016 – 0.040 mm
- Wear limit:	0.03 mm	0.04 mm

Max. weight difference within engine:
- New: ....4 grams
- Wear limit: ....10 grams

M115 and M102 Petrol Engines

Piston Pins:

Pin diameter:	25.996 – 26.000 mm	23.995 – 24.000 mm
Piston pin running clearance:		
- In small end bush:	0.012 – 0.022 mm	0.007 – 0.018 mm
- In piston:	0.002 – 0.022 mm	0.002 – 0.012 mm

Piston Rings:

Piston Ring Gaps:

- Upper rings:	0.35 – 0.55 mm	0.30 – 0.55 mm
- Wear limit:	1.0 mm	1.0 mm
- Centre rings:	0.30 – 0.55 mm	0.25 – 0.45 mm
- Wear limit:	0.8 mm	0.8 mm
- Lower rings:	0.25 - 0.40 mm	0.25 – 0.50 mm
- Wear limit:	0.8 mm	0.8 mm

Side Clearance in Grooves:

- Upper rings:	0.05 - 0.08 mm	0.05 – 0.085 mm
- Wear limit:	0.15 mm	0.15 mm
- Centre rings:	0.03 - 0.06 mm	0.010 – 0.030 mm
- Wear limit:	0.10 mm	0.10 mm
- Lower rings:	0.03 - 0.06 mm	0.10 – 0.045 mm
- Wear limit:	0.10 mm	0.010 – 0.045 mm

Connecting Rods

Distance from centre small end bore to		
centre big end bore:	149.05 – 148.95 mm	144.95 – 145.05 mm
Width of con rod at big end bore:	31.88 – 31.84 mm	27.857 – 27.890 mm
Basic bore diameter		
of big end bore:	55.60 – 55.62 mm	51.60 – 51.619 mm
Basic bore diameter of		
small end bore:	29.000 – 29.02 mm	27.000 – 27.090 mm
Small End Bush:		
- Outer diameter:	29.090 – 29.058 mm	27.050 – 27.090 mm
- Inner diameter:	26.012 – 26.018 mm	24.007 – 24.013 mm

Max. twist of connecting rods: .... 0.10 mm per 100 mm
Max. bend of connecting rods: .... 0.03 mm per 100 mm
Max. weight difference in same engine: .... 5 grams (per set)
Connecting Rod Bolts:
- Thread: .... M10 x 1
- Diameter of stretch neck: .... 8.4 mm (M115), 8.0 mm (M102)
- Min. diameter of stretch neck: .... 7.2 mm (both engines)

Connecting rod bearing details: .... See under "Crankshaft"

10.5.1. PISTONS – REMOVAL AND INSTALLATION

The removal of the pistons are pushed out towards the top of the cylinder bores, using a hammer handle after connecting rod bearing caps and shells have been removed. Before removal of the assemblies note the following points:

- Pistons and cylinder bores are graded in three diameter groups and marked with the numbers 0, 1 and 2. The class number is stamped into the upper face of the cylinder block, next to the particular cylinder bore, as shown in Fig. 10.11. The class number of the piston must always be identical with the letter stamped next to the cylinder bore. Piston diameter, the class number and the last two numbers of the piston spare part number are stamped into the piston crown, An arrow, indicating the fitting direction, is also stamped into the piston crown.

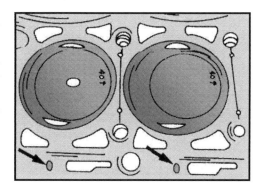

Fig. 10.11 – The marking of the piston size in the cylinder block face.

•   The piston crown of the individual engine is of a different shape. On normally compressed engines, the piston crown is flat. The piston crown of the low compression engine has a step. Pistons can therefore not be interchanged between normal and low compression engines.

Pistons can be removed as follows:

•   Mark each piston and the connecting rod before removal with the cylinder number. This can be carried out by writing the cylinder number with paint onto the piston crown. Also mark an arrow, facing towards the front of the engine (the arrow in the piston crown will be covered by the carbon deposits). When removing the connecting rod, note the correct installation of the big end bearing cap. Immediately after removal mark the connecting rod and the big end bearing cap on the same side. This is best done with a centre punch (cylinder No. 1 one punch mark, etc).

•   Mark the big end bearing shells with the cylinder number. The upper shells have an oil drilling (to lubricate the piston pin).

•   Remove the bearing caps and the shells and push the assemblies out of the cylinder bore. Any carbon deposits on the upper edge of the bores can be carefully removed with a scraper.

•   Remove the piston pin snap rings. A notch in the piston pin bore enables a pointed drift to be inserted, as shown in Fig. 1.27, to remove the rings. Press the piston pins out of the pistons. If necessary heat the piston in boiling water.

•   Remove the piston rings one after the other from the pistons, using a piston ring pliers if possible. If the rings are to be re-used, mark them in accordance with their pistons and position.

10.5.2.   MEASURING THE CYLINDER BORES

The instructions given in section 1.3.1.2 also apply to these engines. Fig. 1.28 can be referred to for details.

The piston clearance must, however, be noted if measurements are carried out. This is between 0.016 to 0.040 mm in the case of the M102 engine, but 0.025 to 0.035 mm in the case of the M115 engine. The max. running clearance of 0.04 mm (M102) or 0.08 mm (M115) must not be exceeded.

10.5.3.   CHECKING PISTONS AND CONNECTING RODS

Pistons and connecting rods are checked in a similar manner as described in Section 1.3.1.3. for the diesel engine. The values given in Section 10.5.0 must be used.

10.5.4.   PISTONS AND CONNECTING RODS - ASSEMBLY

If new pistons are fitted, check the piston crown markings to ensure the correct pistons are fitted. If the original pistons are refitted, arrange them in accordance with the cylinder number markings.

Fig. 10.12 – Piston and connecting rod of the M102 engine must be aligned as explained below. Different for the M115 engine.

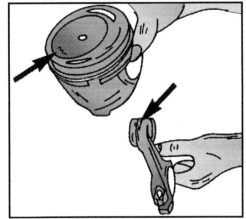

- Insert the connecting rod into the piston and align the two bores. Make sure that the arrow in the piston crown and the oil splash bore on the small end are facing towards the front of the engine, as shown in Fig. 10.12 for an M102 engine. In the case of the M115 engine the arrow in the piston crown must face towards the front and the oil bore towards the R.H. side of the engine.

- Fit the circlips on both sides of the piston, making sure of their engagement around the groove. Move the piston up and down to check for free movement.

- Using a pair of piston ring pliers, fit the piston rings from the top of the piston, starting with the bottom ring. The two compression rings could be mixed up and care should be taken.

10.5.5.   PISTONS AND CONNECTING RODS - INSTALLATION

The installation is carried out in the same manner as described for the diesel engines covered earlier on. The connecting rod nuts are tightened to 4.0 – 5.0 kgm (30 – 36 ft.lb.) and from the final position by a further 90° - 100° Re-check the connecting rod markings and the piston installation direction once more after all piston/connecting rod assemblies have been fitted.

With a feeler gauge measure the side clearance of each big end bearing cap on the crankpin. A clearance of 0.50 mm must not be exceeded. On a new engine the clearance is between 0.11 – 0.23 mm.

10.6.   Cylinder Block

10.6.0.   Technical Data

Cylinder Bore Diameter: ....93.750 – 93.772 mm (M115), 95.498 – 95.528 mm (M102)
Oversize 1: ....94.150 – 94.172 mm (M115), 95.998 – 96.028 mm (M102)
Oversize 2: ....94.550 – 94.572 mm (M115), 96.498 – 96.528 mm (M102)
Max. wear, longitudinal and across: ....0.10 mm
Max. out-of-round or taper of bores:
    New condition: ....0.013 mm (M115), 0.007 mm (M102)
    Wear limit: ....0.05 mm
Measuring point for bores: ....Upper edge, centre and lower edge,
                                       in longitudinal and transverse
                                       direction

Crankcase

Cylinder block height, new:
- M115 engines:..242.80 – 242.90 mm
- M102 engine: ....292.45 – 292.55 mm
Cylinder block height, minimum: ....242.50 mm (M115), 292.23 mm (M102)
Permissible unevenness of:
  Upper crankcase face: ....0.03 mm
  Lower crankcase face: ....0.04 mm
Difference between upper and lower sealing face: ....0.10 mm (0.004 in.)

The instructions given for the 616/617 engines apply in general also to the four-cylinder petrol engines. The main oil gallery of the M102 engine is closed off with an M16 plug, which can be removed to clean the gallery bore (Allen key is used).
The bearing bores for the intermediate shaft can be measured in the cylinder block. We recommend to have the work carried out in an engine shop.

10.7. Crankshaft and Bearings, Flywheel
10.7.0. TECHNICAL DATA

All dimensions in metric units.
Machining tolerances:
Max. out-of-round of journals: ....0.005 mm (M115), 0.0025 mm (M102)
Max. taper of journals:...0.010 mm
Max. taper of crankpins: ....0.010 mm (M115), 0.015 mm (M102)
Max. run-out of main journals*:
- Journals Nos. II and IV:...0.07 mm
- Journals No. III: ....0.10 mm

   *   Crankshaft placed with Nos. I and V journals in "V" blocks.

Main Bearing Journal Diameter:
- Nominal diameter:..............69.96 – 69.95 mm (M115), 57.950 – 57.965 mm (M102)
- Repair size: .... Enquire at dealer
Width of fit bearing, std.:...................... 34.00 – 34.03 mm (M115), 28.50 – 28.521 mm

Crankpin Diameter:
- Nominal dimension:..................51.96 – 51.95 mm (M115), 47.955 – 47.965 (M102)
- Repair size: .... Enquire at dealer

Width of Crankpins:
- Nominal Dimension:............... 32.00 – 32.10 mm (M115), 28.00 - 20.04 mm (M102)

Bearing Running Clearances:
- Main bearings:........................ 0.031 - 0.068 mm (M115), 0.025 – 0.045 mm (M102)
- Big end bearings: .... 0.031 - 0.068 mm (M115), 0.030 – 0.050 mm (M102)
   Wear limit: ....0.080 mm (M115), 0.070 mm (M102)

Bearing End Float (all engines):
- Main bearings:................................ 0.10 - 0.22 mm (M115), 0.06 – 0.22 mm (M102)
- Big end bearings: .... 0.12 - 0.26 mm (M115), 0.11 – 0.23 mm (M102)
- Wear limit - Main bearings: .... 0.30 mm
- Wear limit - Big end bearings: .... 0.50 mm

Connecting Rod Bolts:
- Thread:...M10 x 1
- Tightening torque: ....4.0 – 5.0 kgm + 90° - 100°

10.7. 1. REMOVAL AND INSTALLATION

The engine must be removed to take out the crankshaft. The removal of the crankshaft takes place in the manner described in Section 1.3.3.1 (page 33) for the diesel engines. The crankshaft end float must be checked before the shaft is removed. The crankshaft bearing caps are marked with the numbers 2, 3, 4 and 5 (in the centre of the bearing caps). Cap No. 1 has no identification number. No. 1 cap is situated on the crankshaft pulley side.

10.7.2. Inspection of Crankshaft and Bearings

The operations are carried out in the same manner as described for the 616/617 diesel engines, but note the differences when checking the main bearing running clearance:
Check the main bearing and big end bearing running clearance as follows:
- Bolt the main bearing caps without shells to the crankcase, oil the bolt threads and fit each cap. In the case of the M115 engine tighten the bolts to 9.0 kgm (65 ft.lb.). In the case of the M102 engine tighten the caps to 9.0 kgm (65 ft.lb.) and from the final position a further 90° - 100°. Bearing caps are offset and can only be fitted in one position.
- Referring to Fig. 1.39 measure the bearing bores in directions A, B and C and write down the results. If the basic diameter is exceeded (see Section 10.7.0.), the bearing cap and/or the cylinder block must be replaced.
- Remove the bearing caps and refit them, this time with the well cleaned bearing shells. Re-tighten the bolts as specified.
- Measure the diameter of each bearing in accordance as shown in Fig. 1.39 and write down the results. Deduct the journal diameter from the bearing diameter. The resulting difference is the bearing running clearance, which should be between the values specified in the technical data above.
- Check the big end bearing clearances in a similar manner, but bolt the bearing caps to the connecting rods. Tighten the nuts to the value given in the technical data. The bearing clearance should be between the values given in the technical data in Section 10.7.0.

Selection of bearing shells is rather complicated, and we advise you to take the cylinder block to an engine shop, if the above measurements have revealed that new bearing shells are necessary.

10.7.3. Crankshaft - Installation

The installation of the crankshaft of an M115 engine is identical with the operations for the six-cylinder engine, covered later on in the manual, with the difference that the main bearing caps are tightened to 9.0 kgm (65 ft.lb.).
The following instructions apply to the M102 engine only:
- Thoroughly clean the bearing bores in the crankcase and insert the shells with the drillings into the bearing bores, with the tabs engaging the notches. Fit the thrust washers to the centre bearing, with the oil grooves towards the outside. Use the two forefingers to hold the thrust washers against the bearing cap and fit the cap in position.
- Lift the crankshaft in position and fit the bearing caps with the inserted shells (again shells well oiled and locating tabs in notches). Fit the two thrust washers to the centre bearing cap, as shown in Fig. 1.42, again with the oil groove towards the outside. Place this cap in position, guiding the two thrust washers in order not to dislodge them. Use the forefingers, as shown in Fig. 1.42, to hold the washers.
- Check the numbering of the bearing caps and fit the well oiled bolts. Tighten the bolts from the centre towards the outside in several steps to a torque reading of 9.0 kgm (65 ft.lb.) and from this position a further 90° – 100°.
- Rotate the crankshaft a few times to check for binding (hard spots).
- Re-check the crankshaft end float as described during removal. Attach the dial gauge to the crankcase as shown in Fig. 1.37. The remaining operations are carried out in reverse order to the removal procedure. The various sections give

detailed description of the relevant operations, i.e. piston and connecting rods, rear oil seal flange, timing mechanism, flywheel and clutch or drive plate, oil pump, oil sump and cylinder head.

10.7.4.   Flywheel or Drive Plate (Automatic)

The flywheel and drive plate for an injection engine have two 55° segments machined into the rear face, located opposite each other. Together with a position indicator, fitted into the crankcase, these segments transmit the speed signal to the ignition switch unit. Fig. 10.13 shows where the segments are located on the flywheel. Fig. 10.14 shows where the position indicator is situated on the cylinder block (M102 engine shown).

Both flywheel and drive plate can be replaced with the engine fitted without re-balancing the crankshaft. Proceed as follows:

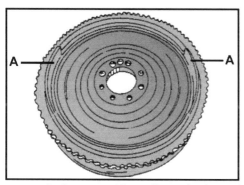

Fig. 10.13 – The location of the two segments (A) in the rear face of the flywheel.

*   Remove the transmission (Section 4.1).
*   Counterhold the flywheel in a suitable manner and remove the clutch after having marked its relationship to the flywheel.   Remove the drive plate in a similar manner.   8 bolts are used to secure the flywheel. A hole has been drilled between two of the bolts and a similar hole is drilled into the crankshaft. These two holes must be aligned when the flywheel or the drive plate is fitted.

Fig. 10.14 – The arrow shows the bore where the position indicator is fitted to the crankcase.

*   Remove the flywheel or the drive plate. Distance washers are used in the case of the drive plate, which can also be removed.
*   Measure the diameter of the mounting bolts at their smallest section. If less than 8.0 mm (M102) or 8.1 mm (M115), replace the bolts. The measurement is carried out as shown earlier on for the connecting rod bolts.

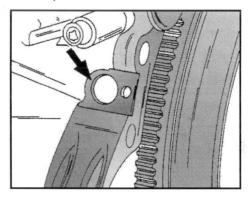

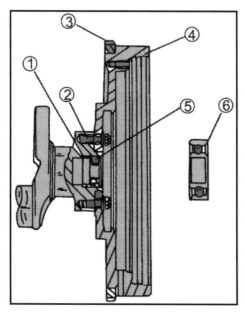

Fig. 10.15 – Sectional view of the crankshaft rear end.
1   Spacer ring
2   Stretch bolt
3   Starter ring gear
4   Flywheel
5   Closing cover
6   Ball bearing

*   If the flywheel or the starter ring gear looks worn, take the wheel to your dealer to have the flywheel re-machined and/or the ring gear replaced.

Fit the flywheel or the drive plate with the alignment bores in line. Fit a distance washer underneath and on top of the drive plate. Tighten the bolts evenly across to 3.0 – 4.0 kgm (22 – 29 ft.lb.) and from this position a further 90° – 100°.

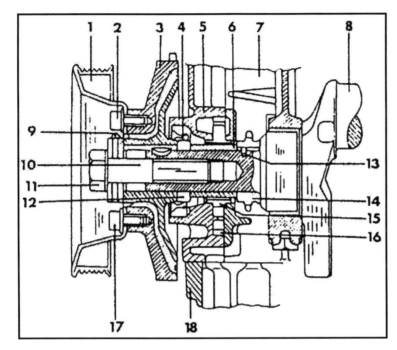

Fig. 10.16 – Sectional view of the crankshaft end without A/C system.
 1 Crankshaft pulley
 2 Bolt, M8 x 16
 3 Vibration damper
 4 Oil seal
 5 Timing cover
 6 Oil pump drive sleeve
 7 Crankcase
 8 Crankshaft
 9 Spring discs
10 Woodruff key
11 Bolt, M18 x 1.5 x 75 mm
12 Spacer ring
13 Dowel pin, 3 x 5 mm
14 Crankshaft sprocket
15 Inner gearwheel, oil pump
16 Outer gearwheel, oil pump
17 Bolt, M8 x 10
18 Oil pump

The angle is important to give the stretch bolts their correct tension.

Engines for manual transmissions have a ball bearing in the end of the crankshaft, illustrated in Fig. 10.15. A retaining ring is used to hold the bearing in position and must be removed to withdraw the ball bearing with a suitable puller, as already shown in Fig. 1.45.

10.7.5.   Crankshaft Pulley and Vibration Damper

The injection engine is fitted with a vibration damper. The carburettor engine has a crankshaft pulley and a hub. The hub, vibration damper or the crankshaft pulley can be replaced without balancing the crankshaft. The mounting bolts for the crankshaft pulley are off-set, allowing the fitting of the pulley in one position only. Two different types can be found:

Fig. 10.17 – Sectional view of the crankshaft end when an A/C system is fitted.
 1 Flange
 2 Bolt, M6 x 13
 3 Ball bearing
 4 Closing cap
 5 Stretch bolt, M18 x 1.5
 6 Spacer ring
 7 Retaining ring
 8 Bolt, M6 x 13
 9 Crankshaft pulley
10 Spring discs
11 Woodruff key
12 Oil seal
13 Timing cover
14 Oil pump drive sleeve
15 Crankcase
16 Crankshaft
17 Dowel pin. 3 x 5 mm
18 Crankshaft sprocket
19 Inner gearwheel, oil pump
20 Outer gearwheel, oil pump
21 Hub with rubber element

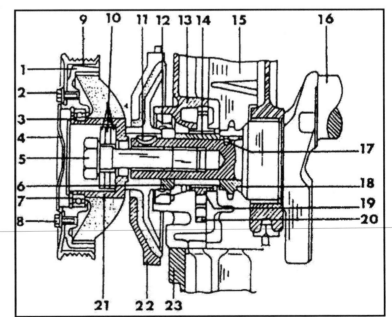

22 Vibration damper
23 Oil sump

In the case of vehicles without air conditioning system, the pulley is secured with six bolts and a thrust washer to the vibration damper. The complete assembly is secured by means of an M18 x 1.5 x 75 bolt. The tightening torque of the bolt is 27 – 33 kgm (195 – 238 ft.lb.). Fig. 10.16 shows a sectional view of the crankshaft front of this type of drive.

In the case of models with air conditioning system, the pulley is attached to the crankshaft by means of a coupling. The coupling consists of a hub with a rubber section and a steel ring flange, a ball bearing and a closing cover. Fig. 10.17 shows a sectional view of this type of drive. Irregular rotation of the crankshaft at low revs and during the cutting-in of the A/C compressor are absorbed by the coupling, resulting in a slipless drive of the single belt. The complete assembly is fitted to the front end of the crankshaft by means of an M18 x 1.5 x 75 bolt. The bolt is tightened to 2.0 kgm (14.5 ft.lb.) and then twice by 90°.

Remove the parts as follows, but note that a puller is required to remove the damper:

M102 Engine

- Remove the fan cowling and the fan, release the tension of the drive belt and remove the single belt.
- Engage a gear and apply the handbrake to lock the engine against rotation. In the case of a vehicle with automatic transmission remove the starter motor and lock the starter motor ring gear in a suitable manner.
- Remove the centre bolts from the vibration damper and remove the damper or the hub together with the crankshaft pulley, using a suitable puller. To do this, unscrew the pulley and attach the puller to the inside of the hub or the damper and withdraw. Make a note of the fitting position of the three spring discs, as they must face the same way during installation.

Before installation fit the crankshaft pulley to the vibration damper or to the hub, depending on the model year and tighten the socket head bolts to 1.0 kgm (7.2 ft.lb.).

- Turn the crankshaft until the Woodruff key is visible and push the damper or the hub over the key and the shaft end. Place the three spring discs over the centre bolt, coat the bolt threads with engine oil and fit the bolt. Tighten the bolt to the value given for the two types of drive. The crankshaft must again be locked against rotation.
- The remaining operations are carried out in reverse order.

M115 Engine

The crankshaft pulley and the balancing disc can be removed on this engine. As a new balancing disc must be re-balanced before installation you will have to have the work carried out in a workshop. If a new disc is required. The removal of the crankshaft pulley is a straight-forward operation after removal of the radiator and the drive belt. The balance disc can be removed in a similar manner as described above, if for example the front oil seal for the crankshaft requires replacement.

The removal of the balancing disc requires a two- or three arm puller. Before the disc is removed mark the crankshaft and the disc at opposite points to ensure installation of the disc in its original position.

10.7.6.   Rear Crankshaft Oil Seal

M115 Engine

The engine must be removed to replace the oil seal, as the seal is located in a groove in the rear crankshaft main bearing cap. Remove the seal with a screwdriver out of the groove. The installation is carried out as described for the 616/617 engines. Details can are described on page 35.

M102 Engine

The oil seal can be replaced with the engine fitted. The oil seal is located inside a flange which is bolted to the rear of the crankcase. Two dowels locate the flange correctly in relation to the crankshaft centre. The flange is fitted with sealing compound. The transmission and flywheel or the drive plate (automatic) must be removed to replace the oil seal. If only the oil seal needs replacement, lever it out carefully with a screwdriver without damaging the flange. If the oil seal carrier is to be removed, remove the bolts around the outside edge and two bolts from below. Apply two screwdrivers at the points shown in Fig. 10.18 (one on each side) and carefully lever the carrier off the crankcase. The oil seal can now be removed from the inside.

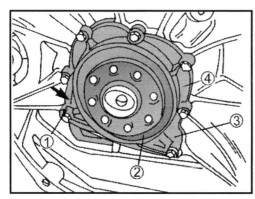

Fig. 10.18 – Rear oil seal carrier in position (M102).
1   Location of dowel pin
2   Oil seal
3   Location of dowel pin
4   Oil seal carrier

Clean the carrier and the crankcase faces and fit a new oil seal to the carrier (removed or still fitted). The sealing lip of the new oil seal is offset to prevent it from running on the same crankshaft area. Fill the space between the sealing lip and the dust protection lip with grease. Coat the carrier face with sealing compound and fit it to the block, with the dowel pins engaged. Slightly tap the carrier in position. Great care must be taken during installation in order not to damage the oil seal.

Fit the bolts. First tighten the lower bolts and then the upper bolts. The torque is 1.0 kgm (7.2 ft.lb.) for all bolts.

Carry out all other operations in reverse order.

10.7.7.   Front Crankshaft Oil Seal

The front crankshaft oil seal is located in the timing cover and can be replaced with the engine fitted. In the case of an M102 engine it is also possible that the oil leak is caused by a leaking timing cover gasket. Note that the oil seal of an M115 engine can be one of two types.

M102 Engine

The vibration damper and the crankshaft pulley must be removed as already described before the oil seal can be replaced (see description earlier on). The oil seal can be carefully removed with a screwdriver. Screw a self-tapping screw into the outside of the seal and apply the screwdriver blade under the screw head. If the spacer ring on the crankshaft shows signs of wear, remove it with a suitable puller.

Thoroughly clean the surrounding parts. Burrs on the timing cover bore can be removed with a scraper. Fill the space between the sealing lip and the dust protection lip with grease and carefully drive a new oil seal into the timing cover and over the crankshaft until the outer face is flush. Refit the vibration damper or the hub as described earlier on.

M115 Engine

Although the removal of the balancing disc is not recommended on this engine, it can be removed in a similar manner as described. The disc and the cranshaft must be marked at opposite points to assure installation in the same position.

The centre bolt of this engine is tightened to 27 – 30 kgm (194 – 21 ft.lb.) during installation.

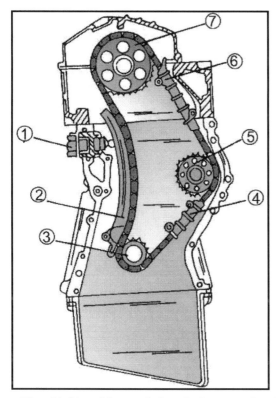

Fig. 10.19 – View of the timing mechanism (M102 engine).
1   Chain tensioner
2   Tensioning rail
3   Crankshaft sprocket
4   Lower slide rail
5   Intermediate shaft sprocket
6   Upper slide rail
7   Camshaft sprocket

10.8.   Timing Mechanism

The component parts covered in this section can be removed with the engine fitted. The arrangement of the timing chain and the other timing gear components are shown in Fig. 10.19 for the M102 engine and Fig. 10.20 for the M115 engine.

The endless timing chain is engaged with the camshaft and the intermediate shaft socket and drives the ignition distributor and in the case of the carburettor engine, the fuel pump.

Fig. 10.20 – View of the timing mechanism (M115 engine).
1   Tensioning rail
2   Chain tensioner
3   Camshaft sprocket
4   Slide rail
5   Intermediate shaft sprocket
6   Chain locking bolt
7   Slide rail
8   Camshaft sprocket

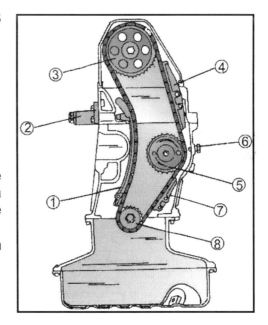

The chain is guided by two slide rails. The tension of the chain is ensured by means of a hydraulic chain tensioner, which is located in the crankcase and pushes onto a tensioning rail.

The camshaft sprocket is secured by means of a centre bolt and located by a Woodruff key.

10.8.0.   Chain Tensioner – Removal and Installation

M102 Engine

• Slacken the drive belt and lift off the belt. To do this, slacken the tensioning device as described in the "Cooling" section for this engine.

• If a separate drive belt for the alternator is fitted, remove the adjuster bar, swing it upwards and push the alternator towards the outside.

• Remove the plug (1) in Fig. 10.19 and remove the sealing washer underneath the plug head. Fig. 10.4 shows the removal of the chain tensioner. Items (1), (2) and (3) must be removed.

M115 and M102 Petrol Engines

- Insert a 17 mm Allen key into the chain tensioner and unscrew it from the cylinder block. Remove the thrust bolt out of the chain tensioner housing. A new chain tensioner is supplied together with the thrust bolt as a complete unit.

To refit the tensioner, screw it into the cylinder block and tighten to 1.0 kgm (7.2 ft.lb.). All other operations are carried out in reverse order. The plug is tightened to 7.0 kgm (51 ft.lb.).

M115 Engine

- Drain the cooling system and disconnect the coolant hose from the thermostat housing. Unscrew the thermostat housing and place it to one side.
- Unscrew the chain tensioner and withdraw it.

Before the chain tensioner is fitted it must be filled with oil. The operations are described on pages 126 and 127, as they are the same as in the case of the 602/603 diesel engines.

10.8.1. Timing Chain – Removal and Installation

The replacement of the timing chain is carried out in general as described for the other engines covered earlier on. We recommend that you refer to the section dealing with the 2.8 litre engine for certain details and illustration. The following operations must be carried out before the chain can be replaced.

- Remove the air cleaner.
- Remove the cylinder head cover and unscrew the spark plugs.
- Remove the chain tensioner (M102 engine) or push back the chain tensioner plunger (M115 engine).

10.8.2. Tensioning Rail – Removal and Installation

The location of the tensioning rail can be taken from Fig. 10.19 (M102) or 10.20 (M115). The timing cover must be removed in the case of an M102 engine. The plastic coating of the tensioning rail can technically speaking be replaced, but must be heated to 65° C in water before it is fitted to the rail – workshop. Remove the rail as follows, noting that the radiator, the cooling fan, the crankshaft pulley and the cylinder head cover must be removed. Note that a special tool is required to remove the rail of an M115 engine. Read the instructions first.

- Remove the timing cover (M102) and the chain tensioner as described earlier on.
- Using paint, mark the relationship between the timing chain and the crankshaft sprocket in a similar manner as shown in Fig. 1.12 for the camshaft sprocket and mark the camshaft sprocket and timing chain as shown. In the case of an M115 engine rotate the crankshaft until the groove in the balancing disc is opposite the bearing bolt for the tensioning rail.
- Counterhold the camshaft as shown in Fig. 10.5 for the engine in question and remove the camshaft sprocket bolt. Remove the sprocket.
- In the case of the M102 engine swivel the tensioning rail towards the inside and withdraw it from the pivot pin. In the case of the M115 withdraw the bearing pin for the tensioning rail with the special extractor as shown on page 43 for one of the diesel engines (see also Fig. 1.55). Without extractor it is possible to screw a bolt of suitable diameter into the bearing bolt and try to withdraw the bolt.
- In the case of the M102 engine check the plastic coating for wear or damage and replace it or have it replaced if necessary or fit a new tensioning rail. In the case of the M115 the tensioning rail and the bearing bolt must be replaced if the wear is excessive. On this engine also make sure to obtain the correct tensioning rail.

- The installation is a reversal of the removal procedure. In the case of the M115 engine coat the outside of the bearing bolt with sealing compound, arrange the tensioning rail in the correct position and fit the bearing bolt, again using the slide hammer.
- Fit the camshaft sprocket, counterhold the camshaft and tighten the camshaft sprocket bolt to 8.0 kgm (58 ft.lb.). When fitting the timing chain to the camshaft sprocket and the crankshaft sprocket make sure that the paint marks are in line, as shown in Fig. 1.12.

10.8.3.   Slide Rails – Removal and Installation

The position of the slide rails is shown in Figs. 10.19 and 10.20 for the two engines. To remove a slide rail, a slide hammer with a suitable, threaded adapter is required, to remove the bearing bolts. The bolt is screwed into the end of the bearing bolt and the impact hammer (slide hammer) attached to the end of the bolt (Fig. 1.55). Provided that these tools can be obtained, the rails can be removed as described below. Remove the upper slide rail as follows:

- Disconnect the battery, drain the engine coolant, remove the air cleaner and the cylinder head cover.
- In the case of the M102 engine it is of advantage to remove the thermostat housing. To do this, slacken the hose clamps at the housing (one at the bottom and one at the side) and withdraw the hose from the thermostat housing cover. At the top of the housing remove the hollow bolt, connecting the vent pipe and also the hollow bolt at the other end of the pipe. Unscrew the thermostat housing screws and remove the housing. Also remove the engine lifting bracket.
- **In the case of the M102 engine:** Unscrew the plug for the hydraulic chain tensioner and the camshaft sprocket. Operations have already been described.
- Screw the 6 mm bolt mentioned above into the bearing bolts (one at the top and one at the bottom) and attach a slide hammer to the end of the extraction bolt. Hit the weight of the slide hammer against the stop until the bearing bolts are free. Remove the slide rail. Note that the slide rail of the M115 engine can have two bores and you will have to find out which bolt is the bearing bolt.

If the bearing bolts need replacing, take the old one to your parts supplier to make sure an identical one is obtained, as bearing bolts have been changed at some stage. Fit the slide rail as follows:

Coat the bearing bolts on the flange with sealing compound, fit the slide rail in position and insert the bearing bolts. Fit the 6 mm bolt and the slide hammer to the end of the bearing bolt and knock the bolt in position, this time hitting the weight of the slide hammer towards the front. Fit the second bearing bolt in the same manner. Counterhold the slide rail during the bearing bolt installation with a screwdriver to prevent distortion. A locating nose in the bearing bolt bore of the slide rail will engage in the locating groove in the upper bearing bolt when the bolt is in position.

The remaining operations are carried out in reverse order. Pay attention to the paint marks on timing chain and camshaft sprocket when the parts are refitted. Fit the thermostat housing with a new gasket (M102 engine) and refit the cylinder head cover.

Replace the lower slide rail (4) in Fig. 10.19 (M102) or (7) in Fig. 10.20 (M115) as follows:

- **In the case of the M102 engine** remove the timing cover as described and remove the slide rail from the two bearing bolts. Fit the new slide rail in position and refit the timing cover.

In the case of the M115 engine the operations are more complicated:
- Remove the intermediate shaft as described below.

- Remove the closing plug with the bearing bolt, located near the oil filter next to the crankshaft pulley.
- Remove the lower bearing bolt with the special extractor or in the manner described for the tensioning rail (see also Fig. 1.55). Note which bore of the rail is used to secure the rail, if the rail has two bores.
- Remove the slide rail through the opening for the intermediate shaft sprocket.

Coat the bearing bolt on the flange with sealing compound, fit the slide rail in position and insert the bearing bolt. Fit the bolt as described above. Counterhold the slide rail during the bearing bolt installation with a screwdriver to prevent distortion. A locating nose in the bearing bolt bore of the slide rail will engage in the locating groove in the lower bearing bolt when the bolt is in position.

Fit the upper bearing bolt, making sure that the correct bore in the rail is used, if the rail has two bores.

Carry out the remaining operations in reverse order.

10.8.4.   Intermediate Shaft – Removal and Installation

The intermediate shaft sprocket of an M102 engine is pressed onto the intermediate shaft, which in turn is mounted in the timing cover and the cylinder block. The shaft is held in position by a keeper plate, inserted into a groove in the shaft and bolted to the cylinder block. The distributor drive gear is fitted to the front of the intermediate gear, The fuel pump drive cam is fitted to the shaft in the case of a carburettor engine. Now shafts are supplied together with the sprocket. Fig. 10.21 shows a sectional view of the fitted shaft.

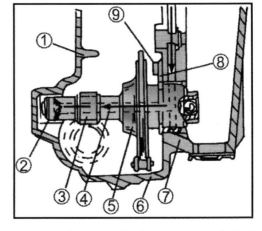

Fig. 10.21 – Intermediate shaft of an M102 engine (injection version).
1   Timing cover
2   Bearing bush in timing cover
3   Distributor drive gear
4   Intermediate shaft
5   Intermediate shaft sprocket
6   Crankcase
7   Bearing bush in crankcase
8   Keeper plate
9   Screw, M5 x 18 mm

The intermediate shaft of the M115 engine is located in a bush, which is secured with a locking bolt. The shaft must be removed together with the bush with an impact (slide) hammer. Access to the locking bolt is possible after removal of a closing plug. A drive shaft for the distributor drive must be removed before you can obtain access to the intermediate shaft.

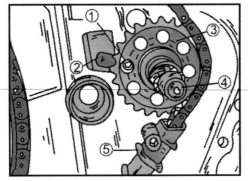

Fig. 10.22 – The intermediate shaft sprocket in fitted position.
1   Socket head bolt
2   Keeper plate
3   Intermediate shaft sprocket
4   Intermediate shaft
5   Slide rail

Removal of the shaft can be carried out as follows:

M102 Engine
- Remove the timing cover. If fitted, remove the fuel pump.
- Remove the chain tensioner as described earlier on.

- Referring to Fig. 10.22 withdraw the slide rail (5) from the two bearing bolts.
- Mark the crankshaft sprocket and the timing chain at opposite points as shown in Fig. 1.12 for the camshaft sprocket.
- Remove the socket bolt (1) in Fig. 10.22 through one of the holes in the sprocket and withdraw the keeper plate (2) from the side of the sprocket.
- Rotate the crankshaft slightly against the direction of engine rotation, to slacken the timing chain on the intermediate sprocket and withdraw the intermediate shaft. The crankshaft must be rotated by applying a 27 mm socket and a ratchet to the crankshaft damper bolt. Disconnect the green cable connected to the distributor from the ignition control unit (pull off the plug). Make sure that the timing chain remains in mesh with the camshaft sprocket as the crankshaft is rotated.

The installation is a reversal of the removal procedure. Make sure that the paint marks on crankshaft sprocket and timing chain are in line before the timing cover is refitted.

M115 Engine

The removal and installation of the intermediate shaft of this engine cannot be recommend as it is rather complicated with the engine fitted to the vehicle. With the engine removed you can remove the shaft as follows with the cylinder head cover removed:

- Rotate the engine until the No. 1 piston is at top dead centre in the firing position.
- Grip the drive shaft in the opening for the distributor with a pair of pliers and withdraw it. **During installation** arrange the drive slot parallel with the engine. The wider segment must be on the side of the engine.
- Push back the pressure plunger of the chain tensioner.
- Remove the closing plug on the crankcase and remove the two slide rails as already described.
- Unscrew the intermediate shaft sprocket. A screwdriver is then inserted behind the sprocket and the shaft is levered to the rear until the sprocket is free and can be removed towards the top.
- In the opening for the closing cover remove the L.H. screw. The intermediate shaft is withdrawn together with the front bearing bush, using an impact hammer, similar as shown in Fig. 1.55 for the slide rail bearing bolts.

Fit the intermediate shaft as follows:
- Insert the shaft with the bearing bush (well oiled) and turn the bearing bush so that the lock washer is located in its groove and the lock screw can be fitted.

Fit the intermediate shaft sprocket as follows:
- Fit both slide rails.
- Unscrew the chain lock bolt (6) in Fig. 10.20.
- Fit the distributor drive shaft, noting the instructions above.
- Pull the timing chain towards the top and check that the distributor drive shaft is in the correct position. If this is not the case, move the chain by one tooth on the intermediate shaft sprocket.
- Fit the camshaft sprocket, noting the colour marking (Fig. 1.12) and fit and tighten the bolt to 8.0 kgm (58 ft.lb.).
- Tighten the chain lock screw (6) in Fig. 10.20 and carry out all other operations in reverse order. The cylinder head cover is tightened to 1.5 kgm (11 ft.lb.).

10.8.5. Camshaft and Rocker Mechanism – M102

Section 10.3.2 should be read before the camshaft is removed. The camshaft is removed towards the top after the rocker shaft brackets and the camshaft sprocket have been removed.

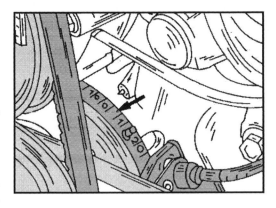

Fig. 10.23 – The engine is set to the T.D.C. firing point.

If the camshaft is replaced, also replace the rocker arms and the rocker shafts. Remove as follows:

• Remove the air cleaner and the cylinder head cover.

• Rotate the engine until the piston of No. 1 cylinder is at top dead centre on the firing stroke. Check the timing mark in the camshaft is in line with the edge of the cylinder head and that the TDC mark in the crankshaft pulley is aligned with the ignition pointer on the timing case as shown in Fig. 10.23. Rotate the crankshaft by applying a 27 mm socket and a ratchet to the crankshaft pulley bolt. Before rotating the crankshaft disconnect the green cable from the distributor at the ignition control unit (follow the cable and withdraw the plug).

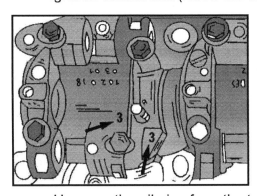

Fig. 10.24 – The rocker shaft bearing brackets and the cylinder head are marked with numbers 1 to 4 (arrows). No. 1 is at the front end.

• Mark the camshaft sprocket as shown in Fig. 1.12.

• Unscrew the chain tensioner plug as described earlier on and remove the spring.

• Counterhold the camshaft as shown in the L.H. view of Fig. 10.5 and remove the sprocket bolt.

• Unscrew the oil pipe from the top of the engine.

• Remove the rocker shaft bearing brackets four bolts each bracket). Use a plastic mallet to tap against the brackets if they are difficult to remove.

• Lift the camshaft out of the bearing bores. Remove the spacer ring and the Woodruff key from the end of the camshaft end.

If the camshaft is to be refitted, follow the notes given during the overhaul of the cylinder head for any of the other engines. Check the bearing journals and the bearing bores for excessive wear. The following notes refer to the rocker shaft bearing brackets and should be noted before installation:

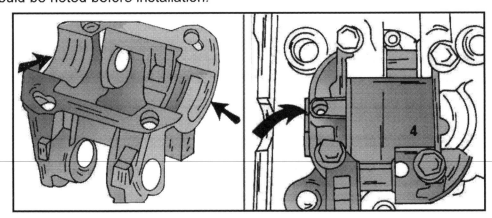

Fig. 10.25 – The two arrows in the L.H. view show the bearing points for the front rocker shaft bearing bracket. The arrow in the R.H. view shows the oil hole for the oil pipe connection (bearing bracket No. 4).

• All bearing brackets are located by means of two dowel sleeves.

160

- The bearing brackets are different. A number in the bracket and the cylinder head indicates where the bracket is to be fitted (see Fig. 10.24). Bearing brackets can also be identified through the following:
- The front bearing bracket (marked "1") has two bearing points (Fig. 10.25, L.H. view).
- The centre bearing brackets (marked "2" and "3") are identical apart from their numbering.
- The rear bearing bracket (marked "4") has a connecting hole for the oil pipe (Fig. 10.25. R.H. view).
- The brackets must be fitted so that all numbers are on the R.H. side (seen in the direction of drive).
- New bearing brackets have no numbers. The relevant number should be stamped into the bracket or marked in an other manner for future use. Never replace more than one bearing bracket as this could lead to binding of the camshaft.
- The rocker arms (levers) are mounted individually on a short shaft, which engages on both sides into bearing brackets (Fig. 10.26).

Fig. 10.26 – View of the fitted rocker arms (arrows). The oil pipe can also be seen.

- The rocker arm shafts must be pulled out with a slide hammer and a threaded 8 mm bolt, 150 mm long. Clamp the rocker arm assembly into a vice, screw the bolt into the rocker arm shaft and attach the slide hammer to the bolt. Hit the weight against the stop. If no slide hammer is available, pull out the shaft with the screwed-in bolt. New rocker arm shafts must be lubricated with oil before installation. Push the shafts in position.

Refit the camshaft and the rocker assemblies as follows:

- Generously lubricate the camshaft bearing journals with engine oil and insert the camshaft into the bearing bores. Rotate the camshaft until the timing mark is aligned as shown earlier on.
- Fit the rocker shaft bearing brackets in accordance with the markings in the cylinder head and brackets, checking that both are on the same side. Tighten the bearing bracket bolts to 2.1 kgm (15 ft.lb.).
- The remaining operations are a reversal of the removal procedure. Fit the camshaft sprocket with the wider boss facing the camshaft. Tighten the bolt to 8.0 kgm (58 ft.lb.). Check that the paint mark in the timing chain and the camshaft sprocket are aligned after installation.

10.8.6.   Rocker Arms – M115

The rocker arms must always be fitted to their original position. If rocker arms require replacement always check the camshaft as a new shaft may have to be fitted. Remove the rocker arms as follows:

- Remove the cylinder head cover.
- Free the tension spring of the rocker arms with a screwdriver or remove it with a pair of pliers. The camshaft must be rotated so that the rocker arm is free of tension (cam toe points upwards). Do not rotate the camshaft by applying a spanner to the camshaft sprocket bolt.
- Push the valve spring cap carefully downwards, using a valve lifter as used for the removal of the valves and lift out the rocker lever.

M115 and M102 Petrol Engines

The installation is a reversal of the removal procedure. The contact area of the rocker arm on the valve end must be lubricated with oil. Adjust the valve clearances as described in the section given below.

10.8.7. Adjusting Valve Clearances (if applicable)

The adjustment of the valve clearance is described in the same manner as described later on for the 2.8 litre six-cylinder engine, with the difference that the crankshaft must be rotated each time by half a turn to close the valves of the four cylinders in turn (commencing on cylinder No. 1).

10.8.8. Hydraulic Valve Clearance Compensating Elements

All information given for the 602/603 diesel engine are also valid for the M102 engine as their construction is the same. This also applies to the checking and the removal and installation of the elements.

10.9. Tightening Torque Values

Cylinder Head Bolts – M102 Engine:
- 1st stage:..7.0 kgm (50.5 ft.lb.)
- 2nd stage: ....90° angle tightening
- 3rd stage: ....90° angle-tightening

Cylinder Head Bolts – M115 Engine, M10 thread:
- 1st stage:..3.0 kgm (22 ft.lb.)
- 2nd stage: ....5.5 kgm (40 ft.lb.)
- 3rd stage: ....Re-tighten to 5.5 kgm, temperature 80° C

Cylinder Head Bolts – M115 Engine, M12 thread:
- 1st stage:..7.0 kgm (50.5 ft.lb.)
- 2nd stage: ....10.0 kgm (73 ft.lb.)
- 3rd stage: ....Re-tighten to 10.0 kgm, temperature 80° C

Cylinder head bolts (in timing case): .... 2.5 kgm (18 ft.lb.)
Cylinder head cover bolts:...1.5 kgm (11 ft.lb.)

Connecting Rod Bearing Caps:
- 1st stage:.. 4.0 – 5.0 kgm (29 - 36 ft.lb.)
- 2nd stag: .... Angle-tighten 90° – 100°

Main Bearing Cap Bolts:...9.0 kgm (65 ft.lb.)
Camshaft sprocket bolt:...8.0 kgm (58 ft.lb.)
Plug for chain tensioner:...7.0 kgm (50.5 ft.lb.)
Alternator mounting bracket: ....4.6 kgm (33 ft.lb.)
Inlet manifold support stay to manifold:...2.3 kgm (16.5 ft.lb.)
Exhaust manifold to cylinder head: ....2.1 kgm (15 ft.lb.)
Exhaust manifold to exhaust pipe flange:...3.0 kgm (22 ft.lb.)
Exhaust pipe to gearbox bracket:...2.0 kgm (14.5 ft.lb.)

Vibration damper or hub with crankshaft pulley
  to crankshaft (M102): ....30.0 kgm (216 ft.lb.)
Balance disc to crankshaft (M115):......................... 27.0 – 33.0 kgm (194 - 238 ft.lb.)
Spark plugs: ....1.5 kgm (11 ft.lb.)
Oil drain plug: ....3.0 kgm (22 ft.lb.)
Timing cover to cylinder block (M102):...2.3 kgm (16.5 ft.lb.)
Ignition distributor to timing cover (M102): ....2.3 kgm (16.5 ft.lb.)
Oil pipes to transmission (A/T): ....2.5 kgm (28 ft.lb.)

Flywheel or driven plate:
- 1st stage:..3.0 – 4.0 kgm (22 – 30 ft.lb.)

- 2nd stage:.. Angle-tighten by 90° – 100°
Inlet manifold to cylinder head:...1.0 kgm (7.2 ft.lb.)
Bolt for T.D.C. transmitter (sensor): ....0.6 kgm (4.5 ft.lb.)
Oil sump to cylinder block: ....1.0 kgm (7.2 ft.lb.)
Earth strap to chassis:...2.3 kgm (17.0 ft.lb.)
Coolant drain plug (block): ....2.8 kgm (20 ft.lb.)

11   M110 PETROL ENGINE (6 Cylinder)

Although not identical, both engine types are described in this section. Important differences are given whenever necessary.

11.0.   General Technical Data

Fitted Engine (model 280 GE):   M110
Type of fuel system: With mechanically controlled fuel injection system (CIS system)

Number of Cylinders: Six
Arrangement of cylinders: In-line
Arrangement of valves: Overhead
Valve Clearances
- Engine cold – Inlet valves   0.10 mm
- Engine cold – Exhaust valves   0.25 mm
- Engine warm – Inlet valves   0.15 mm
- Engine warm – Exhaust valves   0.30 mm

Cylinder bore: 86.5 mm
Piston stroke: 78.80 mm
Capacity: 2746 cc
Compression Ratio: 8.0 : 1
Max. B.H.P. (DIN):   114.5 kW (156 BHP) at 5250 rpm
Max. Torque: 22.6 kgm at 4250 rpm
Crankshaft bearings   7
Cooling system   Thermo system with water pump, thermostat, cooling fan with electro-magnetic clutch, tube-type radiator

Lubrication   Pressure-feed lubrication with gear-type oil pump, driven with chain from crankshaft. With full-flow oil filter

Air cleaner   Dry paper element air cleaner

11.1.   Engine – Removal and Installation

It is recommended to remove the engine together with the transmission and then to separate the transmission from the engine. Remember that the engine/transmission assembly is a heavy unit and a suitable hoist or hand crane is required to lift the engine out of the engine compartment. The removal and the installation is carried out in general as described for the four-cylinder petrol engines in Section 10.1. The main difference perhaps is the separation of the propeller shaft from the flange at the rear of the transmission and the disconnection of the electrical leads connected to the transmission, incl. the speedometer drive cable. Also disconnect the fluid hose for the clutch operation from the pipe.

11.2.   Engine – Dismantling and Assembling

General instructions to be observed during the dismantling of the 616/617 engines. Refer to section 1.1.

11.3.   Engine - Overhaul

11.3.0.   Cylinder Head and Valves – Technical Data

Cylinder Head:

Cylinder head height:	93.9 – 94.0 mm (min. 93.1 mm)
Max. Distortion of Cylinder Head Faces:	
- Longitudinal direction:	0.08 mm
- Across the face:	0.00 mm
Max. deviation of faces between upper and lower scaling faces (parallel to each other)	0.10 mm

Valves

Valve Head Diameter:	
- Inlet valves:	45.10 – 45.30 mm
- Exhaust valves:	39.90 – 39.10 mm
Valve seat angle:	45°
Valve Stem Diameter:	
- Inlet valves:	8.970 – 8.955 mm
- Exhaust valves:	8.960 – 8.935 mm
Valve Length:	
- Inlet valves:	114.80 – 115.20 mm
- Exhaust valves:	117.80 – 118.20 mm
Valve Seat Width:	
- Inlet valves:	1.8 to 2.5 mm
- Exhaust valves:	1.5 – 2.0 mm

Valve Seats

Valve seat width:	
- Inlet valves:	1.8 to 2.5 mm
- Exhaust valves:	1.5 – 2.0 mm
Valve seat angles:	45°
Upper correction angle:	15°
Lower correction angle:	60°

Valve Springs

Outer diameter, inner springs:	22.0 – 22.4 mm
Outer diameter, outer springs:	33.8 – 34.1 mm
Wire diameter, inner springs:	2.50 mm
Wire diameter, outer springs:	4.60 mm
Free length, inner springs:	45.0 mm
Free length, outer springs:	49.5 mm

Valve Guides

Inlet Valve Guides:
- Outer diameter – Std.:   14.03 – 14.05 mm
- Outer diameter – Repair size 1:   14.21 – 14.23 mm
- Outer diameter – Repair size 2:   14.41 – 14.43 mm
- Inner diameter: 9.00 – 9.015 mm
- Max. inner diameter: 9.025 mm
- Basic bore in cylinder head:
   Std.:   14.020 – 14.040 mm
   Repair size 1:   14.200 – 14.220 mm
   Repair size 2:   14.400 – 14.420 mm
- Interference fit of valve guides:
   Std.:   0.01 – 0.04 mm

Exhaust Valve Guides:
- Outer diameter – Std.:   15.03 – 15.05 mm
- Outer diameter – Repair size 1:   15.21 – 15.23 mm
- Outer diameter – Repair size 2:   15.41 – 15.43 mm
- Inner diameter: 9.00 – 9.015 mm
- Max. inner diameter: 9.025 mm
- Basic bore in cylinder head:
   Std.:   15.020 – 15.040 mm
   Repair size 1:   15.200 – 15.220 mm
   Repair size 2:   15.400 – 15.420 mm
- Interference fit of valve guides: 0.01 – 0.04 mm

Valve Clearances   See Section 11.0

Camshaft
Camshaft end float: 0.17 – 0.44 mm

11.3.1.   CYLINDER HEAD – REMOVAL AND INSTALLATION

The cylinder head must only be removed when the engine is cold. The removal takes place together with the inlet manifold and the exhaust manifold. New cylinder head gaskets are wrapped in plastic and must only be unwrapped just before the gasket is fitted. The cylinder head can be removed with the engine fitted and these operations are described below. Read the instructions before commencing the operations, as a make-shift tool must be prepared to refit the head.

Remove as follows:

- Place the engine bonnet into vertical position, disconnect the battery and drain the cooling system.
- Remove the air cleaner.
- If A/C is fitted remove the compressor without disconnecting the hoses/pipes and place it to one side.
- Remove both covers at the front of the camshaft housing.
- Disconnect all coolant, fuel and vacuum hoses and the electrical cables to the cylinder head or any other unit on the head which cannot be removed together with the head.
- Remove the regulating shaft for the throttle operation.
- Disconnect the oil return hose from the cylinder head.

- Free the oil dipstick tube for the automatic transmission from the clamp on the side of the cylinder head and carefully bend it to one side.
- Remove the coolant between thermostat housing and water pump. Also disconnect another pipe from the pump.

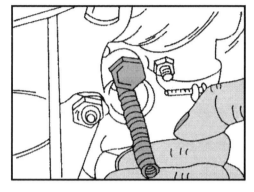

Fig. 11.1 – Removal of the chain tensioner.

- Rotate the engine until the piston of No. 1 cylinder is at top dead centre in the firing position. A 27 mm socket can be applied to the crankshaft pulley bolt to rotate the crankshaft. Never attempt to rotate the crankshaft by applying a socket to the camshaft timing wheel bolt. Mark the camshaft sprocket and the timing chain in a similar manner as shown in Fig. 1.12.
- Remove the plug shown in Fig. 11.1. The plug closes off the chain tensioner. Remove the spring and take out the sealing ring.

Fig. 11.2 – Counterhold the camshafts as shown when slackening or tightening the camshaft sprocket bolts.

- Unscrew the camshaft sprocket bolts. To counterhold the camshaft against rotation, use an open-ended spanner, applied to the camshaft as shown in Fig. 11.2.
- Remove the upper slide rail from the camshaft housing (see description later on), push both camshafts towards the rear and withdraw the camshaft sprockets.
- Remove the timing chain sprocket below the inlet camshaft and the chain guide rail from the cylinder head. Both operations are described later on.
- Unscrew the cylinder head bolts in reverse order to the one shown in Fig. 11.3. A special multi-spline bit (10 mm) and an extension is required. A normal Allen key is not suitable, as it will damage the bolt heads. Some earlier engines use socket head bolts and must be removed with an Allen key.

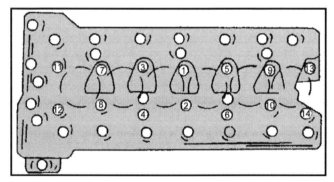

Fig. 11.3 – Tightening sequence for the cylinder head bolts (M110 engine).

- Remove the M8 bolts in the timing chain case by means of a 6 mm Allen key. A suitable extension is required to reach the bolts. If possible use a magnet to take the bolts out of the timing case to prevent them from dropping into the case.
- Pull the timing chain upwards and push the tensioning rail towards the centre of the engine.
- Lift off the cylinder head. If a hoist or lifting equipment is available hook a rope to the two lifting eyes and lift off the head.
- Immediately after removal clean the cylinder head and block surfaces of old gasket material.
- If necessary overhaul the cylinder head as described in section 11.3.3 after dismantling it.

Install the cylinder head as follows:

- Place a new cylinder head gasket in position. Two dowel pins in the crankcase will guide the gasket and the cylinder head.
- Prepare two pieces of wood with dimensions 15 x 35 x 240 mm and place them over the cylinder head gasket. Place one piece at the front and one piece at the rear over the gasket.
- Lower the cylinder head in position with the host or lifting equipment until it rests on the two pieces of wood and engage the timing chain and the tensioning rail.
- Lift the front end of the cylinder head and remove the wood towards the exhaust side. Then lower the head until it engages with the dowel pin.
- Lift the rear end of the cylinder head and remove the wood towards the exhaust side. Again lower the head until it engages with the dowel pin.
- Coat the threads of the cylinder head bolts with oil. Insert the cylinder head bolts and tighten them with the correct bolt wrench as follows, using the diagram in Fig. 11.3.
- Tighten the bolts in several stages to 4.0 kgm (30 ft.lb.), using the correct multi-spline bit.
- Re-tighten the cylinder head bolts in the same order, but this time to 7.0 kgm (50.5 ft.lb.). Allow the engine to stand for at least 10 minutes.
- Fit the three socket head bolts to the inside of the timing chain chamber and tighten them to 2.5 kgm (18 ft.lb.).

Fig. 11.4 – Sectional view of the inlet camshaft drive end.
1   Securing bolt
2   Spring discs
3   Spacer bush
4   Bearing location
5   Spacer ring
6   Camshaft sprocket
7   Woodruff key
8   Camshaft
9   Camshaft housing

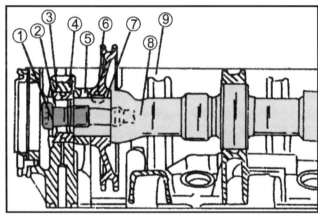

- In the order shown tighten each cylinder head bolt to the final torque of 11.0 kgm (79 ft.lb.), if socket head bolts are used. If multi-spline head bolts are used, tighten them by 90° and from this position once more by 90°. To obtain the correct angle, place the tommy bar in parallel with the cylinder head and tighten each bolt until it is at right angle to the head. The torque wrench must not be used.

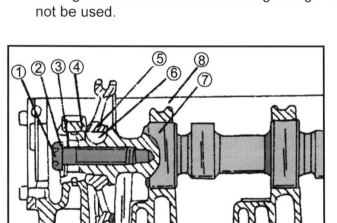

Fig. 11.5 – Sectional view of the exhaust camshaft drive end.
1   Securing bolt
2   Spring discs
3   Spacer bush
4   Bearing location
5   Camshaft sprocket
6   Woodruff key
7   Camshaft
8   Camshaft housing

Proceed as follows:
- Rotate both camshafts to check them for easy rotation.

- Lift up the timing chain and place it over the guide sprocket and refit the sprocket (described later on).
- Fit the inlet camshaft sprocket with the spacer ring. Coat the spacer bush with engine oil and insert it. Fig. 11.4 shows a sectional view of the camshaft end with the various parts.

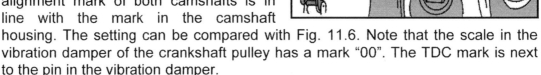

Fig. 11.6 – The alignment marks in the camshafts must be in line as shown.

- Fit the camshaft sprocket bolts with the washers, but do not tighten them yet. Check that the paint marks on sprockets and timing chain are again in line.
- Make sure that the piston of No. 1 cylinder is still at top dead centre and the alignment mark of both camshafts is in line with the mark in the camshaft housing. The setting can be compared with Fig. 11.6. Note that the scale in the vibration damper of the crankshaft pulley has a mark "00". The TDC mark is next to the pin in the vibration damper.
- Fit the slide rail to the camshaft housing and fit and tighten the solid chain tensioner.
- Rotate the crankshaft to set the engine to the ignition timing point. Mark "00" must be aligned.
- Fit the camshaft sprocket bolts and tighten the bolts to 8.0 kgm (58 ft.lb.). Counterhold the camshaft as shown in Fig. 11.2.
- Refit the rocker arms.
- Fit the chain tensioner.
- Adjust the valve clearances.
- The remaining operations are carried out in reverse order to the removal procedure. Finally adjust the drive belt tension.

Notes after Installation:
A re-adjustment of the valve clearances is not necessary.
A re-tightening of the cylinder head bolts is not necessary.

11.3.0.2.   Cylinder Head - Dismantling

The following description assumes that the cylinder head is to be replaced. If only a top overhaul is asked for, ignore the additional instructions. The cylinder head must be removed.

It should be noted that a replacement of the camshaft(s) also requires the replacement of the rocker arms. Camshaft bearing journals can be re-ground as two repair size bearings are available. This is of course a job for an engine shop. Proceed as follows during dismantling:

- Remove all auxiliary parts from the cylinder head, including the inlet and exhaust manifolds, rocker arms, spark plugs, sensors, etc.
- Remove the camshaft housing. To do this, remove the housing securing bolts and lift off the housing together with the fitted camshafts. Withdraw the camshafts towards the rear. The removal of the camshaft housing can also be carried out with the engine fitted. The operations are described in the section dealing with the timing drive.
- Valves are held in position by valve cotter halves. A valve lifter, as shown in Fig. 11.7, is required to compress the springs. Remove the cotter halves with a pair of

pointed pliers. The removal of the valves is described on page 106 for one of the diesel engines.

Fig. 11.7 – Removal of valves.

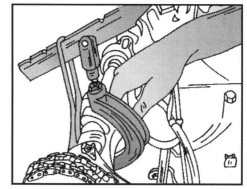

- Remove the spring cup, valve spring and valve stem oil seal. Remove valve stem oil seals carefully with a screwdriver or a pair of pliers.
- Remove the valves one after the other out of the valve guides and pierce them in their fitted order through a piece of cardboard. Write the cylinder number against each valve if they are to be re-used.

11.3.3. CYLINDER HEAD – OVERHAUL

The instructions given for the engines covered earlier on also apply to these engines, using any necessary data as given in Section 11.3.0.

11.3.4. CYLINDER HEAD – ASSEMBLY

The assembly of the cylinder is a reversal of the dismantling procedure. Fit the valves as explained for the diesel engines 602/603 covered earlier on. The camshaft and the rocker shaft installation is covered under its own heading.

11.4. Pistons and Connecting Rods
11.4.0. Technical Data

All dimensions are given in metric units.

Pistons
Diameter – Std.:..85.98 mm
    Repair size 1:..86.48 mm
    Repair size 2:..86.98 mm

Piston Running Clearance:
- New:...0.025 – 0.035 mm
- Wear limit..0.08 mm

Max. weight difference within engine:
- New:..4 grams
- Wear limit :...10 grams

Piston Pins:
Pin diameter: ....22.995 – 23.000 mm
Piston pin running clearance:
- In small end bush:.....................................0.007 – 0.018 mm
- In piston:..0.002 – 0.012 mm

Piston Rings:
Piston Ring Gaps:
- Upper rings:...............................0.30 – 0.45 mm (wear limit 1.0 mm)
- Centre rings:..............................0.30 – 0.45 mm (wear limit 0.8 mm)

M110 Petrol Engine

- Lower rings:... 0.25 – 0.40 mm (wear limit 0.8 mm)

Side Clearance in Grooves:
- Upper rings:... 0.050 – 0.085 mm (wear limit 0.15 mm)
- Centre rings:.. 0.015 - 0.050 mm (wear limit 0.10 mm)
- Lower rings:... 0.010 - 0.042 mm (wear limit 0.10 mm)

Connecting Rods
Width of con rod at big end bore:..27.857 – 27.890 mm
Basic bore diameter of big end bore:..51.600 – 51.619 mm
Basic bore diameter of small end bore:.......................................26.000 – 26.021 mm

Small End Bush:
- Outer diameter: ....27.050 – 27.090 mm
- Inner diameter: ....23.007 – 23.013 mm
Max. twist of connecting rods:..0.10 mm per 100 mm
Max. bend of connecting rods:..0.040 mm per 100 mm
Max. weight difference in same engine:.. 5 gram (per set)
Connecting Rod Bolts:
- Thread:... M10 x 1
- Diameter of stretch neck :... 8.4 mm
- Min. diameter of stretch neck: .... 8.0 mm
Connecting rod bearing details:.. See under "Crankshaft"

11.4.1.   PISTONS, CYLINDER BLOCK, etc.

All information given for the four-cylinder petrol engines, i.e. removal, measuring the cylinder bores, checking of pistons and connecting rods and installation are carried out in the same manner. Fig. 10.11 shows where the piston size is marked into the cylinder block. All data given in section 11.4.0 must be used.

11.5.   Crankshaft

The removal and installation of the crankshaft is carried out in a similar manner as described for the diesel engines described in section 1 under the heading in question. The main bearing caps are tightened to 8.0 kgm (58 ft.lb.).

11.5.1.   Flywheel or Drive Plate (Automatic)

Figs. 1.43 shows the end of the crankshaft together with the flywheel and the driven plate respectively, as fitted to the 616/617 engines. The same applies to this engine. Always check the height of the old flywheel before fitting a new one.
Both flywheel and drive plate can be replaced with the engine fitted, without the need to re-balance the crankshaft. Proceed as described with the removal and installation for the diesel engines specified above.

11.5.2. Crankshaft Pulley, Vibration Damper

The engine is fitted with a crankshaft pulley and a vibration damper. The damper can be replaced without re-balancing the crankshaft. The crankshaft pulley can only be fitted in one position to the damper (secured with 6 bolts), as the threaded bores are offset.

- Remove the parts as described for the 616/617 diesel engines (page 37) until the crankshaft pulley has been removed and the centre bolt of the vibration damper has been slackened.

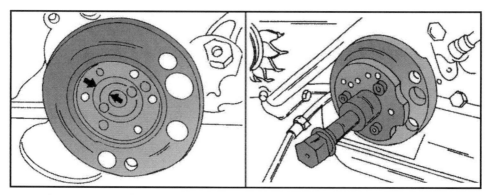

Fig. 11.8 – Marking the balancing disc and the crankshaft before removal of the disc in the L.H. view. The R.H. view shows the removal of the balancing disc.

- Mark the balancing disc and the crankshaft with a centre punch as shown in Fig. 11.8 and remove the disc with a suitable puller. The R.H. view of Fig. 11.8 shows the puller used in a workshop. Make a note of the fitting position of the three spring discs on the bolt, as they must face the same way during installation.

The crankshaft pulley has a certain diameter. If replaced, quote the engine type and number.

The installation of the crankshaft pulley and the hub or the vibration damper proceed as follows:

- Fit the balancing disc to the crankshaft end with the holes for the dowel pins in line.
- Fit the balancing disc with the M18 bolt, with the four spring discs fitted (curved side towards the bolt head). Drive in the two dowel pins.
- Tighten the centre bolt 40.0 kgm (288 ft.lb.). The crankshaft must still be locked against rotation.
- Fit the vibration damper and the crankshaft pulley.
- The remaining operations are carried out in reverse order.

11.5.3.   Rear Crankshaft Oil Seal

The engine must be removed to replace the oil seal, as the seal is located in a groove in the rear crankshaft main bearing cap. Remove the seal with a screwdriver out of the groove. The installation is carried out as described for the 616/617 engines. Details are described on page 35.

11.5.4.   Front Crankshaft Oil Seal

The front crankshaft oil seal is located in the timing cover and can be replaced with the engine fitted.

The vibration damper and the crankshaft pulley must be removed as already described before the oil seal can be replaced (see description earlier on). The oil seal can be carefully removed with a screwdriver. Screw a self-tapping screw into the outside of the seal and apply the screwdriver blade under the screw head. If the spacer ring on the crankshaft shows signs of wear, remove it with a suitable puller.

Thoroughly clean the surrounding parts. Burrs on the timing cover bore can be removed with a scraper. Fill the space between the sealing lip and the dust protection lip with grease and carefully drive a new oil seal into the timing cover and over the crankshaft until the outer face is flush. Refit the vibration damper or the hub as described earlier on.

11.6.   Timing Mechanism

The component parts covered in this section can be removed with the engines fitted. The arrangement of the timing chain and the other timing gear components are shown in Fig. 11.9.

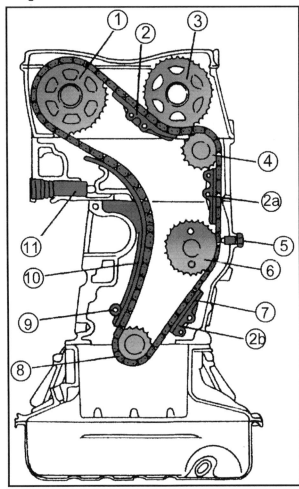

Fig. 11.9 – Timing chain and chain drive in fitted position.
1.   Exhaust camshaft sprocket
2.   Slide rail
3.   Inlet camshaft sprocket
4.   Guide sprocket
5.   Lock bolt
6.   Intermediate shaft sprocket
7.   Timing chain
8.   Crankshaft sprocket
9.   Bearing bolt for tensioning rail
10.   Tensioning rail
11.   Hydraulic chain tensioner

The endless timing chain is engaged with the camshaft sprockets, the intermediate shaft sprocket, a guide sprocket and the crankshaft sprocket. The chain is guided by two slide rails. The tension of the chain is ensured by means of a hydraulic chain tensioner, which is located in the crankcase and pushes onto a tensioning rail. The camshaft sprockets are fitted by means of a bolt and located by a Woodruff key. Technical data concerning the camshaft are given in Section 11.3.0.

11.6.0.   Chain Tensioner – Removal and Installation

- Drain the cooling system and disconnect the battery. The battery can also be removed to create more room.
- Unscrew the chain tensioner plug with a 17 mm socket head wrench (Fig. 11.9 shows the location of the tensioner) and remove the compression spring.
- The chain tensioner is withdrawn with a 10 mm socket head wrench. To do this, rotate the tensioner towards the right.

The chain tensioner must be dismantled before it can be refitted to set the pressure plunger into the installation position to prevent the timing chain from being excessively tensioned. A new chain tensioner is supplied together with the plunger.

The installation is a reversal of the removal procedure. Fit the tensioner plug with a new sealing ring and tighten it to 5.0 kgm (36 ft.lb.).

11.6.1.   Removal and Installation of Timing Chain

Fig. 11.9 shows the arrangement of the timing chain. The replacement of the timing chain is a complicated operation. The description for the removal and installation, is however, given for the 616/617 engines and can be carried out in a similar manner on these engines.

Two slide rails guide the chain on one side, a long tensioning rail, operating in conjunction with the hydraulic chain tensioner, is fitted to the other side.

11.6.2. Tensioning Rail - Replacement

The location of the tensioning rail can be taken from Fig. 11.9. The plastic coating of the tensioning rail can technically speaking be replaced, but must be heated to 65° C in water before it is fitted to the rail – workshop. Remove the rail as follows, noting that the radiator, the cooling fan, the crankshaft pulley and the cylinder head cover must be removed. The compressor must be removed if A/C is fitted and placed to one side without disconnecting the pipes or hoses. Also note that an impact hammer is required to remove the bearing pin for the rail.

- Remove the cylinder head cover as already described.
- Remove the rocker arms of the R.H. camshaft (exhaust camshaft).
- Rotate the crankshaft until the piston of No. 1 cylinder is at TDC and remove the crankshaft pulley and vibration damper and the chain tensioner as described earlier on.
- Using paint, mark the relationship between the timing chain and the camshaft sprockets, similar, as shown in Fig. 1.12 and mark the camshaft sprocket and chain as shown in this illustration.
- Counterhold the R.H. camshaft as shown in Fig. 11.2 and remove the camshaft sprocket bolt. Remove the sprocket without disengaging the timing chain.
- Remove the slide rail (see below).
- Withdraw the bearing pin with the impact hammer and a threaded insert, as shown in Fig. 1.55 and lift out the tensioning rail towards the top.
- Check the plastic coating for wear or damage and replace the rail if necessary.

The installation of the tensioning rail is a reversal of the removal procedure. Coat the bearing bolt on the flange with sealing compound. Fit the tensioning rail in position and insert the bearing bolt. Fit the 6 mm bolt and the slide hammer to the end of the bearing bolt and knock the bolt in position, this time hitting the weight of the slide hammer towards the front.

Engage the camshaft sprocket with the timing chain and fit and tighten the camshaft sprocket bolt to 8.0 kgm (58 ft.lb.). The camshaft must be held against rotation (Fig. 11.2). When fitting the timing chain to the camshaft sprocket make sure that the paint marks are in line.

11.6.3. Slide Rails - Removal and Installation

The position of the slide rails (2), (2a) and (2b) is shown in Fig. 11.9. An impact hammer, together with a M10 threaded bolt of 100 mm in length is required to remove the slide rail bearing bolts. The 10 mm bolt is screwed into the end of the bearing bolt and the impact hammer (slide hammer) attached to the end of the bolt. Provided that these tools can be obtained, the rail can be removed as described below. Proceed as follows to replace the slide rail (2) in the camshaft housing.

- Remove the cylinder head cover.
- Withdraw the two bearing pins with the impact hammer and a threaded insert, as shown in Fig. 1.55 and lift out the slide rail.

Install as follows:
- Coat the bearing bolt on the flange with sealing compound.

- Fit the slide rail in position and insert the bearing bolt. Fit the 10 mm bolt and the slide hammer to the end of the bearing bolt and knock the bolt in position, this time hitting the weight of the slide hammer towards the front. Counterhold the slide rail during the bearing bolt installation with a screwdriver to prevent distortion.
- Refit the cylinder head cover.

Remove and install the slide rail (2a) in Fig. 11.9 in the cylinder head as follows:

- Remove the radiator and the chain tensioner or the spring in the tensioner.
- Mark the position of the camshaft sprockets and the timing chain and remove the slide rail from the camshaft housing as described above.
- Use a piece of wire to secure the guide sprocket (4) to the timing chain and withdraw the bearing pin with a slide hammer as described above. A 10 mm bolt is used. Withdraw the guide sprocket.
- Withdraw the slide rail bearing pin with the impact hammer and a M10 threaded insert, as shown in Fig. 1.55 and pull out the slide rail with a piece of wire.

The installation is a reversal of the removal procedure. Coat the bearing bolt on the flange with sealing compound.

Remove and install the slide rail (2b) in Fig. 11.9 in the crankcase head as follows. The removal is more complicated as the radiator, the oil sump and the crankshaft pulley with the vibration damper must be removed as described. The slide rail in the camshaft housing and the guide sprocket must also be removed as described above.

11.6.4. Guide Sprocket - Removal and Installation

The guide sprocket can be removed after removal of the slide rail in the camshaft housing as described during the removal of the slide rail (2a). After installation check that the paint marks on camshaft sprocket and timing chain are in line.

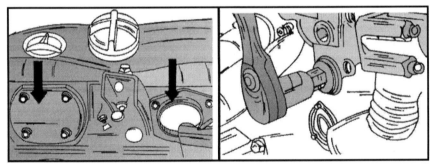

Fig. 11.10 – The arrows in the L.H. view show the location of the two camshaft housing covers. Only the R.H. cover must be removed. The R.H. view shows the removal of the chain tensioner.

11.6.5. Camshaft Housing - Removal and Installation

Bolts with multi-spline heads or socket heads can be used. Different tightening torques apply. A new gasket for the housing is required.

- If an A/C system is fitted remove the compressor and place it to one side, all hoses, pipes connected.
- Drain the cooling system and disconnect the upper coolant hose between engine and radiator.
- Referring to Fig. 11.10 (left) and remove the R.H. cover from the front of the camshaft housing.
- Remove the rocker shafts.
- Prevent the R.H camshaft from rotating as shown in Fig. 11.2 and undo the sprocket securing bolt.

- Rotate the engine until the piston of No. 1 cylinder is at top dead centre in the firing position, i.e. the mark "00" must be opposite the pointer. A 27 mm socket can be applied to the crankshaft pulley bolt to rotate the crankshaft. Never attempt to rotate the crankshaft by applying a socket to the camshaft timing wheel bolt.
- Remove the chain tensioner (Fig. 11.10, R.H.) and the spring and the slide rail located in the camshaft housing (2 in Fig. 11.9).
- Push the R.H. camshaft to the rear until the sprocket can be removed. Then push the shaft back to its original position.

Fig. 11.11 – Tightening sequence for the camshaft housing/cylinder head bolts. Slacken in reverse order.

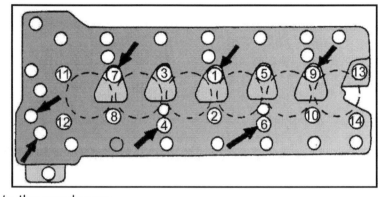

- Refer to Fig. 11.11 and slacken the M8 bolts in reverse order. Do not slacken the 5 cylinder head bolts and the two M8 bolts, marked with the arrows. These secure the cylinder head to the crankcase.
- Lift off the camshaft housing together with the camshafts.

The installation is carried out as follows. Clean the cylinder head and camshaft housing faces and place a new gasket in position. Place the camshaft housing over the cylinder head. Lubricate the threads and the underside of the bolt heads with oil and tighten the bolts as follows, depending on the type in question.

- *If bolts with multi-spline head are used.* Tighten all bolts in the order shown in Fig. 11.11 to 11.0 kgm (79 ft.lb.) and then the bolts 2, 3, 5, 8, 10, 11, 12, 13 and 14 twice by a quarter of a turn. Then tighten the lower bolts 1, 4, 6, 7 and 9 again to 11.0 kgm.
- *If bolts with socket head are used.* Tighten all bolts in the order shown in Fig. 11.11 to 7.0 kgm (50.5 ft.lb.). Again tighten all bolts in order to 11.0 kgm (79 ft.lb.), but the bolts 1, 4, 6, 7 and 9 must be slackened before they are re-tightened.
- Tighten the M8 bolts to 2.5 kgm (18 ft.lb.). One of the M8 bolts can only be reached when the camshaft sprocket is removed, i.e. the bolt near bolt (12) in the illustration.
- After tightening of the bolts check that the camshafts can be rotated easily.
- Fit the camshaft sprocket over the R.H. camshaft, making sure that the paint marks are in line. Also fit the slide rail to keep the timing chain in position.
- Lubricate the spacer sleeves with engine oil and slide it into the camshaft housing. Fit and tighten the sprocket securing bolt (8.0 kgm). Prevent the shaft from rotating as shown.
- The remaining operations are carried out in reverse order.

11.6.6. Adjusting the Valve Clearances

The valve clearance is checked between the rocker arm face and the cam for the respective valve, shown by the arrow in Fig. 11.12, using a feeler gauge. The feeler gauge must have a tight fit. To obtain the correct valve position for the check, rotate the camshaft until the point of the cam is facing downwards, i.e. the round section of the cam must face towards the rocker arm. The following text describes the checking and adjusting with the engine fitted. Mercedes workshops use a special spanner (110 589 00 01 00) to adjust the valve clearance. The clearance is adjusted on a cold engine (0.10 mm inlet valves, 0.25 mm exhaust valve). Different values apply if the

Diesel Injection System

clearance check is carried out on a warm engine (0.15 mm inlet valves, 0.30 mm exhaust valves).

Fig. 11.12 – Sectional view of the valve/cam arrangement of the six-cylinder engine.
1 Tensioning spring
2 Valve adjusting screw
3 Threaded bush
4 Thrust ring

The valves should be checked, and if necessary adjusted, at intervals of 12,000 miles. Proceed as follows:

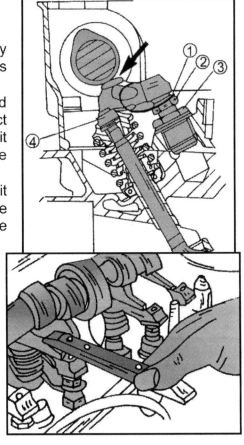

- Remove the air cleaner and the cylinder head cover. Switch off the ignition and disconnect the green cable from the ignition control unit (withdraw the plug) and withdraw the centre cable from the ignition distributor.

- Use a 27 mm socket and a ratchet, place it over the crankshaft pulley bolt and rotate the engine until both valves of No. 1 cylinder are closed.

Fig. 11.13 – Checking the valve clearances with a feeler gauge. Note the position of the cam.

- Apply the special wrench and rotate the valve adjusting until the correct valve clearance has been obtained. As already mentioned, the clearance is checked by inserting a feeler gauge into the gap shown in Fig. 11.13. A good indication for a correct clearance is if the feeler gauge will enter without binding, then bends slightly and "jumps" into the gap.

- Rotate the engine until the next set of valves are fully closed and check and/or adjust as described above. Proceed in the same manner until all valves are adjusted.

- Carry out all other operations in reverse order to the removal procedure.

11.7.   Tightening Torque Values

All tightening torque values are given whenever applicable.

12   DIESEL INJECTION SYSTEMS

Absolute cleanliness is essential during any repairs or work on the diesel fuel injection system, irrespective of the nature of the work in question. Thoroughly clean union nuts before unscrewing any of the injection pipes.

Injection pump and injectors are the main components of the fuel injection system. The injection system is basically the same for all engines, but is based on the OM602 and OM603 engines. The system is fitted with a pneumatically controlled idle speed increase (PLA) and have an electronically controlled idle speed regulation system (ELR). Again we will refer to these systems later on.

A fuel lift pump sucks the fuel out of the tank and delivers it via a fuel filter to the suction chamber in the injection pump. The injection pump delivers the fuel through high-pressure pipes to the injectors and injector nozzles. Diesel injection systems operate on the principle of direct injection or indirect injection. The Mercedes diesel works with indirect injection, i.e. pre-combustion chambers are used in the cylinder head. The fuel is injected into these pre-combustion chambers which are connected to the main combustion chambers. The combustion of the fuel commences in the pre-combustion chamber. Through the resulting pressure increase, the burning fuel particles are pushed into the main combustion chamber and complete the combustion.

The fuel injection pump is a piston pump and is fitted to the L.H. side of the cylinder block and is driven from the timing chain. A pump element, consisting of cylinder and piston, serves each of the engine cylinders.

A governor is fitted to the rear of the injection pump. The governor consists of a system of levers and springs and a centrifugal mechanism, fitted to the rear of the injection pump camshaft. A vacuum unit for the switching off of the engine, a vacuum unit for the idle speed increase (if applicable) and a stop lever on the side of the governor all act on the governor. The injection pump cannot be repaired or overhauled and an exchange pump or a new pump must be fitted in case of malfunction or damage.

The adjustment of the injection timing and also the removal and installation of the injection pump requires certain special tools and these operations cannot not be undertaken if these are not available. The removal and installation should therefore be left to a workshop. However, the operations are described in Section 12.2.

12.0.   Precautions when working on diesel injection systems

Whenever repairs are carried out on a diesel fuel injection system, whatever the extent, observe the greatest cleanliness, apart from the following points:

- Only carry out work on diesel injection systems under the cleanest of conditions. Work in the open air should only be carried out when there is no wind, to prevent dust entering open connections.
- Before removal of any union nut clean all around it with a clean cloth.
- Removed parts must only be deposited on a clean bench or table and must be covered with a sheet of plastic or paper. Never use fluffy shop rags to clean parts.
- All open or partially dismantled parts of the injection system must be fully covered or kept in a cardboard box, if the repair is not carried out immediately.
- Check the parts for cleanliness before Installation.
- Never use an air line to clean the exterior of the engine when connections of the injection system are open. With the availability of air compressors which can be plugged into a cigar lighter socket, you may be tempted to use air for cleaning.
- Take care not to allow diesel fuel in contact with rubber hoses or other rubber parts. Immediately clean such a hose if it should happen accidentally.

12.1.   Fuel Filter

The fuel filter element should be replaced approx. every 40,000 miles. A further filter is fitted upstream of the fuel lift pump and should also be replaced at the same time.

The fuel filter can be removed towards the bottom after unscrewing the bolt in the centre. The vacuum line for the brake servo unit must be removed from the filter base.

Diesel Injection System

Thoroughly clean the bottom bowl, if the filter housing remains on the engine, and fit a new filter insert. Always replace the sealing ring. Make sure that the seal is correctly located underneath the head of the centre bolt.

12.2.   Injection Pump – Removal and Installation

602/603 Engines

A special tool is required to fit the injection pump. This tool (refer to the description) must be obtained before the pump is removed. Also available must be a 27 mm socket (to rotate the crankshaft), a 14 mm ring spanner, with a slot cut into the ring to undo the injection pipe union nuts and a serrated wrench to rotate the injection pump shaft. Provided these tools can be obtained, proceed as follows:

*   Disconnect the battery earth cable, remove the radiator and the fluid coupling for the cooling fan, as already described.

Fig. 12.1 – Disconnect the vacuum hoses from connections (1) and (2).

*   Disconnect the injection pipes and the fuel pipes from the injection pump and carefully bend them to one side. Seal the open connections and fuel hoses at the injection pump in suitable manner, by pushing push-on caps over the connections. Make absolutely sure that no dirt can enter the open connections.
*   Rotate the engine (apply the socket mentioned above to the crankshaft pulley) until the piston of No. 1 cylinder is at top dead centre and then slightly further until the 15° mark in the crankshaft pulley/vibration damper is in line with the pointer.
*   Remove the single drive belt and the tensioning device as described in Section "Cooling System".

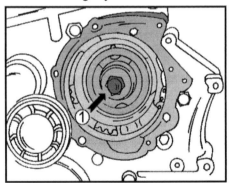

Fig. 12.2 – The bolt (1) with left-hand thread secures the injection timing advancer to the front of the injection pump.

*   Remove the timing chain tensioner as described for these engines.
*   Disconnect the vacuum connections from the vacuum unit for the idle speed increase and from the unit for the stop control. The two hoses are shown in Fig. 12.1, but must, of course, be located.
*   Disconnect the regulating rod for the accelerator control from the injection pump.
*   Remove the exhauster pump from the front of the engine (this pump is your vacuum supply for the various vacuum-operated units).
*   Remove the bolt (1) in the centre of the injection timing advancer (Fig. 12.2). The crankshaft must be locked against rotation. **Note that the bolt has left-hand thread,** i.e. the bolt must be slackened in the direction you would normally tighten a bolt.
*   Remove the pump securing bolts and the bolt securing the support bracket and withdraw the pump towards the rear.

Refit the injection pump in the following order. If the special tool mentioned cannot be obtained, you will be able to have the commencement of injection adjustment carried out in a workshop.

- Check that the engine is still in the position described above. Otherwise make the necessary corrections, by carefully turning the crankshaft with the 27 mm socket. Remember that the timing chain is engaged with the wheel.

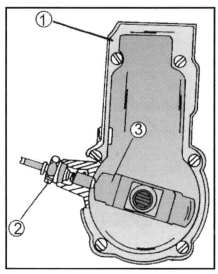

Fig. 12.3 – Locking the governor inside the injection pump, using the special locking pin.
1   Injection pump
2   Locking bolt
3   Governor

- Remove the plug from the side of the injection pump at the position shown in Fig. 12.3. The serrated wrench 601 589 00 08 00 must now be used to rotate the pump until the lug (3) of the governor rotor is visible. In this position insert the locking tool 601 589 05 21 00, as shown in the illustration. Hand-tighten the nut of the locking bolt. If the tools can be obtained, carry out the operation by studying Fig. 12.3. **Read the note below.**

- The injection pump can now be refitted. Tighten the pump flange bolts to 2.0 - 2.5 kgm (14.5 - 18 ft.lb.). Immediately remove the locking pin from the injection pump and refit the plug. Tighten the plug to 3.0 - 3.5 kgm (22 - 25 ft.lb.).

NOTE: Immediately after fitting the pump in position remove the locking pin from the side of the pump. The pump can be seriously damaged if this is forgotten.

- Re-connect the injection pipes one after the other. Make sure to engage the threads properly before the union nuts to 1.0 – 2.0 kgm (7.2 – 14.5 ft.lb.).
- All other operations are carried out in reverse order.

Checking the Start of Injection Delivery
The start of the injection delivery can be checked in various ways, but every method requires the use of special tools. For this reason we recommend to have the work carried out in a workshop.

NOTE: Whenever possible have the idle speed adjusted at a Dealer who has the necessary equipment to do it. Remember that a correct idle speed can save you fuel.

616/617 Engines
The adjustment of the injection pump is only possible on a test stand. It is therefore not recommended to remove the pump of the two engines in question.

12.3.   Injectors
12.3.0.   REMOVAL AND INSTALLATION

- Disconnect the battery earth cable.
- Remove the plastic clips securing the injection pipes and disconnect the fuel pipes. Also disconnect the leak-off hoses from the injectors (slacken hose clamps).

Diesel Injection System

- Unscrew the injector pipes. A suitable ring spanner can be cut for this purpose. Slide the open gap over the injection pipe and slacken the union nuts. If an ordinary open-ended spanner is used, take care not to damage the union nuts.
- Unscrew the injectors with the special tool available for this purpose or use a long 27 mm socket. Take out the injector sealing gaskets and the nozzle plates. Injector nozzle plates must be replaced once an injector has been removed.

The installation of an injector is a reversal of the removal procedure. Tighten them to 7 - 8 kgm (50 - 60 ft.lb.). Attach the injector pipes and tighten the union nuts to 1.0 - 2.0 kgm (7.2 – 14.5 ft.lb.). Make sure that none of the injector pipes is tightened under tension or strain.

12.3.1. INJECTOR REPAIRS

A special test pump is required to check the injectors. If a faulty injector is suspected, take the set to a specialist and have them checked and their injection pressure adjusted. Different injectors are fitted to the various engines. Check with your parts supplier against the engine number to make sure that the correct injectors are fitted.

12.4. Glow Plugs

The glow plug system consists of the glow plugs, the glow time relay and the warning lamp in the instrument panel.

When the ignition is switched on, the glow plug relay will receive current via terminal "15". A relay directs the current from the plus terminal "30" via a fuse (80 amps) to the glow plugs. The glow plugs receive a voltage of at least 11.5 volts and a current of 30 amps, which is however, reduced to 8 to 15 amps by means of a regulator, thereby preventing burning out of the plugs. The glow plugs heat up to 90° C within 10 seconds and can reach a temperature of 1180° C after 30 seconds.

The glow plug time relay determines the operating time of the glow plugs. This relay senses the outside temperature, i.e. at very low temperatures, for example – 30° C, the plugs can glow as long as 25 seconds. During the summer months, however, glowing time may be as little as 2 seconds. If the engine is not started immediately after the warning light has gone "off", the current feed will be interrupted through a safety circuit. Subsequent starting of the engine will switch in the glow plug circuit via starter motor terminal "50".

The glow time relay is located in the engine compartment and is protected with a cover. The connectors and the 80 amp fuse are accessible after removal of the cover. The warning lamp circuit, the relay and the safety circuit are controlled by the relay. If the vehicle has been built as model year 1989 or later, the 80 amp fuse is replaced by an electronic short-circuit fuse. The current supply will be interrupted in case of a short circuit. Again this arrangement is not fitted to all vehicles.

Glow plugs of most engines have the Part No. 0 250 201 001, but as there are also other glow plugs used in the engines covered in this manual, we advise you to check with your parts supplier.

The glow plugs are fairly hidden below the tubes of the inlet manifold and a socket and extension are required to reach them. A ratchet is of advantage.

Unscrew all nuts from the glow plugs and take off the connecting line. The nuts cannot be fully removed. Unscrew the glow plug with the special wrench, available for this purpose, or use an ordinary long socket of the correct size.

Before installation of a glow plug, clean out the plug channels and the holes in the pre-combustion chambers with a reamer. Again a special reamer is used by Mercedes workshops. Pack the flutes of the reamer with grease when reaming out the plug channels. The installation of the glow plugs is a reversal of the removal procedure. Plugs are tightened to 2.0 kgm (14.5 ft.lb.). Do not over-tighten the cable securing nuts.

12.4.1. FAULTS IN THE GLOW PLUG SYSTEM

Difficult starting of the engine can in many cases be traced back to the glow plug system. Failure for the warning light to light up will obviously indicate a fault in the system which may be traced with a few simple operations. If a 12 volt test lamp can be made available and you have some experience with electrical systems. First remove the cover from the glow plug relay. Glow plug problems are always difficult to diagnose and we recommend to have the work done in a workshop dealing with Bosch injection pumps.

12.5.   Idle Speed Adjustment

A professional adjustment of the idle speed can only be carried out with the Bosch Digital Tester and the impulse transmitter 601 589 04 21 00. The tester is plug into the diagnostic plug and the impulse transmitter receives the information from the T.D.C. sender unit above the flywheel.

12.6.   Adjusting the Throttle Control

Before carrying out any adjustments check the throttle operating linkage for freedom of movement and the operating cable for freedom of movement or damage. All swivel points must be lubricated with graphited grease. Check and if necessary the throttle control as follows:

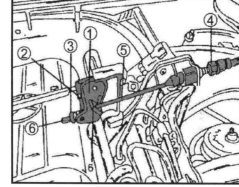

Fig. 12.4 – The throttle valve operation.
1   Angled lever
2   Connector
3   Spring
4   Adjusting nut
5   Operating cable
6   Guide piece

• Refer to Fig. 12.4 and disconnect the operating cable. To do this, remove the slotted guide piece (6) from the angle lever (1) and withdraw the cable.

Fig. 12.5 – Details for the throttle control adjustment when an automatic transmission is fitted.
1   Connecting link
2   Slotted lever
3   Guide lever
4   Roller

• On a vehicle with automatic transmission disconnect the adjustable connecting link (1) in Fig. 12.5 from the relay lever (3). Check if the adjuster lever on the injection pump is resting against the speed stop. Re-connect the connecting link to the lever, adjusting it if necessary to eliminate any tension. Check that the roller (4) is resting without tension against the end stop, again without tension (arrow in Fig. 12.5).

• Move the angled lever (1) in Fig. 12.4 in direction "full load", at the same time ensuring that the adjusting lever on the pump is also against the full load stop. If necessary move the adjustable ball joint pin (2) in the slot of the relay lever (3) and retighten the nut (Fig. 12.6).

- If a manual transmission is fitted, check if the adjusting lever on the fuel injection pump is resting against the speed full load stop and re-connect the operating cable.
- Ask a helper to depress the accelerator pedal to its floor stop if a manual transmission is fitted or to the stop of the kick-down switch if an automatic transmission is fitted and check that the lever on the injection pump is resting against its stop. If necessary adjust the adjusting nut (4) in Fig. 12.4 to move the operating cable.

Fig. 12.6 – Adjusting the throttle operating linkage on a vehicle with manual transmission.
1   Connecting link
2   Ball joint head
3   Guide lever
4   Lever

- Slowly have the accelerator pedal released to bring the throttle control to the idle position and check that the trunnion (2) in Fig. 12.4 contacts the spring (3), but without tension. If tension is felt, the cable must be adjusted from the inside of the vehicle.

12.7.   Pneumatic Idle Increase

Both engines operate with this system. The idle speed increase acts via vacuum onto the idle speed stop in the governor. If the engine temperature is less than 30° C (manual transmission) or 17° C (automatic transmission), the idle speed will increase by approx. 100 rpm.

Faults in the idle speed increase is mainly due to a defective vacuum unit. As the injection pump must be partially dismantled to replace the unit, you will need the assistance of a Mercedes dealer or Bosch service station to rectify the fault.

12.8.   Air Cleaner

The air cleaner is made of plastic and consists of three parts, the air cleaner case, the air cleaner cover, connected to which is the large air intake hose and the air cleaner element, inserted between the two mentioned parts. The air filter housing is connected by means of rubber sleeves to the inlet manifold tubes.

The removal and installation of the air cleaner presents no major problems, but the following points should be noted:

- Remove the air intake hose between the intake and the air cleaner cover.
- Free the fuel pipe from the air cleaner cover and spring back the air cleaner cover clips to remove the cover.
- Remove the air cleaner element to clean it or to replace it. Filter elements must not be cleaned with any fluids. Only compressed air should be used to blow out a dirty element. Always clean the case before fitting a new element. Filter elements are not the same for all engines. Always quote the engine number and the model year. Elements are supplied by Bosch, Knecht, Mann and Purolator. There is no special recommendation which one should be fitted, but insist on an element as used by Mercedes.

12.9. Electronic Idle Speed Regulation (602/603 Engines)

There is more or less nothing you can do on this type of system, fitted on engines with automatic transmission and air conditioning system.

Again a brief description of the operation for the technically minded.

The system consists basically of an engine speed sensor on the flywheel starter ring gear and an electronic control unit. A setting magnet is fitted to the rear of the injection pump, taking the place of the vacuum unit, fitted to other pumps. The speed sensor detects the engine speed and feeds this information to the control unit. The control unit evaluates the information received and compares between the nominal idle speed and the actual speed received. The idle speed is kept at a constant level by the setting magnet, irrespective of the engine load at the time. A coolant temperature sensor, fitted into the cylinder head (near the injection pipes), detects temperatures of less than 60° C and increases the idle speed to a pre-determined value, If necessary.

Due to the electronic regulation of the idle speed you will find that there is no speed variation. The idle speed can be adjusted, if necessary, but we feel that this operation should be left to a Mercedes workshop.

12.10. Fuel Feed Pump

The fuel feed pump is fitted to the side of the injection pump and sealed-off with a gasket. The opening for the fuel pump will allow the oil to drip out of the injection pump, when the pump is removed. Avoid contamination.

The pressure pipe to the injection pump (at the top) is secured with a union nut, the feed hose at the side is secured with a hose clamp. To remove the pump, disconnect the fuel lines and unscrew the pump. Fit the pump with a new gasket and correct the oil level in the pump.

12.11. Fuel Pre-heater

A heat exchanger is fitted into the feed line to the heating system to pre-heat the diesel fuel for easier combustion in cold condition. A thermostatic control unit is inserted into the fuel lines which directs the fuel to the fuel pump in dependence of the fuel temperatures. Up to a fuel temperature of +8° C, the fuel will flow through the heat exchanger and is warmed-up. Between temperature of +8° C and +25° C a variable operation takes place, i.e. the fuel passes partially through the heat exchanger. As soon as the fuel temperature increases above 25° C, the fuel by-passes the heat exchanger and is no longer pre-heated.

We recommend that faults in the fuel pre-heating system should be investigated in a workshop.

13 PETROL INJECTION SYSTEMS

Two different fuel injection systems are fitted to the petrol engines covered in the manual. A KA fuel injection system is fitted to the M115 and the M110 engines. Although different in constructions, the basic principle of operation is the same. The system fitted to the M102 engine is of the type CIS-E. The following description gives in brief an inside view of the injection systems. The idle speed and the CO content can only be adjusted on engines with the KA fuel injection system.

Petrol Injection System

M115 and M110 Engines

The KA injection system is a mechanically controlled system which is not driven by the engine (A = Antriebslos – without drive). Contrary to the intermittent injection of similar Mercedes-Benz systems, the fuel is injected continuously (K = Kontinuierlich – Continuously), i.e. the fuel is injected to the injection valves irrespective of the firing order of the engine. The injected amount of fuel depends on the amount of air sucked in by the engine, which is metered by an air mass meter. Fig. 13.1 shows the major component parts of the system, irrespective of the number of cylinders.

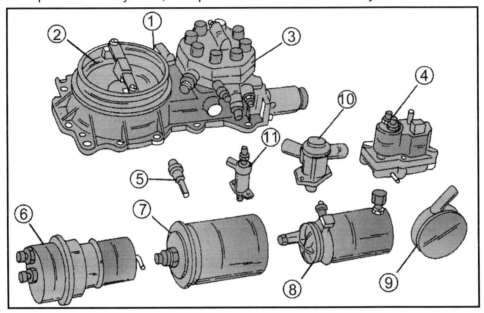

Fig. 13.1 – Component parts of the fuel injection system (KA).

1 Mixture regulator	5 Injection valves	9 Intake air damper
2 Air flow meter	6 Fuel accumulator	10 Auxiliary air valve
3 Fuel distributor	7 Fuel filter	11 Cold start valve
4 Warm-up regulator	8 Fuel pump	

The fuel is supplied from the electric fuel pump via a suction damper from the fuel tank and is directed through the fuel filter to the fuel distributor in the mixing chamber. A pressure regulator in the distributor keeps the pressure continuously at 5.4 bar. Excess fuel is re-directed to the fuel tank. The fuel pump receives current supply when the starter motor is operated and as long as the engine is running.

The mixture regulator consists of the air flow meter with a sensor plate and the fuel distributor. A pressure compensating valve is fitted in the centre of the fuel distributor. The valve remains closed as long as the pressure in the fuel system is maintained.

The air flow meter measures the air drawn in by the engine via an air flow sensor plate, which is raised and lowered by the intake air. The movement of this plate is transmitted via a lever to the control plunger of the control plunger in the fuel distributor. The control pressure, acting on the control plunger, counteracts this movement The combined movement controls the fuel amount directed to the injector valves.

The fuel is directed through the injection pipes to the injection valves, which are designed to open at a pressure of 3.6 bar and inject the fuel continuously before the inlet valves of the cylinders. When the inlet valves open, the fuel/air mixture is injected into the cylinder.

A fuel accumulator is fitted into the pipe system next to the fuel pump into the pipe system. The accumulator contains a fuel supply of 20 c.c. of fuel and enables an immediate operation and delivery of the fuel pump.

The fuel filter is also located next to the fuel pump and contains a fine-mesh filter element. Both ends are fitted with a connection. If the filter or the fuel pump is replaced, make absolutely sure the plastic sleeve is fitted between these units and the bracket, to prevent corrosion. The filter can be removed after taking out the screws. When fitting the filter observe the direction of flow, indicated on the filter by an arrow.

The electro-magnetically operated injector valves meter and atomise the fuel. The valves consist of a valve body with a spring-loaded nozzle and a magnetic armature. If the magnet is energised, the nozzle will lift between 0.1 to 6.0 mm from its seat and fuel can enter through a calibrated ring groove. If current supply to the magnet is cut off, the spring will return the nozzle back into its seat.

Temperature switches are fitted to measure the temperature of the coolant and the intake air temperature in order to adapt the amount of fuel injected into the engine in accordance with the prevailing temperatures.

The electro-magnetic cold start valve is fitted to the intake tube and is connected to the fuel line. The valve is controlled from the ignition/starter switch and a thermo time switch. The switch is inserted into the engine cooling system.

The auxiliary air valve is heated electrically and is in operation during the warm-up period of the engine. The engine needs during this period, increased fuel supply and the additional air is taken through a small filter from the engine compartment and directed via a control slide to the engine without passing the throttle valve. The valve is temperature-sensitive and meters the air supply in accordance with the requirements. The valve is connected electrically with the fuel pump and the warm-up regulator.

The warm-up regulator controls, as the name says, the warming-up of the engine as long as the engine is cold. The warm-up regulator is also connected to the fuel pump.

Adjusting Idle Speed and CO-Content – M115 and M110 Engines

Idle speed and CO content should only be adjusted by your dealer. A special tool to remove the tamper-proof plug for the CO adjustment screw is required. The idle speed can be adjusted, provided that the following conditions are provided:

Fig. 13.2 – The location of the idle speed adjusting screw.

*   The ignition timing must be properly adjusted, the air intake system must be free of leaks, the engine must have operating temperature, but never adjust the idle speed if the engine is hot, switch off all electrical consumers and check how the engine runs at idle speed.

If these pre-conditions are met, adjust the idle speed as follows:

*   Switch off the air conditioning system. If an automatic transmission is fitted, place the selector lever into the "P" position.
*   Connect a revolution counter suitable for the ignition system fitted in accordance with the instructions of the manufacturer.
*   Check that the throttle valve lever is against its stop and start the engine. Check that the engine runs with 700 to 800 rpm. If this is not the case, refer to Fig. 13.2 and adjust the idle speed accordingly.

Fuel Injection System – M102 Engine

Fig. 13.4 shows a functional diagram of the fuel injection system, showing the relationship between the various component parts. The physical appearance can be taken from Fig. 13.3. The following description refers to Fig. 13.3.

The fuel pump (13) is fitted on the L.H. side, seen in the direction of drive, in front of the rear axle. The pump is an electrically operated roller pump with a damper. The pump has a delivery capacity of 80 litres/hour at a voltage of 12 volts. Fig. 13.5 shows the location of the pump/filter/suction assembly on the vehicle.

Petrol Injection System

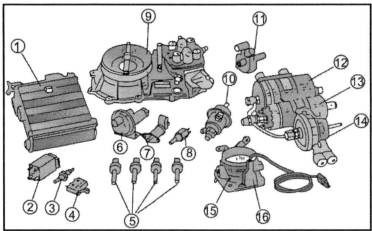

Fig, 13.3 – The component parts of the fuel injection system.

1 Electronic control unit
2 Overvoltage protection
3 Temperature sensor, coolant
4 Micro switch
5 Injection valves
6 Auxiliary air valve
7 Cold start valve
8 Thermo time switch
9 Mixture control unit
10 Pressure regulator
11 Idle air distributor

12 Fuel filter 13 Fuel pump 14 Fuel accumulator 15 Throttle housing 16 Throttle valve switch

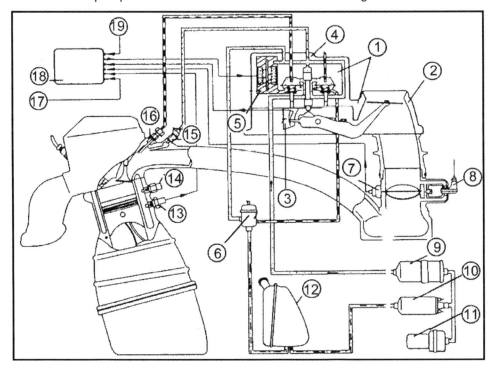

Fig. 13.4 – Functional diagram of the fuel injection system.

1 Mixture control unit
2 Air flow sensor
3 Transmitter, air flow sensor
4 Fuel distributor
5 Electro-hydraulic control unit
6 Diaphragm pressure regulator
7 Auxiliary air valve
8 Auxiliary air valve
9 Fuel filter
10 Fuel pump
11 Fuel accumulator
12 Fuel tank
13 Temperature, coolant
14 Thermo time switch
15 Cold start valve
16 Injection valve
17 Micro switch
18 Control unit
19 From ignition unit

The fuel pump relay (not shown in the illustration) is fitted to the L.H. side of the vehicle in front of the central electrical system. The relay has the following functions: it energises the pump and drives the pump for starting and engine operation, it cuts off the fuel supply as soon as pulses stop arriving via the switch unit terminal TD and it supplies voltage to the auxiliary air valve and regulates the warm-up of the engine.

The fuel accumulator (14) is fitted into the pipe system and is located next to the fuel pump, as shown in Fig. 13.5. The accumulator contains a supply of 20 c.c. and enables immediate operation of the pump.

The fuel filter (12) is also located next to the fuel pump (see Fig. 13.5). It contains a fine filter element. Both filter ends are fitted with a connection. When fitting the filter observe the direction of flow, indicated an arrow on the filter (Fig. 13.5).

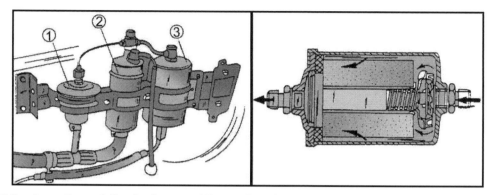

Fig. 13.5 – Location of the fuel pump (1), the fuel filter (2) and fuel accumulator (3). The R.H. view shows the flow direction of the fuel filter (by the arrows).

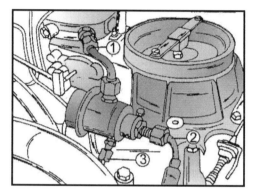

Fig. 13.6 – Connections of the different pipes on the mixture control unit.
1   Supply system pressure
2   Fuel return line
3   Return flow fuel distributor

The diaphragm pressure regulator (10) is fitted at the location shown in Fig. 13.6 and cannot be adjusted. The regulator has the function to pressurise certain section of the fuel system or to release the pressure, when the engine is running or to produce a holding pressure in the system (to re-start the engine) and to hold the pipe connection between the fuel pump and pressure regulator free of pressure, when the engine is switched off.

Fig. 13.7 – Top view of the mixture regulator.
1   Air flow sensor
2   Transmitter for air flow sensor
3   Fuel distributor
4   Electro-hydraulic controlling element

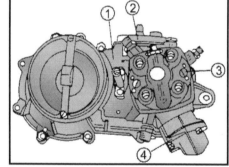

The mixture regulator (9) meters the amount of fuel allowed into the engine in accordance with the incoming air and depending on the operating condition. The mixture regulator, or mixture control unit, consists of an air flow meter with sensor and a fuel distributor with electro-hydraulic control unit. Fig. 13.6 shows a top view of the mixture regulator with the location of the mentioned parts.

The air flow meter measures the air drawn in by the engine via an air flow sensor plate, which is raised and lowered by the intake air. The movement of this plate is transmitted via a lever to the control plunger in the fuel distributor. Fig. 13.7 shows a top view to show the location of the various parts. See also Fig. 13.8.

The fuel distributor is fitted with an electro-hydraulic controlling unit to regulate the mixture. When the engine is running, a constant system pressure of 5.4 kg/sq.cm is present at the fuel inlet. An electrically controlled valve plate is actuated in dependency of the currency intensity and thereby determines the flow rate. The pressure in the lower chambers will change in combination with a fixed orifice (0.3 mm diameter) on the fuel distributor. This change will influence the location of the diaphragm in the fuel distributor, and thereby the fuel quantity flowing towards the injection valve.

The electro-magnetically operated injector valves (5) meter and atomise the fuel. The valves consist of a valve body with a spring-loaded nozzle and a magnetic armature. If the magnet is energised, the nozzle will lift between 0.1 to 6.0 mm from its seat and fuel can enter through a calibrated ring groove. If current supply to the magnet is cut off, the spring will return the nozzle back into its seat.

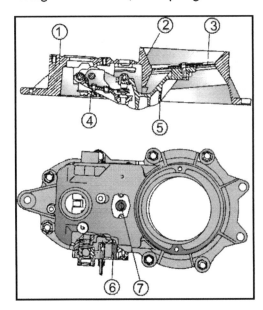

Fig. 13.8 – View of the mixture control unit.
1 Air flow sensor
2 Air funnel (cone)
3 Air flow sensor plate
4 Return spring
5 Adjusting arm
6 Transmitter, air flow sensor
7 Mixture adjusting screw

The temperature switches (2) and (13) consist of temperature sensitive resistors. Temperature switches are fitted to measure the temperature of the coolant and the air intake temperatures in order to adapt the amount of fuel injected into the engine in accordance with the prevailing temperatures. Fig. 13.9 shows the shape of the two switches.

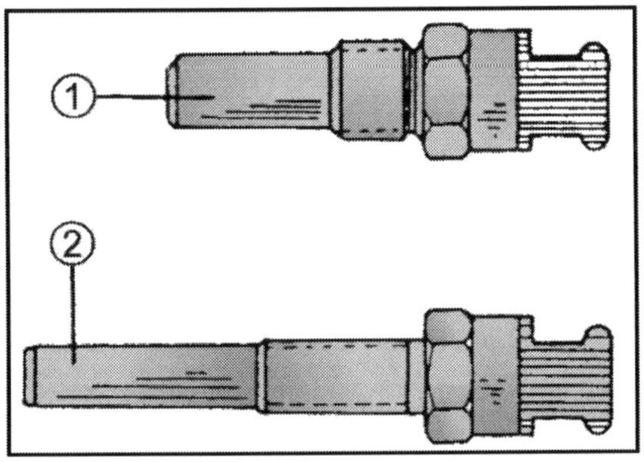

Fig. 13.9 – View of the temperature sensors (1) for the coolant and (2) for the intake air temperature.

The electro-magnetic cold start valve (15) is fitted to the intake tube and is connected to the fuel line. The valve is controlled from the ignition/starter switch and a thermo time switch (14). The switch is inserted into the engine cooling system.

The auxiliary air valve (8) is heated electrically and is in operation during the warm-up period of the engine. The engine needs during this period, increased fuel supply and the additional air is taken through a small filter from the engine compartment and directed via a control slide to the engine without passing the throttle valve. The valve is temperature-sensitive and meters the air supply in accordance with the requirements. The valve is connected electrically with the fuel pump and the warm-up regulator.

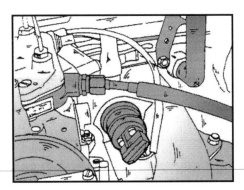

Fig. 13.10 – The location of the idle speed valve.

The electronic control unit (18) controls the warming-up of the engine, the acceleration enrichment, full load enrichment and all other aspects of the day to day running of the fuel injection system.

Adjusting Idle Speed and CO Content

The idle speed is electronically controlled, ensuring consistant speeds under all conditions. Idle speed fluctuations due to additional loads, created by the power-assisted steering or cutting-in of the compressor if an air conditioning system is fitted, will be eliminated. An idle speed air valve, the shape of which is shown in Fig. 13.10, is fitted into the system to control the idle speed.

If consistent faults with the idle speed are experienced, seek the assistance of a Mercedes-Benz dealer, to have the idle speed control system checked over.

14   Electrical System

14.0   Battery

Voltage   12 volts
Polarity   Negative earth
Capacity   72 Ah

Condition of Charge:
- Fully charged   1.280
- Half charged   1.200
- Discharged   1.120

To check the voltage of the battery, use an ordinary voltmeter and apply between the two battery terminals. A voltage of 12.5 volts or more should be obtained.

If a hydrometer is available, the specific gravity of the electrolyte can be checked. The readings of all cells must be approximately the same. A cell with a low reading indicates a short circuit in that particular cell. Two adjacent cells with a low reading indicates a leak between these two cells.

A battery can be re-charged, but the charging rate must not exceed 10% of the battery capacity. The battery must be disconnected from the electrical system. Charge the battery until the specific gravity and the charging voltage are no longer increasing within 2 hours. Add distilled water only. Never add acid to the battery.

The level of the battery electrolyte should always be kept above the top of the plates.

14.1.   Alternator

14.1.0.   ROUTINE PRECAUTIONS

The vehicles covered in this manual employ an alternator and control unit. This equipment contains polarity-sensitive components and the precautions below **must** be observed to avoid damage:

- Check the battery polarity **before** connecting the terminals. Immediate damage will result to the silicon diodes from a wrong connection - even if only momentarily.

- Never disconnect the battery or alternator terminals **whilst the engine is running.**

- Never allow the alternator to be rotated by the engine unless **ALL** connections are made.

- Disconnect the alternator multi-pin connector **before** using electric welding equipment anywhere on the vehicle.

- Disconnect the battery leads if a rapid battery charger is to be used.

- If an auxiliary battery is used to start the engine, take care that the polarity is correct. **Do not** disconnect the cables from the vehicle battery.

14.1.1.   REMOVAL AND INSTALLATION

The alternator is rigidly attached to the engine. Remove as follows:
- Disconnect the battery.

- Disconnect the cable harness by withdrawing the plug at the rear end of the alternator. Also disconnect the single cable.

- Slacken the alternator drive belt as described in the section dealing with the cooling system and lift off the belt.

- Remove the two alternator mounting bolts from the locations shown in Fig. 14.1 and lift out the alternator. It may be necessary to carry out the operations from below the vehicle, if it is difficult to lift the alternator out of the engine compartment from above.

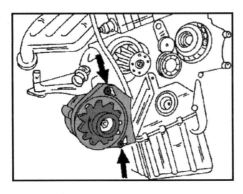

Fig. 14.1 – The alternator mounting bolts. The drive belt has already been removed.

Note: If a 2.5 litre engine is fitted, you may find that the upper mounting screw will interfere with the plastic cooling fan blades when the alternator is removed. If this is the case, first remove the lower bolt and then lift the alternator as shown in Fig. 14.2. Then remove the complete alternator mounting bracket, before the complete unit is removed.

Fig. 14.2 – Removal of the alternator when a 2.5 litre engine is fitted. The alternator is held as shown to remove the mounting bracket (R.H. side).

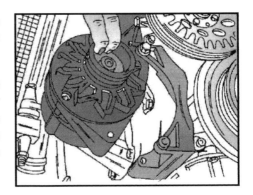

The installation of the alternator is a reversal of the removal procedure. Tighten the alternator mounting bolts to 4.5 kgm (32.5 ft.lb.). If the mounting bracket has been removed tighten the bolts to 2.5 kgm (18 ft.lb.). Take care to make the correct connections. Adjust the drive belt tension.

14.1.3. SERVICING

A Bosch alternator is used on the engines dealt with in this manual. We do not recommend that the alternator or control unit should be adjusted or serviced by the owner. Special equipment is required in the way of test instruments and the incorrect application of meters could result in damage to the circuits.

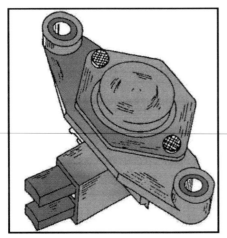

Fig. 14.3 – The ends of the alternator brushes must protrude by at least 5 mm.

The alternator is fitted with sealed-for-life bearings and no routine attention is required for lubrication. Keep the outside of the alternator clean and do not allow it to be sprayed with water or any solvent.

The alternator brush gear runs in plain slip rings and the brushes have a long life, requiring inspection only after a high mileage has been covered. To inspect the brushes, we recommend the removal of the alternator. Take out the two screws from the brush holder assembly and withdraw for inspection. Measure the length of the brushes, shown by "a" in Fig. 14.3. If the protruding length is less than 5.0 mm (0.2 in.) or approaching this length, replace the brushes. New brushes will have to be soldered in position. We would like to point out that it is not an easy operation to guide the brushes over the slip rings when the slip ring cover is being fitted.

14.2.   Starter Motor

A Bosch pre-engaged starter motor is fitted to the models covered in this manual.

14.2.0.   REMOVAL AND INSTALLATION

*   Disconnect the battery earth (ground) cable.
*   Remove the starter motor mounting bolts.
*   Disconnect the starter motor cables from the starter motor solenoid switch. Withdraw the unit from the vehicle. The unit must be guided past the engine crossmember. Tilt the motor so that the solenoid switch is facing downwards and then remove it sideways.

Install in the reverse sequence to removal. Tighten the starter motor bolts to 4.5 kgm (32.5 ft.lb.). Make sure that the mating faces are clean before bolting up. Re-connect the wires and the battery terminals. Tighten the nut to 2.5 kgm (18 ft.lb.).

14.2.1.   SERVICING

It may be of advantage to fit an exchange starter motor if the old one has shown faults. Exchange starter motors carry the same warranty as new units and are therefore a far better proposition.

The following repairs can, however, be attempted without any problems:

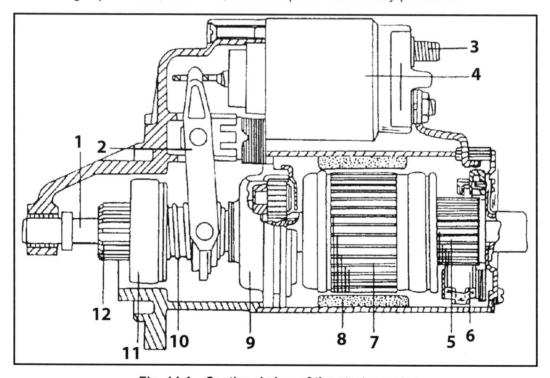

Fig. 14.4 – Sectional view of the starter motor.

1 Armature shaft	5 Commutator	9 Planetary gear
2 Engagement lever	6 Carbon brush	10 Engagement spring
3 Terminal, battery cable	7 Armature	11 Free wheel clutch
4 Solenoid switch	8 Permanent magnet	12 Starter motor pinion

Electrical System

Solenoid Switch

- Disconnect the cable between the solenoid switch and the starter motor terminal.
- From the front of the solenoid switch remove the bolts and withdraw the switch from the starter motor, at the same time disengaging the engagement lever from the starter motor drive.
- Refit the new switch in reverse order.

Starter Motor Brush Replacement

- Unscrew and remove the cover from the rear of the starter motor.
- Remove the two screws securing the commutator bearing cover.
- Remove the "C" clip from the rear end of the armature shaft (screwdriver), remove the sundry parts and withdraw the cover from the starter motor yoke. If necessary insert a screwdriver to get the parts apart. Remove the shims.
- Remove the brushes from their holders. The brush leads are either screwed-on or soldered. If they are soldered, you will have to be familiar with a soldering iron. Otherwise take the unit to an auto electrical repair shop to have the bushes replaced.
- Replace the brushes as applicable and re-assemble the starter motor in reverse order.

14.2.2. Starter Motor Faults

Following are a few tips to locate faults in the starting system before the starter motor is replaced:

- *When the key is turned to the starting position, the starter motor turns very slowly, nothing happens and starts to crank the engine and stops:* If the warning lights in the instrument panel are nearly or fully extinguished, check the battery. Loose or corroded cables on the starter motor, bad earth connection are other causes. If the battery has been connected previously, check the terminals for good contact. Use a jumper lead or get a tow-start to start the engine.

- *If the warning lights in the instrument panel remain "on" and a faint click is heard from the area of the starter motor,* it is possible that the engagement plunger of the solenoid switch is sticking. Use a heavy spanner and knock against the outside of the switch. Sometimes this will free the plunger. Other causes are worn starter motor brushes or defective contacts in the solenoid switch. In both cases remove the starter motor to replace the bushes and/or the solenoid switch. If the warning lights remain "on" and no click can be heard, check the cable connections between battery and starter motor.

- *If the starter motor is heard to operate without cranking the engine,* suspect a damaged solenoid switch, or the engagement mechanism, the starter motor pinion of the flywheel teeth are damaged. Try to engage a gear, push the vehicle backwards and forwards a few times and try the starter motor again. Otherwise fit a new starter motor.

- *If the starter motor "spins" after the engine has started and the key has been turned to the normal position,* a sticking solenoid switch is mostly the cause for the fault (contacts fail to open). The ignition switch can also be damaged. *Immediately switch off the engine.*

- If the starter motor pinion "spins" after starting the engine (howling noise), switch off the engine immediately. In most cases a new starter motor will be necessary.

14.3. Headlamps
14.3.0.   Headlamp/Side Light Bulb - Replacement

All front bulbs are fitted to the rear of a light unit. An "H4" headlight bulb is replaced as follows:

- Open the bonnet and from the rear of the headlight unit remove the rubber cover.
- Withdraw the multi-plug connector from the headlamp bulb, push the bulb holder towards the inside, at the same time turning it anti-clockwise. Remove the bulb when the bulb holder is free.
- Fit the new bulb into the holder. Do not touch the bulb with your fingers. The bulb has a locating tab which must engage properly. Push the bulb holder in position and turn it clockwise.
- To replace the side light bulb, push it down and at the same time turn it anti-clockwise.

14.3.1.   Replacing a Headlamp Unit

The headlamp units are attached from the outside by means of screws to the front section of the vehicle. Headlamp surround must be removed to take out the headlamp. Remember that the headlamps must be adjusted. We recommend to have the replacement of a headlamp and the adjustment carried out at a dealer.

15.   FUEL SYSTEM - CARBURETTOR

15.0.   Technical Data

Carburettor type: .... Stromberg 175 CDTU
Float needle valve: .... 2.25 mm
Brake caliper bolts (guide bolts): .... 3.3 kgm (24 ft.lb.)
Idle speed: .... 800 – 900 rpm
CO content: .... 1.0 – 2.0 %
Oil for piston damper: .... As in automatic transmissions (ATF)

Short description: The designation 175 CDTU signifies that the carburettor has a suction bore of 1.75 in., is working under constant depression (CD) and has a temperature-controlled starting device.

15.1.   Carburettor – Removal and Installation

- Disconnect the crankcase ventilation hose and the vacuum hose from the air cleaner.
- Disconnect the connector plug from the from the choke heater. Place the cables to one side.
- Free the rubber sleeve on the carburettor and remove it.
- Pinch the fuel feed and return hoses with a suitable clamp and disconnect the hoses. The self-locking fuel hoses must not be pulled off, but pushed off carefully with screwdriver. Looking at the carburettor, the feed hose is on the right (black marking) and the return hose to the fuel tank on the left (green marking).
- Disconnect a black hose from the side of the carburettor.

Carburettor Fuel System

- Release any vacuum in the cooling system by opening the radiator cap for a short moment and then clamp-off the hoses leading to the carburettor with suitable clamps.
- Disconnect the ball joint for the throttle operation and disconnect the regulating rod from the carburettor throttle lever.
- Undo the earth cable and the carburettor securing screws and lift off the carburettor. Remove the insulating flange, the protective shield and the gaskets. Check the parts for re-use as they are removed. Immediately cover the opening of the intake manifold to prevent entry of foreign matter.

The installation is a reversal of the removal procedure, noting the following points:

- Always replace the gaskets. Make sure that the gaskets cannot cover the ventilation bores in the carburettor.
- Make sure to re-connect the vacuum hoses correctly.
- The fuel hoses are marked with arrows and must be connected accordingly.
- Replace any cooling hoses if no longer in good condition.
- Tighten the carburettor securing bolts to 5.0 kgm (36 ft.lb.).
- Start the engine and check the idle speed. Adjust if necessary.

15.2.   Carburettor Adjustments

Some of the adjustments which may be possible by simple means are described below. Any other operations should be left to a dealer.

Float Adjustment

A gauge is normally required to adjust the float level, but a depth gauge can also be used. The carburettor must be removed.

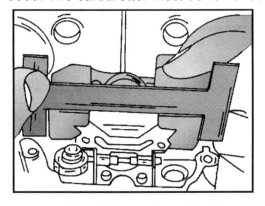

Fig. 15.1 – Measuring the float level.

Remove the float chamber. To do this, unscrew the screws and detach the float chamber. To facilitate the operation, slacken the locknut securing the fuel shut-off valve and unscrew the valve approx. 5 mm. Withdraw the temperature controlled compensating element together with the fuel jet.

Carefully push the float towards the bottom until the spring-loaded ball in the float needle valve is **fully depressed**. In this position measure the distance from the top of the float to the contacting face, as shown in Fig. 15.1, which should be 16 to 17 mm. If correction is necessary, check if the sealing washer under the float needle valve still has a thickness of 1.5 mm. Otherwise carefully bend the lug of the float (float removed). Both floats must be level. Refit all parts in reverse order.

Idle Speed and CO Content

The idle speed can only be adjusted correctly if ignition, valve clearance and other criteria relevant to the perfect running of the engine are properly adjusted. A CO content meter and revolution counter must be connected in accordance with the instructions of the manufacturer. Proceed as follows:

- Start the engine and allow it to warm-up to operating temperature. Check the oil level in the piston damper and check the throttle lever and the choke valve for freedom of movement.

Fig. 15.2 – View of the throttle valve lever with location of the adjusting screws. Do not mix-up screw (2) and (3).

1   Connecting rod
2   Warm-up speed screw
3   Idle adjusting screw
4   Throttle valve lever

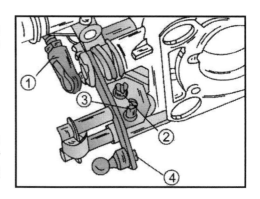

- Check the idle speed. If the speed is within 800 to 900 rpm, there are no further adjustments necessary. Otherwise adjust the idle speed.

Fig. 15.3 – Position of the CO adjusting screw (1) at the bottom of the carburettor.

- Unscrew the screw (3) in Fig. 15.2 or screw it in, until the engine runs with the given speed. Switch on the headlamps to check if the engine runs with the same idle speed.

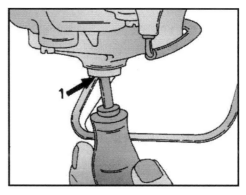

- Connect the CO meter and start the engine. Check the CO reading which should be between 1.0 to 2.0%. If this is not the case, adjust the CO adjusting screw at the bottom of the carburettor at the position shown in Fig. 15.3. Unscrewing the screw will reduce the CO content, screwing it in will increase the CO content. After each adjustment re-check the idle speed and the CO content. A tamper-proof locking cap is fitted over the screw after completed adjustment.

16.   SERVICING AND MAINTENANCE

Most of the maintenance operations can be carried out without many difficulties. In many cases it is, however, better to have certain maintenance operations carried out in a workshop as experience and special equipment, for example test instruments, are required to carry out a certain job. Most important are the regular inspections and checks which are described below. Operations to be carried out after a certain mileage are described later on in this section and the text will advise when specific jobs should be left to a Mercedes Dealer.

16.0.   Regular Maintenance

Oil Level Check: Check the engine oil level every 500 miles. With the vehicle standing on level ground, remove the oil dipstick and wipe it clean with a clean rag or a piece of tissue paper. Re-insert the oil dipstick and remove once more. The oil level must be visible between the upper and the lower mark on the dipstick. If the oil level is below the lower mark, top-up with engine oil of the correct viscosity. The oil quantity between the two marks is approx. between 5.0 and 3.5 litres and from the actual level indicated you will be able to tell how much oil is missing. Never overfill the engine - the level must never be above the upper dipstick mark.

Checking the Brake Fluid Level: - The brake fluid reservoir is in the engine compartment on the driver's side. The reservoir is transparent and it is easy to check whether the fluid level is between the "Min" and "Max" mark. If necessary, top-up to the "Max" mark with the correct brake fluid.

Checking the Brake Lights: The operation of the brake lights can either be checked with the help of another person or you can check it by yourself by driving the vehicle backwards near the garage door. Operate the brake pedal and check if the reflection of the brake lights can be seen on the garage door by looking through the rear view mirror.

Checking the Vehicle Lights: In turn check every vehicle light, including the horn and the hazard warning light system. Rear lights and reversing lights can be checked in the dark in front of a garage door, without leaving the vehicle.

Checking the Tyre Pressures: Check the tyre pressures at a petrol station. Pressures are different for the various models. Either your Operators Manual or tyre charts will give you the correct pressures.

If continuous speeds of more than 100 mph are anticipated, increase the tyre pressure by 0.2 kg/sq.cm. (3 psi.).

Checking the Coolant Level: See Section 1.7.1. Never open the radiator filler cap when the engine is hot.

Checking the Fluid Level in the Automatic Transmission: The fluid level should be checked at regular intervals to ensure the correct operation of the transmission:

- Apply the handbrake and place the gear selector lever into the "P" position. Start the engine and allow to idle for 1 to 2 minutes.
- Remove the oil dipstick from the transmission and read off the fluid level. The level must be between the "Min" and "Max" mark when the transmission is at operating temperature; the level may be up to 10 mm (0.4 in.) below the "Min" mark if the transmission is cold.
- If necessary top-up the transmission with ATF fluid through the fluid dipstick tube. A funnel is required. Use only the fluid recommended for the transmission.

16.1.   Service every 6,000 Miles

Changing the Engine Oil and Oil Filter: Some petrol stations will carry out an oil change free of charge – You only pay for the oil. The same applies to the oil filter (there may be a small extra charge), but not every petrol station will be able to obtain a Mercedes filter. To change the filter yourself, refer to Page 51.

Lubrication Jobs: Apart from the engine lubrication there are further lubrication points which should be attended to. These include the throttle linkage and shafts (only grease the swivel points), the engine bonnet catch and the hinges (use a drop of engine oil) and perhaps the door mechanism.

16.2.   Additional Service Every 12,000 Miles

Checking the Idle Speed: If the engine no longer idles as expected, have the idle speed checked and if necessary adjusted at your Dealer.

Air Filter Service: Remove the air filter element for cleaning.

Checking the Brake System: If no trouble has been experienced with the brake system, there is little need to carry out extensive checks. To safeguard for the next 6,000 miles, however, follow the brake pipes underneath the vehicle. No rust or corrosion must be visible. Dark deposits near the pipe ends point to leaking joints. Brake hoses must show no signs of chafing or breaks. All rubber dust caps must be in position on the bleeder valves of the calipers. Insert a finger underneath the master cylinder, where it is fitted to the brake servo unit. Moisture indicates a slightly leaking cylinder.

The brake pads must be checked for the remaining material thickness as has been described in Section "Brakes" for the front and rear brakes.

Adjusting the Parking Brake: Adjust the parking brake as described in Section "Brakes" under the relevant heading.

Brake Test: A brake test is recommended at this interval. You will decide yourself if the brakes perform as you expect them to. Otherwise have the brakes tested on a dynamometer. The read-out of the meter will show you the efficiency of the brake system on all four wheels.

Checking the Wheel Suspension and Steering: In the case of the front suspension remove both wheels and check the shock absorbers for signs of moisture, indicating fluid leaks.

Check the free play of the steering wheel. If the steering wheel can be moved by more than 25 mm (1 in.) before the front wheels respond, have the steering checked professionally.

Check the rubber dust boots of the track rod and drag link ball joints. Although rubber boots can be replaced individually, dirt may have entered the joints already. In this case replace the ball joint end piece.

Check the oil level in the mechanical steering. Remove the filler plug and check if the oil level is up to the filler plug bore hole. If necessary top-up with the recommended oil.

If a power-assisted steering is fitted, check the fluid level in the reservoir. Refer to Section 7.1.2. for details. If steering fluid is always missing after the 12,000 miles check, suspect a leak somewhere in the system - See your dealer.

Tyre Check: Jack up the vehicle and check all tyres for uneven wear. Tyres should be evenly worn on the entire surface. Uneven wear at the inner or outer edge of front tyres points to misalignment of the front wheel geometry. Have the geometry measured at your dealer. Make sure that a tread depth of 1.6 mm is still visible to remain within the legal requirements. Make sure to fit tyres suitable for your model, mainly if you buy them from an independent tyre company.

Re-tighten Wheel Bolts: Re-tighten the wheel bolts to 18.0 kgm (130 ft.lb.). Tighten every second bolt in turn until all bolts have been re-tightened.

Checking the Cooling System: Check all coolant hoses for cuts, chafing and other damage. Check the radiator for leaks, normally indicated by a deposit, left by the leaking anti-freeze. Slight radiator leaks can be stopped with one of the proprietary sealants available for this purpose.

Checking the Clutch: Check the clutch operation. The fluid reservoir should be full. If it is suspected that the clutch linings are worn near their limit, take the vehicle to a dealer. A gauge is used to check the protrusion of the slave cylinder push rod. It is a quick check and may prevent the clutch driven plate to wear down to the rivets.

Checking the Anti-freeze: The strength of the anti-freeze should be checked every 12,000 miles. Petrol stations normally have a hydrometer to carry out this check. Make sure that only anti-freeze suitable for Mercedes engines is used.

Checking the Manual Transmission Fluid Level: Refer to Section 3.3. on page 72.

Checking the Rear Axle Oil Level: Remove the filler plug and check the level.

16.3.   Additional Service every 36,000 Miles

Automatic Transmission Oil and Filter Change: These operations should be carried out by a Dealer.

Air Cleaner Element Change: Refer to the engine in question.

Diesel Oil Filter Change: Replace the fuel filter as described for the engine in question.

Fault Finding Section

Clutch: The wear of the clutch driven plate should be checked by a dealer with the special gauge available.

16.4. Once every Year

Brake Fluid Change: We recommend to have the brake fluid changed at your dealer. Road safety is involved and the job should be carried out professionally. If you are experienced with brake systems, follow the instructions in the "Brakes" section to drain, fill and bleed the brake system.

16.5. Once every 3 Years

Cooling System: The anti-freeze must be changed. Refer to Section "Cooling System" to drain and refill the cooling system.

FAULT FINDING SECTION

The following section lists some of the more common faults that can develop in a motor car; both for petrol and diesel engines. For the purpose of this manual, references to diesel engines are of course, first and foremost, as vehicles with petrol engine require technical assistance for many of the faults. The section is divided into various categories and it should be possible to locate faults or damage by referring to the assembly group of the vehicle in question.

The faults are listed in no particular order and their causes are given a number. By referring to this number it is possible to read off the possible cause and to carry out the necessary remedies, if this is within the scope of your facilities.

ENGINE FAULTS

Fault	Causes
Engine will not crank:	1, 2, 3, 4
Engine cranks, but will not start:	5, 6, 7, 8
Engine cranks very slowly:	1, 2, 3
Engine starts, but cuts out:	5, 6, 9, 10
Engine misfires in the lower speed ranges:	5, 6, 9, 11
Engine misfires in the higher speed ranges:	5, 6, 11, 12
Continuous misfiring:	5, 6, 7, 10 to 15, 21, 22
Max. revs not obtained:	5, 6, 12, 22
Faulty idling:	5, 6, 8 to 11, 13, 15, 16, 21 and 22
Lack of power:	3, 5 to 11, 13 to 15, 22
Lack of acceleration:	5 to 8, 12, 14 to 16
Lack of max. speed:	5 to 8, 10, 12, 13 to 15, 22
Excessive fuel consumption:	3, 5, 6, 15 ,16
Excessive oil consumption:	16 to 19
Low compression:	7, 11 to 13, 16, 20 to 22

CAUSES AND REMEDIES

1. Fault in the starter motor or its connection. Refer to "Electrical Faults".
2. Engine oil too thick. This can be caused by using the wrong oil, low temperatures or using oil not suitable for the prevailing climates. Depress the clutch whilst starting (models with manual transmission). Otherwise refill the engine with the correct oil grade, suitable for diesel engines.

3. Moveable parts of the engine not run-in. This fault may be noticed when the engine has been overhauled. It may be possible to free the engine by adding oil to the fuel for a while.

4. Mechanical fault. This may be due to seizure of the piston(s), broken crankshaft, connecting rods, clutch or other moveable parts of the engine. The engine must be stripped for inspection.

5. Faults in the glow plug system. Refer to "Glow Plug Faults".

6. Faults in the fuel system. Refer to "Fuel Faults".

7. Incorrect valve timing. This will only be noticed after the engine has been re-assembled after overhaul and the timing belt has been replaced incorrectly. Re-dismantle the engine and check the timing marks on the timing gear wheels.

8. Compression leak due to faulty closing of valves. See also under (7) or leakage past worn piston rings or pistons. Cylinder head gasket blown.

9. Entry of air at inlet manifold, due to split manifold or damaged gasket.

10. Restriction in exhaust system, due to damaged exhaust pipes, dirt in end of exhaust pipe(s), kinked pipe(s), or collapsed silencer. Repair as necessary.

11. Worn valves or valve seats, no longer closing the valves properly. Top overhaul of engine is asked for.

12. Sticking valves due to excessive carbon deposits or weak valve springs. Top overhaul is asked for.

13. Cylinder head gasket blown. Replace gasket and check block and head surfaces for distortion.

14. Camshaft worn, not opening or closing one of the valves properly, preventing proper combustion. Check and if necessary fit new camshaft.

15. Incorrect valve (tappet) clearance. There could be a fault in the hydraulic tappets.

16. Cylinder bores, pistons or piston rings worn. Overhaul is the only cure. Fault may be corrected for a while by adding "Piston Seal Liquid" into the cylinders, but will re-develop.

17. Worn valve guides and/or valve stems. Top overhaul is asked for.

18. Damaged valve stem seals. Top overhaul is asked for.

19. Leaking crankshaft oil seal, worn piston rings or pistons, worn cylinders. Correct as necessary.

20. Loose glow plugs, gas escaping past thread or plug sealing washer damaged. Correct.

21. Cracked cylinder or cylinder block. Dismantle, investigate and replace block, if necessary.

22. Broken, weak or collapsed valve spring(s). Top overhaul is asked for.

GLOW PLUG FAULTS

Check a suspect glow plug as follows:
*   Remove the glow plug lead from the rear glow plug and from the remaining plugs the bus bars.
*   Connect a 12 volts test lamp to the plus terminal of the battery and with the other lead of the lamp touch in turn the connecting threads of each glow plug. The faulty plug is detected when the test lamp does not light up.

Further faults in the glow plug system can develop in the glow plug relay. Check as follows:
*   Disconnect the electrical lead from the glow plug on the flywheel end and connect a test lamp between the lead and a good earthing point.

Fault Finding Section

- Disconnect the electrical lead from the coolant temperature sender unit and move away from earth.
- Turn the ignition key to the "glowing" position and observe the test lamp. The lamp should light up for approx. 25 - 30 sec. and then switch off.
- Turn the ignition switch "off" and then again to the "glowing" position. The test lamp must light up once more.
- Hold the disconnected lead from the temperature sender unit against earth. The test lamp must switch off.
- Turn the ignition switch "off" and then again to the "glowing" position. The test lamp should light up.
- Operate the starter motor and check that the test lamp remains "on".
- If the above tests cannot be carried out satisfactory, see your dealer.

LUBRICATION SYSTEM FAULTS

The only problem the lubrication system should give is excessive oil consumption or low oil pressure, or the oil warning light not going off.

Excessive oil consumption can be caused by worn cylinder bores, pistons and/or piston rings, worn valve guides, worn valves stem seals or a damaged crankshaft oil seal or leaking gasket on any of the engine parts. In most cases the engine must be dismantled to locate the fault.

Low oil pressure can be caused by a faulty oil pressure gauge, sender unit or wiring, a defective relief valve, low oil level, blocked oil pick-up pipe for the oil pump, worn oil pump or damaged main or big end bearings, In most cases it is logical to check the oil level first. All other causes require the dismantling and repair of the engine. If the oil warning light stays on, switch off the engine IMMEDIATELY, as delay could cause complete seizure within minutes.

COOLING SYSTEM FAULTS

Common faults are: Overheating, loss of coolant and slow warming-up of the engine:
Overheating:

1. *Lack of coolant:* Open the radiator cap with care to avoid injuries. Never pour cold water in to an overheated engine. Wait until engine cools down and pour in coolant whilst engine is running.
2. *Radiator core obstructed by leaves, insects, etc.:* Blow with air line from the back of the radiator or with a water hose to clean.
3. *Cooling fan not operating:* Check fan for proper cut-in and cut-out temperature. If necessary change the temperature switch or see your Dealer.
4. *Thermostat sticking:* If sticking in the closed position, coolant can only circulate within the cylinder head or block. Remove thermostat and check as described in section "Cooling".
5. *Water hose split:* Identified by rising steam from the engine compartment or the front of the vehicle. Slight splits can be repaired with insulation tape. Drive without expansion tank cap to keep the pressure in the system down, to the nearest service station.
6. *Water pump belt torn:* Replace and tension belt.
7. *Water pump inoperative:* Replace water pump.
8. *Cylinder head gasket blown:* Replace the cylinder head gasket.

Loss of Coolant:
1. *Radiator leaks:* Slight leaks may be stopped by using radiator sealing compound (follow the instructions of the manufacturer). In emergency an egg

can be cracked open and poured into the radiator filler neck.
2.   Hose leaks: See under 5, "Overheating".
3.   Water pump leaks: Check the gasket for proper sealing or replace the pump.

Long Warming-up periods:
1.   Thermostat sticking in the open position: Remove thermostat, check and if necessary replace.

DIESEL FUEL SYSTEM FAULTS

Engine is difficult to start or does not start:	1 to 13
Engine starts, but stops soon afterwards:	14 to 20
Engine misfires continuously:	1 to 13
Bad idling:	14 to 20
Black, white or blue exhaust smoke:	21 to 29
Lack of power:	30 to 39
Excessive fuel consumption:	40 to 47

CAUSES AND REMEDIES

1.   Fuel tank empty. Refuel.
2.   Pre-glowing time too short. Operate until warning light goes "off".
3.   Cold starting device not operated. Pull cable and push in after approx. 1 mm.
4.   Glow plug system inoperative. Refer to "Glow Plug Faults".
5.   Electro-magnetic cut-off device, loose or no current. Check cable to cut-off at top of injection pump. Ask a second person to operate ignition key and check if a "click" is heard. Either interrupted current supply or defective cut-off device.
6.   Air in fuel system. Operate starter motor until fuel is delivered.
7.   Fuel supply faulty. Slacken the injection pipes at injectors, and check if fuel is running out. Other faults: kinked, blocked or leaking injection pipes blocked fuel filter, tank breathing system blocked. Wrong fuel for cold temperatures.
8.   Injection pipes refitted in wrong order after repair.
9.   Injection timing of pump out of phase: Have the adjustment checked and corrected.
10.   One or more injectors faulty, dirty or incorrect injection pressure. Have injectors repaired or replace them.
11.   Injection pump not operating properly. Fit an exchange pump or have it repaired.
12.   Valves not opening properly.
13.   Compression pressures too low. See item "8" under "Engine Faults".
14.   Idle speed not properly adjusted. Adjust.
15.   Throttle cable not properly adjusted or sticking. Re-adjust or free-off.
16.   Fuel hose between filter and pump not tightened properly. Tighten connections.
17.   Rear mounting of injection pump loose or cracked. Tighten or replace.
18.   See items 6, 7, 9, 11, 12 and 13.
19.   Engine mounting not tightened properly or worn. Tighten or replace.
20.   Sticking accelerator pedal. Free-off pedal.
21.   Engine not at operating temperature. Check exhaust smoke colour again when engine is warm.
22.   Too much acceleration at low revs. Use individual gears in accordance with acceleration.

23. Air cleaner contaminated. Clean or replace.
24. Fuel filter contaminated. Replace.
25. Max. speed adjustment incorrect. Re-adjust.
26. Injectors are dripping. Have them checked or replace faulty ones.
27. Injector nozzles sticking or broken. Replace injector.
28. Injection pressure too low. Have injectors checked and adjusted.
29. See items 9, 11, 12 and 13.
30. Throttle cable travel restricted. Re-adjust. Check that floor mats cannot obstruct pedal movement.
31. Throttle cable not correctly adjusted. Re-adjust.
32. Operating lever loose on pump. Re-tighten.
33. Max. speed not obtained. Re-adjust max. speed or have it adjusted.
34. Injector pipes restricted in diameter (near connections). Disconnect pipes and check that diameter is at least 2.0 mm (0.08 in.).
35. Heat protection sealing gaskets under injectors not sealing or damaged. Remove injectors and check. Replace if necessary. Fit the washers correctly.
36. Injection pressure of injectors wrong. Have them re-adjusted.
37. See items 6, 7, 9, 11 and 13.
38. See item 20.
39. See items 23, 24, 26 and 27.
40. Road wheels dragging. Brakes seized or wheel bearings not running freely.
41. Engine not running "free". Refers to new or overhauled engine.
42. Fuel system leaking. Check hoses, pipes, filter, injection pump, etc. for leaks.
43. Fuel return line blocked. Clean with compressed air if possible.
44. Idle speed too high. Re-adjust.
45. Max. speed too high. Re-adjust.
46. See items 10, 11, 12 and 13.
47. See items 24, 26, 27 and 28.

CLUTCH FAULTS

Clutch slipping:	1, 2, 3, 4, 5
Clutch will not disengage fully:	4, 6 to 12, 14
Whining from clutch when pedal is depressed:	13
Clutch judder:	1, 2, 7, 10 to 13
Clutch noise when idling:	2, 3
Clutch noise during engagement:	2

CAUSES AND REMEDIES

1. Insufficient clutch free play at pedal.
2. Clutch disc linings worn, hardened, oiled-up, loose or broken. Disc distorted or hub loose. Clutch disc must be replaced.
3. Pressure plate faulty. Replace clutch.
4. Air in hydraulic system. Low fluid level in clutch cylinder reservoir.
5. Insufficient play at clutch pedal and clutch release linkage. Rectify as described.
6. Excessive free play in release linkage (only for cable operated clutch, not applicable). Adjust or replace worn parts.
7. Misalignment of clutch housing. Very rare fault, but possible on transmissions with separate clutch housings. Re-align to correct.

8. Clutch disc hub binding on splines of main drive shaft (clutch shaft) due to dirt or burrs on splines. Remove clutch and clean and check splines.
9. Clutch disc linings loose or broken. Replace disc.
10. Pressure plate distorted. Replace clutch.
11. Clutch cover distorted. Replace clutch.
12. Fault in transmission or loose engine mountings.
13. Release bearing defective. Remove clutch and replace bearing.
14. A bent clutch release lever. Check lever and replace or straighten, if possible.
•   The above faults and remedies are for hydraulic and mechanical clutch operation and should be read as applicable to the model in question, as the clutch fault finding section is written for all types of clutch operation.

STEERING FAULTS

Steering very heavy:	1 to 6
Steering very loose:	5, 7 to 9, 11 to 13
Steering wheel wobbles:	4, 5, 7 to 9, 11 to 16
Vehicle pulls to one side:	1, 4, 8, 10, 14 to 18
Steering wheel does not return to centre position:	1 to 6, 18
Abnormal tyre wear:	1, 4, 7 to 9, 14 to 19
Knocking noise in column:	6, 7, 11, 12

CAUSES AND REMEDIES

1. Tyre pressures not correct or uneven. Correct.
2. Lack of lubricant in steering.
3. Stiff steering linkage ball joints. Replace ball joints in question.
4. Incorrect steering wheel alignment. Correct as necessary.
5   Steering needs adjustment. See your dealer for advice.
6. Steering column bearings too tight or seized or steering column bent. Correct as necessary.
7. Steering linkage joints loose or worn. Check and replace joints as necessary.
8. Front wheel bearings worn, damaged or loose. Replace bearing.
9. Front suspension parts loose. Check and correct.
10. Wheel nuts loose. Re-tighten.
11. Steering wheel loose. Re-tighten nut.
12. Steering gear mounting loose. Check and tighten.
13. Steering gear worn. Replace the steering gear.
14. Steering track rods defective or loose.
15. Wheels not properly balanced or tyre pressures uneven. Correct pressures or balance wheels.
16. Suspension springs weak or broken. Replace spring in question or both.
17. Brakes are pulling to one side. See under "Brake Faults".
18. Suspension out of alignment. Have the complete suspension checked by a dealer.
19. Improper driving. We don't intend to tell you how to drive and are quite sure that this is not the cause of the fault.

BRAKE FAULTS

Brake Failure: Brake shoe linings or pads excessively worn, incorrect brake fluid (after overhaul), insufficient brake fluid, fluid leak, master cylinder defective, wheel cylinder or caliper failure. Remedies are obvious in each instance.

Brakes Ineffective: Shoe linings or pads worn, incorrect lining material or brake fluid, linings contaminated, fluid level low, air in brake system (bleed brakes), leak in pipes or cylinders, master cylinder defective. Remedies are obvious in each instance.

Brakes pull to one side: Shoes or linings worn, incorrect linings or pads, contaminated linings, drums or discs scored, fluid pipe blocked, unequal tyre pressures, brake back plate or caliper mounting loose, wheel bearings not properly adjusted, wheel cylinder seized. Rectify as necessary.

Brake pedal spongy: Air in hydraulic system. System must be bled of air.

Pedal travel too far: Linings or pads worn, drums or discs scored, master cylinder or wheel cylinders defective, system needs bleeding. Rectify as necessary.

Loss of brake pressure: Fluid leak, air in system, leak in master or wheel cylinders, brake servo not operating (vacuum hose disconnected or exhauster pump not operating). Place vehicle on dry ground and depress brake pedal. Check where fluid runs out and rectify as necessary.

Brakes binding: Incorrect brake fluid (boiling), weak shoe return springs, basic brake adjustment incorrect (after fitting new rear shoes), piston in caliper of wheel cylinder seized, push rod play on master cylinder insufficient (compensation port obstructed), handbrake adjusted too tightly. Rectify as necessary. Swelling of cylinder cups through use of incorrect brake fluid could be another reason.

Handbrake ineffective: Brake shoe linings worn, linings contaminated, operating lever on brake shoe seized, brake shoes or handbrake need adjustment. Rectify as necessary.

Excessive pedal pressure required: Brake shoe linings or pads worn, linings or pads contaminated, brake servo vacuum hose (for brake servo) disconnected or wheel cylinders seized. Exhauster pump not operating. Rectify as necessary.

Brakes squealing: Brake shoe linings or pads worn so far that metal is grinding against drum or disc. Inside of drum is full of lining dust. Remove and replace, or clean out the drum(s). Do not inhale brake dust.

Note: Any operation on the steering and brake systems must be carried out with the necessary care and attention. Always think of your safety and the safety of other mad users. Make sure to use the correct fluid for the power-assisted steering and the correct brake fluid.

Faults in an ABS system should be investigated by a dealer.

Change the brake fluid in regular Intervals (approx. every 1 year).

ELECTRICAL FAULTS

Starter motor failure:	2 to 5, 8, 9
No starter motor drive:	1 to 3, 5 to 7
Slow cranking speed:	1 to 3
Charge warning light remains on:	3, 10, 12
Charge warning light does not come on:	2, 3, 9. 11, 13
Headlamp failure:	2, 3, 11, 13, 14
Battery needs frequent topping-up:	11
Direction indicators not working properly:	2, 3, 9, 13, 14
Battery frequently discharged:	3, 10, 11, 12

CAUSES AND REMEDIES

1. Tight engine. Check and rectify.
2. Battery discharged or defective. Re-charge battery or replace if older than approx. 2 years.
3. Interrupted connection in circuit. Trace and rectify.
4. Starter motor pinion jammed in flywheel. Release.
5. Also 6, 7 and 8. Starter motor defective, no engagement in flywheel, pinion or flywheel worn or solenoid switch defective. Correct as necessary.
9. Ignition/starter switch inoperative. Replace.
10. Drive belt loose or broken. Adjust or replace.
11. Regulator defective. Adjust or replace.
12. Generator inoperative. Overhaul or replace.
13. Bulb burnt out. Replace bulb.
14. Flasher unit defective. Replace unit.

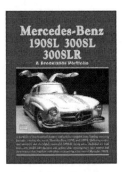

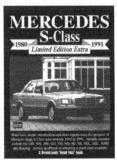

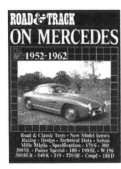

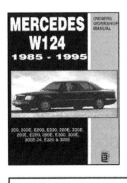

Printed in Great Britain
by Amazon

58473388R00115